P9-CJJ-005

UGLY BEAUTY

Also by Ruth Brandon

FICTION

Caravaggio's Angel
The Uncertainty Principle
Tickling the Dragon
Mind Out
The Gorgon's Smile
Out of Body, Out of Mind
Left, Right and Centre

NONFICTION

Other People's Daughters: The Life and Times of the Governess
People's Chef: Alexis Soyer, a Life in Seven Courses
Automobile: How the Car Changed Life
Surreal Lives: The Surrealists, 1917–1945
The Life and Many Deaths of Harry Houdini
Being Divine: A Biography of Sarah Bernhardt
The New Women and the Old Men: Love, Sex and the Woman Question
The Burning Question: The Anti-nuclear Movement since 1945
Spiritualists: Passion for the Occult in the Nineteenth and Twentieth Centuries
The Dollar Princesses: Sagas of Upward Nobility, 1870–1914
Singer and the Sewing Machine: A Capitalist Romance

UGLY BEAUTY

Helena Rubinstein, L'Oréal, and the Blemished History of Looking Good

RUTH BRANDON

HARPER

An Imprint of HarperCollins*Publishers*
www.harpercollins.com

HarperCollins books may be purchased for educational, business, or sales promotional use. For information, please write: Special Markets Department, HarperCollins Publishers, 10 East 53rd Street, New York, NY, 10022.

FIRST EDITION

Designed by William Ruoto

Library of Congress Cataloging-in-Publication Data

Brandon, Ruth.
Ugly beauty : Helena Rubinstein, L'Oréal, and the blemished history of looking good / Ruth Brandon. — 1st ed.
p. cm.
ISBN 978-0-06-174040-4
1. Rubinstein, Helena, 1870-1965. 2. Helena Rubinstein, inc. 3. L'Oreal (Firm) 4. Beauty, Personal. I. Title.
RA778.B7843 2011
646.7'2—dc22
2010024435

11 12 13 14 15 ID/BVG 10 9 8 7 6 5 4 3 2 1

TO MY UNRETOUCHED FEMALE FRIENDS

CONTENTS

ACKNOWLEDGMENTS

Caroline Davidson, Geoff Garvey, Dr. Lucy Glancey, Abbie Greene and Nick Growse, Nick Humphrey, Sylvia Kahan, David Kuzma at Rutgers University Library Special Collections, Brian Morgan, Luke Shepherd, Ann Treneman, Monica Waitzfelder, Lindy Woodhead, and Randall Wright have given me invaluable help during the writing of this book. I am deeply grateful to them all. My thanks, too, to all at HarperCollins for their professionalism and patience.

I am especially indebted to my agent, Clare Alexander, who was instrumental in shaping this book, and my editor, Ben Loehnen, who sharpened its points.

INTRODUCTION

Everyone has heard of Helena Rubinstein, international queen of cosmetics. Tiny, plump, spike-heeled, bowler hatted, and extravagantly jeweled, she was for many years one of the fixtures of the New York scene, scurrying between her vast apartment on Park Avenue and her salon on Fifth Avenue at Fifty-seventh Street, in one hand an enormous leather bag stuffed with cash, business notes, old tissues, and spare earrings, in the other a paper sack containing a copious lunch. Instantly recognizable to all from the photographs that adorned her advertisements, she was energy personified, at once comic and awe inspiring.

Few, by contrast, have heard of Eugène Schueller—though everyone knows L'Oréal, the firm he founded in Paris in 1909. Like Rubinstein he was born poor; like her, he rode to riches on the back of women's compulsion to beautify themselves. Unlike her, however, neither his name nor his face were familiar to those who bought his hair dyes. Immured within his empire, traveling between factories in the Rolls that was his office on wheels, he shunned personal publicity. So removed was he from society, indeed, that when his wife died and he wished to remarry, the only woman he could find, though he was by then one of the richest men in France, was his daughter's governess.

In 1988, Schueller's business swallowed Rubinstein's. In the normal way of things the takeover would have gone unnoticed except in the business press. But Rubinstein was a Jew, while Schueller, during the German Occupation, had been a leading fascist collaborator. And although they never met during their lifetimes, and both, by then, were long dead, the consequences of this potentially lethal opposition outlived them. The conjunction led to a series of scandals that not only threw a new and sinister light on L'Oréal but threatened the reputations of some of France's most powerful men—up to and including its president himself.

It may seem odd—certainly unexpected—that a history of the beauty business should include an excursion into fascist politics. But cosmetics, unlike clothes, have always been a political hot potato. The stories of Helena Rubinstein and Eugène Schueller show us why this has been so—and continues to be so today.

UGLY BEAUTY

CHAPTER ONE

Beauty Is Power!*

I

"Her life," said *Vogue* of Helena Rubinstein, "reads like a fairy story."[1] It was 1915: Madame (as she was always known) had just opened her first New York salon. Dark-blue velvet covered the walls of its main room, with rose-colored woodwork and sculptures by Elie Nadelman from Madame's own art collection. Each of the many other rooms had its own decorative theme, from a Louis XVI salon to a Chinese fantasy in black and gold and scarlet. The diminutive proprietor, high heels adding a few needed inches to the mere four foot ten nature had allowed her, personally showed the journalists around. However busy she might be, there was always time for journalists. Madame, ever keen to pinch a penny where she could, knew no amount of advertis-

* The title of this chapter is taken from a Helena Rubinstein advertisement that appeared in *Australian Home Journal* in 1907.

ing could equal the boost afforded by a really long interview, with photos, spread over several pages. And such a piece cost nothing at all.

The fairy story in question was a classic rags-to-riches tale. Twelve years earlier, in 1903, Helena Rubinstein, a poor emigrant from Poland, had opened her first beauty salon: a single room in Melbourne, Australia, from which she sold pots of homemade face cream. So great were her marketing skills, such the demand, and so enormous the markup, that within two years she was rich. By 1915 she was a millionaire. She had dazzled London and Paris, and was set to do the same in America.

Fairy stories, however, are more than just dazzling social leaps. They are also dramatizations of our deepest dreams. And in this sense, too, the metaphor was apposite, both for Rubinstein and for her chosen industry. For cosmetics are all about dreams—specifically, the dream of an ideal, time-defying physical self.

Generally speaking, the public acceptance of women's cosmetics has varied according to the social status of their sex. When the Roman poet Ovid, in his *Ars amatoria*, advised women to make sure their armpits didn't smell, that their legs were shaved, to keep their teeth white, to "acquire whiteness with a layer of powder," to rouge if they were naturally pale, "hide your natural cheeks with little patches," and "highlight your eyes with thinned ashes," he was speaking to a society where women had substantial social freedoms in all spheres other than politics. Equally, the heroine of Pope's *Rape of the Lock*, with its famous dressing-table scene enumerating "Puffs, Powders, Patches, Bibles, Billet-doux," was free to take her place as an active player on the social stage. But in societies where a wife's functions are solely to produce children and service her husband, cosmetics are taboo. Saint Paul inveighs against them; the Talmud declares that "a beautiful wife—beautiful without cosmetics—doubles the days of her husband and increases his mental comfort."[2]

The nineteenth century, particularly in Britain, was just such a society: in the words of social commentator William Rathbone Greg, writing in 1862, a woman's function in it was to "complete, sweeten, and embellish the existence of others."[3] But Helena Rubinstein's good fortune, after a century of repression during which no respectable lady could allow herself even a touch of rouge, was to hit a moment when women were poised to claim new freedoms. Her fairy-tale riches—rubies, emeralds, pearls, and diamonds that would not have looked out of place in Ali Baba's cave, sculptures and paintings, apartments and houses in New York, London, Paris, and the Riviera—reflected, in the reassuringly solid form Madame always favored, this surge of empowerment. And since empowerment is the keynote, too, of her own personal story, nothing could be more appropriate than that the first woman tycoon—the first self-made female millionaire—should have amassed her fortune through cosmetics.

Rubinstein's life, as recounted by herself in two memoirs, was a fairy tale in yet another sense: a desirable fiction that had little to do with reality. "I have always felt a woman has the right to treat the subject of her age with ambiguity until, perhaps, she passes into the realm of over ninety," she wrote—she herself being, by then, well into that realm. And ambiguous she was, and remained, not just about her age but about every aspect of her life. Although in the year of her death she finally acknowledged she was born "in the early 1870s, on Christmas Day" (the year was in fact 1872), even then she maintained the story—repeated so often she had perhaps come to believe it—that the family had been well-off. They lived, she said, in a big house near the Rynek, the ancient and splendid market square that is Krakow's city center; her father, a "wholesale food broker," was an intellectual who collected books and fine furniture; she herself had attended a gymnasium, she had for two years been a medical student, and her sisters, too, had attended university.[4]

In fact anyone could tell that Helena had been poor, and hated it, from the extreme pleasure she took in being rich, piling up the bright, shiny goodies with a compulsive delight that never dimmed and that no one born rich could ever experience.

Similarly, it is clear she would have studied medicine if she could. She always projected herself as a qualified scientific professional, was constantly photographed in white lab coats amid test tubes and Bunsen burners, emphasized her products'quasi-medical aspects. She became as knowledgeable in her field as anyone alive. But that field was far from scientific, and such knowledge as she possessed was laboriously gleaned over the years, not formally acquired.

The Rubinsteins actually lived in Kazimierz, Krakow's Jewish ghetto, whose cramped streets, despite restoration as a tourist attraction by the wealthy descendants of the poor Jews who once lived there, still exude a dingy poverty. There, Naftali Herzl Rubinstein, Helena's father, was a kerosene dealer, occasionally selling eggs in the market. His eldest daughter, Chaja, who would become known as Helena, attended a local Jewish school.

She was, like many firstborn children, ambitious and high-achieving, and as the eldest of eight sisters acquired a precociously adult habit of responsibility. When she recounts that her father, "since he had no son . . . fell into the habit of talking over his plans and projects with me,"[5] there is, for once, no reason to doubt her. Many Jewish wives kept the family going by managing a business as well as running a home and raising children, providing the material necessities while their menfolk lived the life of the mind. Yiddish has a special word—*baleboosteh*—for this combination of worldly competence and efficient domesticity, and this, clearly, was clever Chaja's destiny. For a poor girl from her orthodox background (her mother's father was a rabbi), medical school could never have been anything but a dream. A girl's career was marriage. Any activities preceding that were mere time-marking. Afterwards, if her mother's example was anything to go by, she could expect more or less permanent pregnancy: a cramped and frantic life amid an ever-increasing brood of babies.

It was enough to put any intelligent girl off marriage and motherhood for life, and (judging by her later forays into those territories) this was just the effect it had on Chaja. It can be no coincidence that the only Krakow suitor she mentions with enthusiasm was not a possible prospect, as he was not a Jew. Coming from a family like the Rubinsteins, to marry "out" would have been equivalent to death. Had Chaja done so, they would have cut off all contact with her and recited funeral prayers. Instead, her father produced a suitable widower. Chaja refused him, there was an almighty row, and she left the family home, never to return. She took refuge in Vienna with an aunt, her mother's sister. It was her life's defining moment. From now on she would be Helena, and her own woman.

Everything that happened to her subsequently, everything she did, stemmed from this furious decision. It not only reflected her attitude toward the prescribed female life of marriage and motherhood, but would influence her view of what cosmetics were for and what they might do for the wearer. No one was ever less interested in politics, whether of the international or the gender variety, than Helena Rubinstein—on the contrary, throughout her life, until it became impossible, she would shun, in every possible way, the political arena. But this one act catapulted her into it from the outset.

Her Vienna relations, the Splitters, were prosperous furriers. (A photo exists, taken in Vienna, of Helena, aged twenty-one, looking matronly in astrakhan.) Frau Splitter continued, on her sister's behalf, the hunt for a suitable husband. But Helena refused all comers. And since Europe offered no obvious prospects, she decided to move on to a new continent. Three of her mother's Silberfeld brothers had settled in Australia. John was a jeweler in Melbourne; Bernhard and Louis, along with Louis's daughter Eva, a cousin about Helena's age who was married with two small children, kept a general store and a grocery in Coleraine, a small town two hundred miles to the west. The Coleraine family were in need of some extra help, and in the summer of 1896 Helena sailed from Genoa to join them.

Nothing in Europe could have prepared her for the rude life of an Australian small town. She did not get on with her Uncle Louis, who, she hinted in a memoir, made unwelcome advances, and her cousin Eva's marriage was disastrously unhappy. But, speaking no English, she could communicate with no one else: she was stuck with them. In later years Helena conducted her enormous correspondence (even when writing to her sisters) in English, the language of her adult life. But until her arrival in Australia she had spoken only Yiddish and Polish. Her spoken English always remained heavily accented, resounding with Yiddishisms. She described herself as shy, a quality hard to reconcile with her singularly uninhibited approach to business and her constant entertaining. The difficulty, however, seems largely to have arisen from her awkwardness in English. "She uttered in grunts," fashion writer Ernestine Carter recalled[6]—a strange mix of English, French,

Polish, and Yiddish that made her hard to follow and reluctant to strike up conversation with strangers. Surrounding herself with family as she famously did, calling in sister after sister, cousins, nephews, nieces, as the business expanded, she carried her homeland with her, whether to New York, Paris, or London: the archetypical rootless cosmopolitan.

She endured Coleraine for three years. Then, having picked up enough English to operate independently, she decided it was time to make her escape. Revisiting Australia in 1958, she refused to set foot in Coleraine. "No! No! I don't want to go back there," she told Patrick O'Higgins, the aide and companion of her later years. "For what? I was hungry, lonely, poor in that awful place."[7] But the Coleraine years had not been wasted. She knew now that she wanted to start up a business, and knew, too, what that business would be. One reason she was so convincing a beauty counselor was that her exquisite complexion meant she did for a long time look much younger than her real age. This was unusual in Australia, whose harsh climate, with its strong winds and baking sun, is hard on the skin. Her weather-beaten neighbors were admiring. What was her secret?

Helena claimed to have begun by selling her own spare pots of face cream to the local ladies, telling them that she used a formula discovered by some brothers called Lykusky "who had supplied us with it for our personal use ever since I was a little girl." When the supply was exhausted, the legend went, she sent off to Poland to replenish her supplies. This was, on every level, a fantasy. The voyage between Europe and Australia took forty-five days—far too slow if orders had to be fulfilled—and it is unlikely that her own initial supplies would have provided any surplus. But for a natural entrepreneur like Helena, her neighbors' interest was enough to plant an idea—the idea she had been looking for ever since abandoning her father's house and the narrow life it offered. She would start a business selling face cream.

This chance direction was Helena's first great stroke of luck. In all other areas of commerce, women were at a disadvantage, but the beauty business was different. With odd exceptions, such as the French court of Louis XV, where everyone, male and female, whitened their faces (as a sign that they did not lead a lower-class outdoor life) and rouged their cheeks and lips, the misogynistic Christian world had frowned upon cosmetics even where (as in Restoration England) they were widely used. Even when everyone knew that women did use rice powder, or face cream, or rouge, or whitened their skins with the notorious and poisonous ceruse, made from white lead, these preparations still had to be obtained discreetly and applied in strict privacy. Men averted their eyes from such arrangements—and so failed to realize what was obvious to Helena Rubinstein: that half the human race was interested in what she had to sell. Indeed, long after Helena Rubinstein, Elizabeth Arden, and Estée Lauder had all made millions out of cosmetics, men remained noticeably absent from the beauty business. There was Max Factor, but his main specialty was stage makeup, although he did introduce a line of cosmetics to the public in 1920. Otherwise, until the arrival of Charles Revson's Revlon in the 1950s, women entrepreneurs dominated the beauty scene. This was partly because, as *Life* magazine observed in 1941, "Most men do not find an atmosphere conducive to their best work in the tight little matriarchy of the beauty business"[8]—a business Madame described in 1920 as "working for women with women, and giving that which only women can give—an intimate understanding of feminine needs and feminine desires."[9] But the prospect of enormous profits is generally enough to overcome any squeamishness or uncertainty. What gave women the edge in the beauty industry was that, in the beginning at least, this was a huge potential market *of which only women were aware.*

Helena decided to start her business in Melbourne. It was a large city (in 1901 it already had over 500,000 inhabitants), and her uncle John was established there. And—in her second stroke of luck—it proved to be an uniquely propitious location for what she now proposed. Whether or not Australian men disapproved of makeup was of little interest to Australian women—for unlike Europeans, they did not depend on men for their money. In Europe in 1901, respectable women only worked if they had no other means of support. Possible jobs were still effectively limited to dressmaking, millinery, and teaching, either as governesses or in schools. Australia, too, had its dressmakers, milliners, and governesses. But Australian women also worked in other fields, as journalists, telephone switchboard operators, and secretaries, in shops and hotels, in small factories . . . Around 35 percent of Melbourne's breadwinners were women, and 40 percent of working-age women were in paid employment. The Melbourne *Age* coined the phrase "bachelor girls" to describe the young women who, like Helena herself, arrived in the city looking for work—and who constituted an instant customer base. Their wages might be small—the average female wage was only half what men could expect to earn—but this was, nonetheless, their own money, to spend as they pleased.[10]

Unsurprisingly, the beauty-cream business was not a wholly unplowed field. Before the rise of commercial products, most women made their own simple cosmetics. And the fact that this was a familiar domestic craft, with cheap raw materials, made it a tempting, and unintimidating, female business proposition.* Recipes were available in printed compilations in the same way as food recipes, and often using the same ingredients. Skin creams, for example, were made from an emulsion of fat and water, perfumed with scented plant extracts. Women used whatever fat was to hand: milk or cream, goose grease, calf's foot jelly, almond oil, egg yolks. (The egg whites, mixed with lemon juice, could be used to make an astringent face mask.) As it happened, Australia abounded in a particularly suitable fat: this was sheep country, and lanolin, a by-product of sheep's wool, is both cheap and good for the skin. And lots of ladies advertised in the Melbourne papers, offering various treatments for the skin and hair.

The existing Melbourne enterprises, however, were mostly semi-amateur and hand-to-mouth—not at all the kind of business Helena had in mind. But proper business start-ups need capital, and in Australia, as throughout the British Empire, no woman could take out a bank loan under her own name. To start a serious business meant finding someone to underwrite her.

In her unreliable memoir, written sixty years later, Helena identified her Maecenas as a Miss Helen Macdonald, a friend she had made on board ship when she came to Australia, "far from wealthy, but she insisted upon lending me part of her life savings, the two hundred and fifty pounds I would need to start my venture."[11] In fact no such person appears on the relevant passenger list. In another account, she suggested that a Coleraine friend come with her to Melbourne and take a half

* Even today this domestic bias still holds good—arguably, the two most successful contemporary female entrepreneurs are Martha Stewart, with her multimillion-dollar homecrafts empire, and Anita Roddick, with her comparably successful Body Shop chain, both of which began, as it were, at the kitchen table.

share in the business. The offer was declined—surely one of the worst business decisions in history—but perhaps it was this friend who contributed the money.[12] Whatever its provenance, the £250 was forthcoming. It was the only money Helena Rubinstein ever borrowed. Now all that remained was to create a product and sell it.

The first thing was to learn, if she did not already know it, the simple knack of making face cream by emulsifying lanolin and adding essential plant oils to disguise its unpleasant sheepy smell. Some years later she would instruct her London manageress in this process, with a recipe for making blackhead cream:

> *Take one pint of oil, put it into a white basin and take four pints of peroxyde 6 percent and add to the oil or rather the foundation. But you must do it very slowly. You will spoil it if you put in much at a time. You just add a little by little to the oil and stir the whole time. Stir with a knife. The less peroxyde you put in at a time the better and thicker it will get. Add a little rose geranium, to perfume. Also mix.*

Essential oils were expensive—violet perfume cost £25,000 a kilo, "more expensive than diamonds and pearls," but a little went a long way.[13]

Anyone who has made mayonnaise will recognize the method—and indeed, Helena Rubinstein always referred to her workbench as her "kitchen." She adored preparing creams and lotions, and her "kitchen" remained the place she was always happiest. Many years later, when she met her fellow Pole Marie Curie, who had isolated radium by boiling down ton upon ton of pitchblende in a drafty old shed, she startled the distinctly un-domestic Madame Curie by asking what her "cuisine" was like.

With some of the £250 she rented a large, bright room in Melbourne's city center, painted it white, adorned it with curtains made from the unused evening gowns she had brought from Europe, made up some stock, painted a sign announcing "Helena Rubinstein—Beauty Salon," and opened for business. She started out with just one all-purpose face cream, "Crème Valaze."

> *"VALAZE" BY DR LYKUSKI, the most celebrated European Skin Specialist, is the best nourisher of the skin. "VALAZE" will improve the worst of skin in one month. 3/6d. and 5/6d. If posted, 6d. extra.* Available from Helena Rubinstein and company.*[14]

Valaze, "of exceptional value to those who are disfigured with freckles, sun-burn, wrinkles, eczema, blackheads or skin-blemishes of any kind," would remain a central Rubinstein product for the next fifty years.

Although her advertisements emphasized the cream's exotic provenance, specially imported from Poland and "compounded from rare herbs which only grow in the Carpathian Mountains," this description was pure snake oil. Importing someone else's skin cream from Europe to Australia would not just be grindingly slow, it would eat disastrously into the markup. Lots of factors made Helena Rubinstein rich—intelligence, astuteness, hard work, lucky timing. But what made her (and her competitors) so very rich, so fast, was the markup: the difference between cheap raw ingredients and

---

* These prices are in shillings and pence: three shillings and sixpence, five shillings and sixpence, sixpence. There were twenty shillings in a pound and twelve pence in a shilling.

the astounding prices charged for the finished product. A few months before her death, Madame found the original Valaze formula among a heap of old papers in the cellar of her Paris home: it contained only such common raw materials as ceresine wax, mineral oil, and sesame.[15] Psychologically, however, "rare Carpathian herbs" were essential. Then, as now, the beauty industry's real product was magic; and when it came to transforming perfumed fats into magic vials, boring old rose oil or pine-bark extract could never compete with rare Carpathian herbs.

This was Australia's first proper beauty salon, and it aroused enormous curiosity. "People streamed in," Rubinstein remembered. "The majority stayed for advice, and few left without a jar of my hand-labelled cream."[16] This was no small purchase. A milliner earned around £2 a week, a barmaid £1, a dressmaker £3: a pot of Valaze therefore consumed a good proportion of a week's wages. However, one of Helena Rubinstein's early discoveries was that in the beauty business, high prices do not deter sales. On the contrary—if one of her lines failed to sell, Madame would raise the price, and sales would miraculously increase.*

Even as she struggled to keep up with the demand of the walk-in trade, Rubinstein was inundated with mail orders—many of them spurred by an article about the salon in a Sydney newspaper. Newspaper articles were not only free, they were more effective than any number of expensive advertisements. From then on, Rubinstein made it her business to court the press. She studied beauty editors' personal preferences, and in

---

* Similarly, when writer Michael Greenberg was trying to make a living selling discount cosmetics in the Bronx, he found that if the price was too low—say, $3.50—customers got suspicious. When he raised the price to $5, business picked up. (See Greenberg's *Beg, Borrow, Steal: A Writer's Life*.)

later years, when she was due to meet one, always made sure to wear some dispensable item of jewelery—a ring, a bracelet—that she could press upon them as a parting gift. Now she wrote to each customer offering to return their money if they weren't prepared to wait. She had placed a new order with Dr. Lykusky, but it would not arrive for a while. Only one customer asked for her money back. After days and nights of feverish work in the "kitchen," preparing the cream and packing the jars, Miss Rubinstein announced that her stock was replenished, and filled the orders.

She worked eighteen-hour days, and (as she told it sixty years later) "lost many a beau, and missed the fun of being young." The truth was that being young had not been fun—and that work was. "Work has been my best beauty treatment!" she wrote at the end of her life. "It keeps the wrinkles out of the mind and the spirit. It helps to keep a woman young. It certainly keeps a woman alive!"[17] It interested her more than any man ever did. She could never keep a boyfriend for long, Helena recounted of those Melbourne days. Hoping for a night out, they found themselves hefting vats of cream, filling jars, or sticking labels. Even when she met Edward Titus and fell in love—even after they had children—work came first.

The business grew with extraordinary speed. After two years, the original £250 debit had become a credit of £12,000, and larger premises were urgently needed. Helena took a seven-room suite in a new building a little way down the street and began to train up a small staff. Her advertising philosophy was simple: "Fear copy with a bit of blah-blah." Until now women had just had skin, but now they had different varieties of skin: oily, dry, or normal. This distinction sowed profitable uncertainty among her clientele, who demanded, and happily bought, different creams—moisturizing, astringent, bleaching—to combat their newly defined deficiencies. It was a brilliant move. Later, in a similar brainstorm, Helena rebranded and promoted her existing range of creams and lotions as suitable for particular hours of the day or night, making them "Wake-Up Creams," or "Night Creams." An investigation of cosmetics, conducted by the left-wing pressure group Consumer Research in the 1930s, quoted a trade journal that observed: "From a merchandising point of view every manufacturer should . . . avoid 'all purpose' claims, because, even though they could be in part substantiated, it is better to sell a woman four different creams for four different purposes than one cream for all purposes."[18]

A lesser woman might have been satisfied with this unheard-of success. But Helena Rubinstein's secret weapon, the one that set her furthest apart from the small-time habitués of the small ads, was her utter imperviousness to satisfaction. She always needed to move on. And at this point, that would require actual knowledge—dermatological, dietary, even surgical—not available in Australia. In the summer of 1905, confident that the business was established enough to survive her brief absence, she embarked for Europe, and a crash course in the science of beauty.

HER FIRST STOP WAS KRAKOW. For ten years she had bathed its memory in the rosy glow of homesickness. The reality, inevitably, was anticlimactic, but also liberating. "The old town had not moved a pace in my absence. To me who had changed so much in a short while, it seemed indeed to have moved backwards, and to be a bit alien. . . . Home was not the same to me and from that time on I felt my life was in my own hands."[19] Cutting short her visit (she would not see her parents again), she set out on a whirlwind tour of Europe's skin-care specialists, working, as was her habit, day and night, so as not to waste a second of her limited time in Europe. In Paris, where she stayed with her sister Pauline Hirschberg (who would eventually take charge of the Helena Rubinstein Paris salon), she studied dermatology, learning "[the skin's] intricate anatomy and the principles which govern its appearance and health." In Wiesbaden she became acquainted with the then highly experimental science of facial surgery, and learned about metabolism and diet and their relation to health and beauty. In Vienna she met a woman doctor, Frau Doktor Emmy List, who became a good friend and would later come to work for her in London.

Here, at last, was the education she had dreamed of as a girl, albeit in a telescoped version. Described in *My Life for Beauty* as "I think the most stimulating years of my life,"[20] this period in fact lasted two or three months at most. She left Australia in June and returned in September. But for Madame, time was relative. In her later publicity she knocked a decade off her age, simply losing the years in which nothing had happened, and in the same way she extended these life-changing months into the years they psychologically represented. When she told an American interviewer, in 1922, that she "studied medicine in Germany," that (for a week or two) was what she did. The trip to Krakow had disposed, finally and forever, of the Kazimierz daughter; Wiesbaden, Vienna, Paris, Berlin, legitimized the businesswoman. She was no longer in any doubt "that my choice had been right—that this work I had chosen was infinitely preferable to any marriage which my aunt might have destined for me."[21]

When the time came to return to Australia, she did not travel alone, but took with her Ceska, the third-youngest of her sisters, and a cousin, Lola. All but one of the eight Rubinstein sisters would end up working for Helena's company, as would an assortment of cousins. This can be seen as an act of generosity—having discovered the pleasures of the self-sufficient working life, she wanted to extend them to her family. When fashion editor Ernestine Carter, having met the London and Paris Rubinstein sisters, congratulated Madame on her clever family, "she focussed her black gaze on me. 'Better they work,' she said."[22] But family also staved off loneliness. Later, when she became rich, she constantly entertained the famous personalities she encountered in her working life and through her interest in art and fashion. But that was business rather than pleasure, part of the public persona around which the entire Helena Rubinstein operation revolved. For relaxation she relied on her sisters, and endless games of cards.

She opened more salons, and devised a range of wonderful new products: Novena Poudre, a face powder for dry and normal skin; Valaze Herbal Powder for oily skins; Dr. Lykusky's Valaze Blackhead and Open-Pore Paste; Valaze Red Nose Ointment and Powder; Valaze Liquidine . . . "Money flowed in, in a continuous stream," she recalled in her first memoir, *The Art of Feminine Beauty*. "It seemed the whole Australian continent—or, at least, its feminine half—was bent on beautification."[23]

But her visit to Europe had expanded her ambitions. If Krakow had been a backwater, neither was Australia the center of the universe. Europe called, and only one thing held her back: a new acquaintance, Edward Titus.

Titus was a Polish Jew who had known Helena's sisters in Krakow. He had emigrated to America, become a journalist there, and acquired American nationality; now he was traveling around Australia. Arriving in Melbourne, he called in at the salon. For the first and last time in her life, Helena fell in love. "Until then," she said, "most of the people I had known had led rather narrow, humdrum lives; they were afraid of change and suspicious of new ideas. Edward Titus excited my imagination; he was an intellectual, interested in everything, and he had many friends in the literary and artistic world." He took her to theaters and concerts; soon they were seeing a great deal of each other; and one day—to her surprise, she said—he proposed.

"Marriage had never entered into my scheme of things," she wrote at the end of her life.[24] She loved Titus, but she loved her business more; if she married now, would she ever fulfil her ambitions? So she followed her invariable habit when faced with a difficult decision, and fled the country. She packed her bags, withdrew £100,000 from the bank (the equivalent of about $11.7 million today*), and, leaving the Australian business in the safe hands of her sister and cousin, took ship for London.

Until now, moneyed women had been heiresses, rich widows, queens, sometimes even empresses. Helena Rubinstein had become the world's first self-made female tycoon.

* This figure is arrived at using the retail price index—what the equivalent money would buy. But this is only one of several ways of calculating comparative monetary worth. Using, for example, average earnings, the figure would be more like $61.3 million. See http://www.measuringworth.com/ukcompare/result.php#.

II

We cannot all be ladies de Milo, but we can all be the best possible in our individual cases.

Little blots of blemish
In a visage glad
Make the lover thoughtful
And the husband mad.

—Early Rubinstein advertisement

Helena had decided to go to London because it was "the world center of thought, taste, money and beauty."[25] But she knew nobody there, and her first few weeks were lonely. She shared a small flat in Arlington Street with an Australian girl she met on the boat, and spent her days trudging round the West End in search of suitable premises. Eventually she heard that a Georgian house in Grafton Street belonging to Lord Salisbury was for rent. It cost more than she wanted to pay but she took it nonetheless. It was in the right position, and the attic could be converted into a flat for her to live above the shop. Then she returned to Australia, where Titus awaited her, and got married. They at once reembarked for Europe, and a honeymoon on the French Riviera. Madame's pattern for the coming decades was set: constant journeys, and an uneasy juggling of her personal and business lives.

Helena Rubinstein's marriage to Edward Titus might have been designed to provide ammunition for those who—like L'Oréal's founder, Eugène Schueller—felt nothing but bad could come of women entering the world of work. Of course it was no new thing for wives to be richer than their husbands. But until now those wives, and their bank balances, had bolstered, rather than challenged, their fortunate husbands' position in society. High-*earning* wives were something else—a novelty, and not necessarily an agreeable one psychologically.

What was the role of such a person's husband? Whether consort or housekeeper, it was quite evidently subordinate—even now not easy for many, and particularly hard in a culture where men had always been in charge. When Titus proposed, he talked about the business he and Helena would build together.[26] But the business was entirely hers, and always would be. "He claims partnership in everything but everybody knows he has no claim to anything," she complained in 1915.[27]

Put like that, her attitude sounded selfish. But had the situation been the more usual one where the business belonged to the husband, there would not have been—and probably still would not be—any question of the wife claiming partnership as of right. It was only because Titus was a man that he felt it his due. Nor did the situation improve when Helena officially put him on the payroll. He earned his salary—he had a way with words, never her forte, and was good at advertising. But he hated the work, and the lack of independence affronted his self-esteem.

Hers, meanwhile, was dented by his irrepressibly roving eye. Helena was now approaching forty, and her short frame, full of the copious meals she required to keep her energy up, was getting squarer by the year—*brayder vi lenger* (wider than she's long), as her Yiddish-speaking family would have phrased it. Sex appeal had never figured high on the list of her attractions, and her constant hope that Titus might desire her sexually, as she desired him, was always disappointed. During the honeymoon itself, Helena walked into the hotel lobby one morning in "a haze of happiness" and caught him in rapt conversation with a pretty young girl. Humiliated and smarting, she rushed to the nearest jewelers and bought herself a pick-me-up in the shape of a string of fine pearls.

She had found, as a lone woman in the man's world of business, that wearing fine stones gave her confidence,[28] announcing her as a woman of substance. Her self-respect momentarily buoyed, she caught the next train to Paris. By the time Titus caught up with her, however, she regretted her foolish behavior. She still kept the pearls, though, and added to them whenever there was a quarrel. Soon she possessed a good many pearls. "Buying 'quarrel-jewellery' is one of my weaknesses," she would write, still, at ninety-two, using the present tense.[29] By then, gems had become a personal statement, as habitual as the unchanging chignon whose severity they set off.

When the honeymoon was over, Mr. and Mrs. Titus returned to London, where they installed themselves in the Grafton Street attic flat. Then Helena opened her doors and, once again, waited for customers.

It was a nerve-racking moment. Opening a beauty salon in London was a far more complicated affair than opening one in Melbourne. London had no equivalent of the "bachelor girls" who had constituted her Australian clientele. In London, that clientele would have to be drawn from a quite different social stratum—that of well-to-do married ladies with generous dress allowances: a conservative social group, and one that for the past century had been accustomed to consider paint and powder a badge of whoredom. In 1894, the young Max Beerbohm contributed a satirical "Defence of Cosmetics" to the first number of the decadent magazine *The Yellow Book*. The article—which contended, improbably, that "enamelling" would confine women to the home, because the slightest movement would crack the painstakingly applied paint surface—outraged his readers, most of whom, like Max himself, hated cosmetics and would have been mortified had their womenfolk used them.

In fact the piece was a spoof. Max's real view was that "only women of the street resorted to rouge."[30] But the fury he unleashed among the supposedly unshockable readership of *The Yellow Book* showed that this remained a delicate area. And in 1908 the stigma still persisted. Customers came, but only after taking careful precautions. They found the prospect of beautification too tempting to resist, but still worried about the social consequences. "Many a time I watched from an upstairs window as [a customer] arrived, alone, in a covered carriage which dropped her discreetly at the corner of Grafton street," Rubinstein remembered. "There, with her veil lowered, she would wait for a few moments, out of sight, she thought, until the street was free of passers-by. Then came the last few steps to the salon. . . . More than once I wondered what would have happened if any two of my furtive visitors had stepped simultaneously from their carriages and recognized each other."[31]

The new salon did not yet offer eye paint, rouge, or lipstick, though in her attic "kitchen" Helena had begun to experiment with tinted and perfumed powder to supplant the chalky rice powder then in vogue, which gave faces a peculiar whitewashed look. Although Queen Alexandra was rumored to wear cosmetics in the evening, only actresses really knew the art of makeup as it would later develop. They passed on useful tips to the stagestruck Helena, whose memoirs record many London evenings spent at the theater, at that time perhaps the only place where makeup was habitually and openly used. After trying out the new techniques herself, she would pass them on, in turn, to her bolder clients. In her correspondence with

Rosa Hollay, who would become her London manageress in 1914, she mentions a "prep . . . called stage white for arms and neck, it positively does not come off."[32] She also offered skin analysis and facial treatments, including facial peels for bad cases of acne, the province of Frau Doktor List from Vienna.

These treatments were expensive—ten guineas (nearly $1,600 in today's money) for a course of twelve, or £200 ($32,000) for regular weekly visits the year round. But despite the expense, and their initial nervousness, the customers kept coming. Within a year there were over a thousand regular clients on the books, and in London, as in Australia, the money poured in. Later, when life had become less easy, she wistfully looked back to those early days. "We took in before the war about £30,000 a year and expenses were about 7 [thousand],"[33] she told Rosa Hollay in 1923.

In 1909, Helena became pregnant. "I had not consciously longed for motherhood," was how she put it in her memoirs; in fact, her first reaction was fury.[34] Titus, though, was pleased, and in 1912 their first child, a son, Roy, was joined by another, Horace (an anglicization of Helena's father's name, Herzl). "The nursery teas with the boys, the evenings of gaiety with Edward [Titus] and our friends—all of these memories fill me even today with nostalgia," she wrote fifty years later,[35] exhausting the joys of motherhood in three lines before going on to devote several pages to her preferred topic, interior decoration. She was fond enough of her boys in the abstract—various somewhat stilted photographs show them together. But as many career women since have found, not only do the prosaic realities of child care tend to pall beside the constant excitement of a successful professional life, it is famously hard to combine the two. Helena's great rival Elizabeth Arden had no children. Nor, for that matter, did her friend Coco Chanel, the most successful career woman in Paris. Her own summation in

1930 was, "Maternity, I believe, gives a richness to a woman's life which no other satisfaction can replace, yet most women, during this generation at least, are finding that the home and the nursery are not enough."[36] Thirty years later Betty Friedan came to the same conclusion; her book on the subject, *The Feminine Mystique*, would become the catalyst for women's liberation. It is doubtful, however, whether Friedan or anyone else would have recommended subordinating family life to business in quite the single-minded way Helena did.

Despite her domestic ties—or perhaps because of them—this was a period of frenetic traveling for Helena. She visited Australia to keep Ceska up to the mark, and shuttled, when in Europe, between London and Paris. Helped by Titus, a cultured man who knew many writers and artists, she began to buy paintings and sculptures, and developed what would become a lifelong addiction to the Paris couture houses. In Paris, too, she acquired the severe and elegant hairstyle that would henceforth be her trademark, an uncompromising black chignon (later, she had it rinsed blue-black every six weeks) that set her where she would henceforth remain: outside time.

It soon became clear that Paris could use its own Salon de Beauté Valaze. The couture business was becoming an important industry, with houses such as Worth and Lanvin beginning to show collections instead of simply making clothes for individual women, and Helena realized that the couture clients were also, potentially, hers. They needed to know how to make themselves up in a way that would set off their new gowns to maximum effect, and she could show them the way. In 1908 a herbal skin-products business came up for sale on the rue Saint-Honoré. Helena snapped it up, together with its stock, and set about its transformation. In 1911, she established her first factory, just outside Paris at Saint-Cloud, and in 1912, she relocated to France. Her sister Manka took over the London salon, while Helena, Titus, and the boys moved to Montparnasse. Madame had had enough of London and nursery teas.

In Paris, although aristocratic society was every bit as closed and snobbish as in London, the raffish, the artistic, and the talented constituted a glittering *haute bohème*. If you were gifted enough—like Diaghilev, like Picasso, like Chanel—you were lionized even though (like Diaghilev) you were perpetually broke, or (like Chanel) notoriously a *femme entretenue*. And since artists must sell their work in order to live, rich patrons in search of art to buy could also become members of this charmed circle. Madame met everyone, including Marcel Proust—"Nebbishy looking . . . He smelt of moth-balls, wore a fur-lined coat to the ground—How could I have known that he was going to be so famous?" He quizzed her about makeup. "Would a duchess use rouge? Did demimondaines put kohl on their eyes? How should I know?"[37] She preferred Chanel, that rarity of rarities—a self-made woman like herself. Why, Madame once asked the great designer, had she never married the Duke of Westminster, who had been her lover for so many years? "What, and become his third duchess? No," returned Coco, "I am Mademoiselle Chanel and I shall remain so, just as you will always be Madame Rubinstein. These are our rightful titles."[38]

Parisians, unlike Londoners, had no qualms about being seen visiting a beauty salon. Particularly popular was Madame's Swedish masseuse, Ulla. "You know, it wasn't just an ordinary massage, they did little extra things," Madame told Patrick O'Higgins; a hint of what those "extra things" might have been is perhaps to be found in her 1915 request to her London manageress, Rosa Hollay, for some small massage vibrators to be sent to New York, where she had then just opened her first salon.[39] Colette, who had created a scandal when it emerged that she, not her husband Willy, had written the sexy Claudine books, and who received free treatments because of her publicity value, was particularly keen on Ulla's massages. "Massage is a woman's sacred duty," Colette announced after her first visit. "The women of France owe it to themselves—without it, how can they *hope* to keep a lover!"[40] Ulla was soon fully booked, while Colette was so taken with the idea of beauty salons that years later she opened one of her own. (It was not a success. Her clients did not emerge noticeably beautified and did not return.)

In August of 1914 Madame's European progress was interrupted. War was declared—and who knew how it would affect business, or what it would leave in its wake? Fortunately for her, however, one huge potential market remained unaffected. America was booming, and quite remote from the carnage. Titus held American nationality—and so, as his wife, did Helena. Everything pointed westward. She made a quick swoop on her London bank, appointed a new manageress, Rosa Hollay, to look after Grafton Street (where she would soon be joined by Ceska), and in October 1914 sailed with Manka for New York, leaving Titus and the two little boys in Paris to pack up the artworks and follow in her wake.

III

In Australia and Europe, Madame had been a pioneer; in America she was pushing at an open door. A touch of lipstick made a girl feel good. Above all, it made her feel liberated. Participants in the big women's suffrage marches held in New York in 1912 and 1913 were told to wear white shirtwaists—and red lipstick, the badge of independence. Domestic production of manufactured toiletries was nudging $17,000,000.[41] Influential women's magazines such as *Vogue* and *Vanity Fair* were eager to accept beauticians' advertisements and to fill their columns with copy about fashionable persons and doings. And a galaxy of potent new role models was about to enter the public consciousness, as the budding film industry created a goddesshood of idealized beauties for whom heavy makeup was a working necessity. Helena Rubinstein liked to claim that she had taught Theda Bara, the notorious femme fatale who became known as "The Vamp," how to apply her eye makeup. That was dubious, to say the least. What was incontestable was the effect Theda Bara's makeup had on public ideas of what was acceptable and desirable. By the time Helena Rubinstein arrived in New York, every restaurant, hotel, and store of any importance kept a supply of cosmetics in their dressing rooms or bathrooms.

The results of this enthusiasm were not subtle. In 1910, a *New York World* reporter sitting in a café window on Forty-second Street and Broadway noted, "Eyelids can't be painted too blue nor lashes too heavily beaded."[42] Madame was not impressed. "When I first came to America about ten years ago, I was shocked . . . by the number of young girls who were excessively made up," she confided to the *American Magazine*.[43] By contrast she offered a more subtle European exclusiveness. Madame Helena Rubinstein, "the accepted adviser in beauty matters to Royalty, Aristocracy and the great Artistes of Europe," was ready, for a price, to show them how it should really be done. And everyone wanted to learn. Not just rich ladies but "Stenographers, clerks, and even little office girls" would be interested in what she had to offer.[44]

After a continental railroad tour, to pick out the cities they would target, Helena and Manka returned to New York, where

Madame began the now familiar business of locating a suitable site for a salon—her first in the New World. "We haven't found a place yet, it seems to be very very difficult. Indeed there are thousands of places empty as things are not good in general. But as soon as I want one it costs £2500 a year," she grumbled in her first letter to Rosa Hollay (adding: "See that you are economical with everything, even electric light"[45]). She settled upon a house at 15 East Forty-ninth Street, and in February 1915 a half-page advertisement appeared in *Vogue* announcing that "A Famous European 'House of Beauty'" had opened its doors in New York. "At Madame Rubinstein's Maison de Beauté Valaze treatments are administered for the removal of wrinkles, crowsfeet, coarseness of skin, puffiness under the eyes, blackheads, and other complexion defects. The New York salon radiates the same elegance, the same Spirit of Beauty, as her famous salons in London and Paris." Helleu's 1908 etching of Madame looking fey in an aigrette adorned the advertisement. It was the first of what would eventually total twenty-seven portraits by the day's leading artists, from Marie Laurencin to Pavel Tchelitchew, Raoul Dufy to Salvador Dalí, that reflected both Rubinstein's bottomless narcissism and the central role her image played in her business until the very end. In 1955 Picasso sketched her, but never worked up the portrait. "How old are you, Helena?" he asked her, to which she replied, evasive as ever, "Older than you, Pablo."[46] Three years later the British artist Graham Sutherland portrayed her as a *monstre sacré*, a craggy, baton-wielding field marshal weirdly attired in embroidered satin by Balenciaga, with kohl-rimmed eyes and thinning, boot-blacked hair, the whole topped off by a six-strand pearl necklace and Ping-Pong–ball diamond drop earrings. She was then eighty-six. (Sutherland was especially impressed by her makeup skills.

He had made a number of preliminary drawings, but the day he began the actual painting, Madame had a fall. Left with two black eyes, she disguised them by applying copious rouge below them and green eyeshadow above. Sutherland was ecstatic, and at once abandoned all his earlier drawings. "She's a completely different person. It's amazing what really dramatic eye make-up can do!"[47])

Vogue ran two long articles in the months following the New York salon's opening. They extolled the facial treatments of "a certain skin-specialist who has a small and smart establishment on 5th Avenue and gives her personal attention to each and every patron," describing at length the wonders of the new salon and its "moving spirit . . . obviously a continental, and as chic as her charming individuality and Poiret costumes can make her."[48] Then they got down to the real business: all the various balms, lotions, rouges, powders, skin foods, and "beauty grains," together with their prices, which were considerable. The smallest box of powder cost $1 (just over $21 today), while a large pot of cream rouge cost $6.50. In a city where most handbags were sold with specially fitted sets of cosmetic accessories—a powder puff, a rouge box, an eyebrow pencil—how could women possibly be persuaded to spend extra money on Helena Rubinstein's pricey offerings?

The answer was that the high price was an essential part of the treatment. Even if a woman could not afford costly facials and massages, she could still buy indulgence in the form of the same expensive cosmetics rich women used, and vicariously join the wealthy. When a woman paid $6 for a pot of Water Lily Cleansing Cream, "a rejuvenating cream de luxe for the ultra fastidious woman, containing the youthifying essence of Water Lily buds," the mere possession of such a luxury helped her feel both youthified and richer.*

Success, however, created its own problems. Buyers at stores all over the country clamored for her lines, but if Helena Rubinstein products became available in every corner drugstore rather than through her salons, then half the selling value—the half that derived from their exclusivity—would be lost. If the customer paid top prices, she expected the personal attention that went with them. As the advertisements put it, "A visit to [Madame Rubinstein's] sanctum or an inquiry by letter solves many a little heartache that may be due to some shortcoming in appearance. . . ." But Madame could not be everywhere at once, nor could she open a salon in every city in America. How, then, was her special brand of personal service to be maintained?

The solution, she decided, was to set up mini-salons in leading department stores, staffed by specially trained and uniformed women and made worthwhile because the condition of being allowed to stock Helena Rubinstein products was that her whole range had to be carried. When a suitably substantial order was received, Helena or Manka or both would travel to the store to train the sales staff—the famous "Rubinstein ladies"—in the appropriate introduction, promotion, and sales techniques.

"I did not realise what I was letting myself in for!" Madame wrote later. "At night we trained the assistants to be beauty

* A male writer, trying out skin creams in 2010 for the purposes of an article, confirmed this potent effect. "After a few weeks of my trial . . . a habit has formed, and I find myself using the creams and potions without question. I still don't believe my skin looks different . . . but . . . it's not really about skin at all, it's about self-perception. Using skincare products every day starts to become worthwhile largely because I know they are expensive; like most of us I have been conditioned to associate well-being with expenditure, and I feel—against my better judgment—as if I am experiencing luxury." (Michael Hann, "Spot the Difference," *Guardian*, January 25, 2010.)

consultants and teachers, giving them a sound knowledge of my preparations and their use, to be imparted to their assistants, and to customers. For eighteen out of the twenty-four hours we were either travelling between one city and another or actively working. We lived out of our suitcases like actresses in a theatrical touring company."[49] It was hard work, but she loved it. What better way to spend one's life? As she put it, "My only recreation is work."[50] Then and always, it was the literal truth.

Titus, meanwhile, was left holding the babies. "We were naturally very glad to hear from you and of your safe arrival. There is practically a little kindergarten class here," he wrote her in the summer of 1919. The war had ended, and Madame had left for Europe to survey the remnants of her French and English businesses, leaving him in charge not just of Roy and Horace, now aged nine and seven, but Manka's son, Johnnie, and a young cousin, Helena Silberfeld. "With a house so full of children it is difficult to have a little time to oneself."[51] As though she needed telling! Writing at midnight from Paris, where she had occupied a spare hour laying linoleum herself, she commented: "If Mr. Titus had been here I would not have made any progress whatsoever as he wouldn't have allowed me to work."[52]

By 1924 Titus had had enough of this life. When he was unavailable, the boys were looked after by what their mother called "nice women"—the kind of impecunious ladies who in a previous age would have become governesses, and who, like governesses, were both better educated and cheaper than housekeepers, nurses, or maids.[53] Leaving his sons to their uncertain care, he returned to Paris, his favorite city, where he would remain from then on. He had many old friends there, both from prewar days and from New York, which during the war had become a sort of Paris-in-exile.

Artists such as Francis Picabia and the then little-known

Marcel Duchamp, desperate to get away from war-torn Europe, had crossed the Atlantic in 1916 to find themselves American celebrities as a result of the great 1913 Armory Show of modern art. Lionized by wealthy collectors, they took their places at the center of a decadent, nihilistic, and blackly exhilarating whirl in which everyone desperately tried to block out what was happening across the Atlantic. But when the war ended, Paris became once more the center of art and excitement. The exiles returned, and Titus knew them all. With a mortgage from Helena's property company Franc-Am Ltd., he opened a bookshop on rue Delambre. He sold rare books and manuscripts on the ground floor, and ran a small avant-garde publishing house, Black Manikin Press, catering to the anglophone colony, from the rooms above.

Meanwhile, Madame was expanding her repertoire. She began to produce lipstick and other colored cosmetics and became interested, too, in plastic surgery and the famous (and soon to become infamous) monkey-gland extracts, both of which promised more tangible youthifying possibilities than water lily buds. Monkey glands had originally been the province of Dr. Serge Voronoff, who had observed that eunuchs aged faster than men still in possession of their balls and had concluded that grafting pieces of monkey testicle onto human testes might not only increase recipients' potency but might also slow the aging process.* By extension, he was now touting

---

* A cocktail called the Monkey Gland still reminds us of this bizarre (though in its day highly popular) fad. The ingredients are:

1 ounce gin

1 ounce orange juice

1 dash grenadine

1 dash anise (probably originally absinthe; Pernod or Benedictine are often substituted now)

the possibility that grafting monkey ovaries onto women might produce similarly beneficial effects. A Dr. Kapp, whom Helena had met during her initial whirlwind tour of European skin specialists in 1905, and who had since been supplying her with creams and jellies, had become enthusiastic about this idea, and she was anxious to keep him on board. "Put down all sorts of imaginary things every month [i.e., as expenses] and I will take the money and pay Dr Kapp," she instructed Rosa Hollay from New York in 1920. Mrs. Hollay was also to look out for potential surgery guinea pigs. "Do you know anyone who has a scab or a crooked nose or something?"[54]

IV

By 1928, Helena Rubinstein had become a New York institution. The opening of her new salon at 8 East Fifty-seventh Street, on the site of Collis P. Huntington's old mansion, was marked by an article in *The New Yorker*, carefully orchestrated by Madame to enhance her reputation for ice-cool acumen and elegant eccentricity. Her original salon "ranked" (the article reported) "even then, as one of the finest of all such ateliers in New York." But she wanted a better place, and one she owned rather than rented. The palace of the Southern Pacific Railway magnate Collis P. Huntington, recently deceased, caught her eye: she took it instantly, "without pausing to inquire just how many thousands, or hundreds of thousands, of dollars the building could cost. She saw to it later that it wouldn't be too many. Madame is impulsive but canny. . . ." When the salon was finished, she told the interviewer, she had to spend three days in a sanitarium to recover. "Always after the opening of a new salon she has a nervous breakdown; she expects it and looks forward to it. It is part of her schedule."[55]

Decided, imperturbable, astute, *elegant*—such was the public Madame Rubinstein. Her most potent product, as she well knew, was herself. Eagerly scanning Helena Rubinstein's advertisements, emblazoned as they invariably were with pictures of the eponymous founder—ageless, elegant, beholden to no man—women hoped that if they did as she advised, they might become as successful as she was. Salon patrons would often plead for some extra-special beauty cream not available to the general public. If the customer insisted, she would be sold an unlabeled jar for $50, with the whispered assurance that it was "Madame's own cream."[56]

But beneath the visible surface seethed a quite different person, assailed by anxieties, doubts, fury, and hypochondria. She had created this vast sprawling empire ("There are remote cities which have Rubinstein agencies where there are not even Ford agencies," *Vanity Fair* marveled); everyone depended upon her for instructions, for policy, above all for money; and yet she felt, at every moment, as though the whole laboriously constructed edifice might come tumbling down and she would find herself in poverty once more. Her favorite photographs showed her in her white coat in a laboratory, one of the great women scientists of the world engaged in a ceaseless search for more potent ingredients. But she knew, even if she did not choose to remember, that her vaunted medical studies amounted to a two-month tour of visits to selected practitioners. At any moment some prying journalist might find her out and expose her for a quack.

One solution to these constant worries—the solution favored by Titus—was to bow out, sell her business, and live on the proceeds. Eventually the temptation was too much, and on December 11, 1928, Lehman Brothers acquired the American arm of Helena Rubinstein. It netted Madame, who retained the European and Australian interests, a cool $7,300,000—over $84 million today. All her worries should have been at an end.

On the contrary, they got worse. Deprived of the work that had taken up the greater part of her time, she was bored and frustrated. Impotent to intervene, she had to watch as Lehman's sales strategy, which she had endorsed—to expand into a more mid-range market—came unstuck in the wake of the 1929 Wall Street crash. The upmarket end of the trade was unaffected. In fact, sales rose: the first example of the now well-documented "lipstick effect," in which, during hard times, women who otherwise would have bought an expensive outfit buy a nice lipstick instead.* But lower-priced items did less well, and the new range of mass-market goods tainted Helena Rubinstein's upmarket outlets by association. "I knew that they would make a mess of it," she told Patrick O'Higgins. "What do bankers know about the beauty business? Except that it can make money for them. After they bought me out they tried to go mass; to sell my products in every grocery store. Pfft! The idea wasn't bad. But the timing was all wrong."[57]

In October 1930, she became ill—struck with appendicitis in Vienna, Titus said. But this was no mere appendicitis. The following May found her still confined to bed at her sister Ceska's London flat, and boiling with frustration. Ironically, Titus, for the first time in his life, was enjoying considerable professional success. In the spring of 1929 his Black Manikin Press published D. H. Lawrence's *Lady Chatterley's Lover*,

* This effect was seen in New York after the 2001 terrorist attacks, and again during the winter of 2008–9, a time of deep recession, when lipstick sales rose as much as 20 percent, year-on-year. ("Red Alert: Lipstick Wars Are Coming," *Observer*, January 17, 2010.)

which went into three printings within a year. And in 1930 he published another smash hit, the English translation of *Kiki's Memoirs*. Kiki was Man Ray's mistress, and her racy tale came with embellishments by the Montparnasse Americans—saucy photos by Man Ray, and an introduction by Ernest Hemingway. Admittedly, Helena was fabulously wealthy and Titus still relied on her subventions, but for the first time in their married life, with Helena on a low and Titus doing well, the balance tilted his way.

When she fell ill, Titus was kind and attentive, frequently coming over to visit her in London. After all the years of quarrels and separations, was it possible that their marriage might yet be salvaged? They were both over sixty, he pointed out—retirement age, when people think of drawing a pension and putting their feet up. The Lehman deal had given Helena more money than even she could ever spend. Wasn't it time to relax a little?

Depressed by this prospect, she hatched a new plan. The combination of the financial downturn and Lehman's mishandling meant that shares in Helena Rubinstein, Inc., had sunk from $60 to $3. Why not try to buy back control? She could set the business on its feet again, and still be left with a healthy profit. Some of her old board members still remained in place. One of them slipped her a list of shareholders—mostly women—and she wrote to every one, explaining how the business's only chance of survival lay in restoring it to the hands of its creator and convincing them to let her use their proxy votes. Meanwhile she bought whatever shares came on the market, building up a considerable holding.

The whole process had to be conducted discreetly, and for a while it was uncertain whether or not it would succeed. A letter from Titus during this edgy period shows that he, for one, hoped it would not. "Look here, outside of your wounded pride, which is not a wound that can be healed, if you do not win, you will gain something more valuable," he wrote.

> *You have two fine boys, whom you do not enjoy possessing, you have a husband if you would only once begin to really believe in him, who loves you truly and sincerely, whatever his faults are, you finally have yourself, to whom you have never, never given a real chance. These are the only things that substantially matter. The children's life, your life and mine, the combined life of the four of us. Everything else are only things, just things. . . .*[58]

Vain hopes! *Things*, as he should have known, were all that mattered to Helena. An expenditure of $1.5 million, combined with the proxies, netted majority control. Madame was in the saddle once more, with a net profit of $6 million after the sale and buyback. Lehman's furiously issued a communiqué denouncing this brilliant maneuver as "financially illiterate," but she had trounced them handsomely, and recovered her health and happiness in the process. "Ahead of me once more was the lonely treadmill of work," she sighed in her memoir.[59] And with that, miraculously restored, she sailed for New York.

CHAPTER TWO

The Authoritarian

I

> When people say at a dinner-party, "You're so lucky to be in cosmetics!" I say, "Yes, but you had to realize that in 1907."
>
> —Liliane Bettencourt-Schueller, 1987

Rue Saint-Honoré, where Helena Rubinstein opened her first Paris salon in 1908, is one of Paris's most glamorous thoroughfares. But the backstreets that surround it are dark and dingy. Among the least prepossessing is a little corridor, called rue d'Alger, that links rue Saint-Honoré with rue de Rivoli. It was here, however, while Madame bustled about installing her stock and arranging couches and curtains in her new boutique, that the true revolution in cosmetics was taking shape. At the back of number

4's dim courtyard a young chemist named Eugène Schueller had rented a two-room mezzanine to serve as a combination of laboratory, bedroom, and kitchen. He was working to isolate the world's first safe artificial hair dye, and by the time Rubinstein opened her salon, he was almost there. For more than two years he had worked night and day, watching his savings diminish, cooking his food on the Bunsen burner he used for his chemical experiments. Finally he established his formula. He gave it the provisional name L'Auréole, after a hairstyle popular in 1905, the year he had begun his researches. Soon he would change this name to L'Oréal. Eighty years later, his company would swallow Madame's.

Like Helena Rubinstein, Eugène Schueller entered the beauty business at the optimum moment, when the market was ready but still untapped. Like her, it would make him rich. Like her, he spoke to the universal fear of aging, to every woman's dread of wrinkles and grey hairs. But in every other respect, they, like their products, were utterly different.

If you believed Helena Rubinstein's advertising, her various creams and lotions were miracle balms that banished blemishes and left the user's skin blissfully free of wrinkles. And since that was what her customers ached to believe, they convinced themselves that it was true—or, at the very least, that the creams prevented deterioration. There was never any proof, however, that this was actually so. By the 1930s a large number of firms were marketing beauty products of various kinds, and in 1934 the pressure group Consumer Research organized a survey of them, the first attempt at any systematic analysis of what beauty creams did. It showed that most beauty products did not live up to their claims, while some were even dangerous. None of the creams marketed by Helena Rubinstein or her competitors had, Consumer Research reported, any measurable effect on wrinkles, while the notion that skin needed three or four different types of cream—cold cream, cleansing cream, vanishing cream, and skin food—was a myth invented to increase sales. Worse, the glycerine frequently used in vanishing cream was a common allergen that often caused rashes.

Beauticians like Rubinstein and her peers thus trod a wobbly psychological tightrope. On the one hand they shared their customers' profound desire to believe the propaganda. On the other, they knew—none better!—that what went into their products was really nothing but the same old less-than-magical stuff women had always used, repackaged and skillfully sold. The Consumer Research survey therefore filled them with dread. On the day its results were published, in a book called *Skin Deep*, the cosmetics industry threw a party for magazine editors at the Pierre Hotel in Manhattan. The captive audience was harangued for an hour and a half on the wickedness of reformers and consumers' research organizations and the irresponsible anticosmetic prejudice of the American Medical Association. It was magazines' duty, the speaker perorated, to help preserve a million-dollar industry, now irresponsibly imperiled. Meanwhile the worst offenders hastened to change their more offensive products—Max Factor removing barium sulphate colors, which caused rashes, from its lipstick lines, Pond's discontinuing the use of rice starch, which clogged the pores, in its face powder. But there was little they could do to make products such as face creams perform the wonders promised in the advertising copy—and they knew it.

As it happened, they need not have worried. The public bought the book, which swiftly rose up the bestseller charts—and went on with their usual cosmetic routines. No exposé, however painstaking, could outweigh the magical allure of hope. A reader from California spoke for many. *Skin Deep* had "quite shattered my illusions as to the efficacy of cosmetics," she wrote. But despite being "a college graduate and a schoolteacher, I don't really so much believe what saleswomen tell me as I hope that what they tell me will come true."[1] This blind and unquenchable desire—a desire that she herself shared—was the foundation of Madame's fortune.

L'Oréal was a different matter entirely. Like Helena Rubinstein, Eugène Schueller owed his success to both luck and talent. But his talent was for science, and his luck to have been presented with an opening that, left to himself, he would never have espied. In the beauty industry, whose claims routinely bore little if any relation to reality, his product was unique in that both he and his customers knew it would always do precisely what the package promised. L'Oréal worked: it would dye your hair any color you wished—and safely. And this was possible because of perhaps the greatest of all the differences between Eugène Schueller and Helena Rubinstein: he was educated, where she was not. The foundation of her business was folk wisdom; Schueller's business rested on science. What was applicable to hair dye was applicable elsewhere, too. He could make other products, in other industries, and realize *their* possibilities as he had realized L'Oréal's. It was simply a matter of time.

II

EUGÈNE SCHUELLER, BORN IN 1881, was nine years younger than Helena Rubinstein. He, too, came from a poor background. His grandfather was a shoemaker, his father a pastry cook, his mother a baker's assistant. The Schueller family originated in Alsace, the much-disputed Rhineland province on the borders of France and Germany. Eugène's father, Charles, who considered himself French and did not wish to be a German subject, had come to Paris with his wife, Amélie, after the 1870 Franco-Prussian War, when Germany occupied Alsace.

They bought a little patisserie at 124 rue du Cherche-Midi, in Montparnasse, where five sons would be born.* Only one, Eugène, made it past infancy.[2] And for this one surviving child the Schuellers would make any sacrifice. He was bright, and they determined to give him a good education, whatever it might cost. That way he might escape the hand-to-mouth poverty that constrained their own lives, forcing them to work from six every morning (five on Sundays) until ten at night (on Sundays till eleven) 365 days a year.

Young Eugène was expected to take his share of the work. From the age of four he buttered tart tins and shelled almonds before leaving for school in the morning. The habit he then acquired, of early rising in order to lead two or more parallel existences, would remain with him. Later, when he gave lectures or interviews, he often described himself as "Monsieur 6,000 hours" (2,000 hours a year being a normal conscientious working life). "Do you know what a 6,000 hours man is?" he demanded during a 1954 lecture at the Paris École de Commerce. "It's someone who will work more than sixteen hours a day, 365 days a year, without Saturdays, Sundays or holidays."[3]

His daily routine showed what this work involved. He rose at four, and for two hours, in his dressing gown, addressed all the questions raised by colleagues the previous day. Then came an hour's walk in the company of a physical-training instructor, followed by breakfast, when he read the papers. By the time

* Now a small fruit and grocery store.

his secretary arrived at eight a pile of notes and letters awaited her, each with the reply indicated in the margin. This secretary was the object of his pride and admiration: Schueller, possibly because he was rather deaf, could never believe anything was real unless it was written down, and she could take dictation at the speed of light.[4] Another pile had penciled reminders of the replies he would dictate; a third had been read and thought about. Other replies were decided upon while the first batch were dictated. This went on until midday, when his Rolls arrived to take him to the Valentine paint factory at Gennevilliers—one of four businesses he was running in 1954, the year he gave the interview setting out this routine. (The others were L'Oréal, Monsavon soap, and a magazine called *Votre Beauté*.) Office work continued during the drive. At Valentine, he conferred with divisional heads until three p.m., lunching during these discussions on a grapefruit and a cup of tea. Then he left for Monsavon, taking with him a briefcase full of notes, and leaving at five with a second briefcase full. Then it was on to *Votre Beauté* and a third briefcase, and thence to the offices of L'Oréal, where he stayed until nine p.m. He went to bed at midnight, and slept four hours. But even then his work continued: "My best working-time is when I'm asleep," he told business journalist Merry Bromberger. "During the afternoon I often listen to people without knowing how to respond. And then during the night I dream I'm in a meeting at L'Oréal, or in the lab with my chemists, and when I get up in the morning most of the necessary decisions have been made." And so another day began.

He remembered his early life, which had instilled this habit, as "very rough and hard on us." But it produced enough money for his parents to send him to a private school, where he got on well. In 1890, however, the Panama Canal Company, in which his father had invested his small savings, failed. The shop had to close, and there could be no more private school. M. Schueller found a job in a big patisserie at Levallois-Perret, a working-class district on Paris's northwest outskirts, where Eugène attended the local state school.

And here, unexpectedly, Eugène's private education resumed. Levallois abuts rich, leafy Neuilly, where the patisserie supplied a fashionable school, the Collège Sainte-Croix de Neuilly. M. Schueller made a deal with its head: if he made part payment in cakes, he could just afford a place there for his clever son.

It was a life-changing moment—perhaps the most important thing that ever happened to Eugène Schueller. The Collège Sainte-Croix was a feeder school for the elite Lycée Condorcet, and after that the way was open to the highly competitive *grandes écoles*—the Polytechnique, the Centrale, the Ponts et Chaussées, the École Normale Supérieure, whose graduates run France. He was all set to join the ruling class.

He duly made it to Condorcet, where the family scraped together enough to pay the fees. He discovered a bent for science, took his baccalaureate, and was hoping for the École Polytechnique or the École Centrale when his father was wiped out yet again. This time the family, including the sixteen-year-old Eugène, had to return to Alsace, and the German rule they had earlier rejected. His mother kept a market stall, helped by his aunt, whom Eugène remembered watching as she walked to the market barefoot, carrying baskets of goods weighing ten or fifteen kilos on her head. Eugène was apprenticed to a patissier, and also had to help his mother in the market, which he hated. A gifted publicist, he always loathed the business of face-to-face selling.

He endured this life for a couple of years, and then could

bear it no longer. Returning to Paris, he entered the Institute for Applied Chemistry, paying his fees by working nights as a patissier. This was chemistry's heyday: Mendeleyev had recently formulated the periodic table of the elements, and Marie Curie would soon isolate radium. Eugène graduated top of his class, and Victor Auger, one of his professors, who had become a friend, found him an instructor's post at the Sorbonne. The way ahead was clear. He would become a research chemist, and, eventually, a professor. Had he continued on this route, his friend Frédéric Joliot-Curie later remarked, he would undoubtedly have made some significant discovery.[5]

But he found academic life disappointing—"dusty," as he phrased it.[6] The place, he said, felt like a cemetery. No one in France was much interested in science, there weren't enough materials at the lab—even the gas supply was unreliable. And no one seemed to work. Accustomed from childhood to a punishing schedule, he felt cheated by academe's comparatively relaxed pace. Why could one not get into the lab before it officially opened? Why did one have to leave when the bell rang? He would climb in and out through the window before and after hours, sometimes starting work at six a.m., sometimes staying on late into the evening—hours his colleagues inexplicably preferred to spend with their friends and families, or even in bed. He soon left for something less lackadaisical, a job at the Pharmacie Centrale de France, the standard manufacturer of chemical products. He remained there for three years, becoming head of the research laboratory and eventually head of the chemical service and secretary to the editorial board of its publication, the *Grande Revue Scientifique*.

Some of the people he met during this trajectory would remain his friends for life. One was Jacques Sadoul, a friend from Condorcet who later became a Communist, and with whom he would conduct an experimental "free university" before World War I. Another was Fred Joliot, who later became Marie Curie's son-in-law (and who added the Curie name to his own). Joliot and Schueller met at L'Arcouest, a tiny Breton village where the distinguished Sorbonne historian Charles Seignobos kept a cottage. Around the village, in a scatter of houses and rented rooms, a group of all ages known to all as "Sorbonne-sur-mer"—consisting of professors, their families, and their students—passed happy summers sailing, swimming, and living a quasi-communal existence. "A reporter suddenly finding himself in the midst of the peaceful group would have been overjoyed," Marie Curie's daughter, Eve, remembered. "He would have had to take great care not to step on some member of the Institut de France lazily stretched out on the ground, or not to kick a Nobel Prize winner. . . . These customs of children or savages, living half-naked in the water and the wind, were later to become the fashion and to intoxicate all classes from the richest to the poorest. But in those days . . . they aroused the shocked criticisms of the uninitiated. In advance of the fashion . . . we discovered beach life, swimming races, sun-bathing, camping out on deserted islands, the tranquil immodesty of sport."[7]

Eugène became part of the group at the invitation of Victor Auger. It was his first introduction to the notion that life, or parts of it, might be spent having fun, and he adored it. Ever after, recreation, for him, meant L'Arcouest and its pastimes. In 1926 he built himself a luxurious house there on a high spit of land that had once been a beautiful orchard. He kept his own yacht, the *Edelweiss*; Ambre Solaire was invented to counter the sunburn he suffered while sailing it. Sorbonne-sur-mer did not approve. The plot of land had first been noticed, and coveted, by another member of the group, and they found the house pretentious—there was even a colonnade,

Fred Joliot remarked with disgust. Worse, he fenced his estate off, something unheard-of.[8] Schueller didn't care. He might love L'Arcouest and its pastimes, but once he became rich, the simple, communal life was not his idea of pleasure.

The breezy outdoor life at L'Arcouest also set a benchmark for an ideal of feminine beauty. The magazine *Votre Beauté*, which he established in 1933, always included articles on the healthy sporting life, and promoted a tanned and glowing look that related more to fitness and exercise than paint and powder—something rather unusual in the 1930s.

But academic life, even as enjoyed by Sorbonne-sur-mer, was not for him, and in 1905, after only two years as an instructor, he glimpsed a way of escape. A hairdresser came to the Pharmacie Central, offering to pay fifty francs a month to someone who would help him find a safe and reliable artificial hair dye. Schueller eagerly volunteered. A harmless hair dye might not be what Fred Joliot meant by an "important discovery," but it was an interesting problem. Nobody had tackled it before, because hair dye was, as Schueller put it, "such a small part of the scheme of things."[9] That was to say, it was women's frippery and therefore of little interest to male chemists. Indeed, they retained this blind spot even after it became clear that fortunes were to be made in the beauty business. In 1935, the Consumer Research book *Skin Deep* declared, "So far as we have been able to learn, there is no hair dye which is both certainly safe and at the same time effective."[10] In fact, such a hair dye had by then existed for nearly thirty years—but it was available only in France, and no American chemist had concerned himself with this problem.

Schueller discovered that hair dyes were based upon four groups of substances: anilines, silver nitrate, pyrogallic acid, and lead acetate. The first group was the most dangerous. Aniline derivatives are very soluble, going through many intermediate stages before forming the lacquers which give the hair its new color, and some of these derivatives are extremely caustic and may eventually enter the bloodstream, affecting the white cells and giving rise to chemical eczema. Anilines were, nevertheless, the most popular base for hair dyes, because they were easy to prepare. Their dangers were known, but as only 3 to 5 percent of users were adversely affected, they were sold widely. Silver nitrate and lead acetate were less dangerous compounds, though still not altogether safe, but they turned the hair raven-black. "You could see it was artificial a hundred yards away," Schueller remarked. Such blatant artificiality scandalized people: Eugène's own mother would point her finger at a neighbor. "She's using hair dye! And we thought she was a decent woman!" He finished by writing so many articles on the subject for the *Grande Revue Scientifique* that he eventually made a little book out of them: *De l'Innocuité des teintures pour cheveux.* (It is not dated, but since among the author's many listed qualifications—Ingénieur-Chimiste, Diplômé de l'Université de Paris, Ex-préparateur à la Sorbonne, Ex-chef du Laboratoire des Recherches de la Pharmacie Centrale de France—he included "Chevalier de la Légion d'Honneur," it must have been published after World War I, when he received this decoration.)

The hair-dye job meant working at the hairdresser's salon in the evenings, from eight till eleven, at the end of an already unimaginably long day. Eugène's excessive appetite for hard work had not endeared him to his boss at the Institute, and he soon found himself exiled to a factory at Plaine-St.-Denis, out in the northern suburbs. Work there started at 6:30 a.m. There was as yet no Metro. To arrive in time, he had to get up at 4:30 and take a tram. And at the end of the day, the hairdresser's salon was on the other side of Paris.

It was not long before Eugène fell out with the hairdresser—in one account because the hairdresser took no interest in the work, in another because Eugène wanted to claim all the credit for himself. The probable truth was that Eugène's acute business antennae sensed the moneymaking potential of this work, and he preferred to pursue it on his own. The hairdresser, too, must have had some notion of a harmless hair dye's commercial possibilities, else he would not have commissioned the work in the first place. He specialized in hair dyes, and his clients referred to his store of bottles as "the fountain of youth," a phrase potent enough to start the mental cash-registers ringing loud and clear. He had only employed Eugène because he did not know how to make the new product himself and needed a consultant who did. Unfortunately for him, the consultant fate allotted him happened to be that extreme rarity, a brilliant scientist who was also a business genius, and whose sensitivity to potential moneyspinners, and ability to make them spin money, would turn out to surpass that of almost anyone else in France.

The prospect of working for himself with a definite end in view, and of financial independence should he succeed, suited Eugène far better than dreary academic security. He decided to continue his research on his own account, and resigned from the Pharmacie Centrale. His boss was disbelieving. He was still only twenty-six and was already being paid a special salary, 250 francs a month. How could he give it up, just like that?

It was indeed an excellent salary—so much so that during his three years at the Pharmacie he had managed to save 3,000 francs, enough to support him while he perfected his formulas. The only snag was, he'd lent most of the money to a friend who was not just then in a position to pay it back. He resigned anyway, on 800 francs, the capital remaining to him. The two-room apartment on rue d'Alger cost 400 francs a year, which since he had also to eat and buy materials gave him a little less than two years. The dining room became his office, the bedroom his lab. He lived alone, cooked for himself, and slept in a little camp bed until it was crowded out by laboratory equipment, when he took it up to a vacant storage room. "When I think back to those days, I can't imagine how I got through them," he reflected forty years later.

His first product worked well on dead hair in the lab, but proved useless in the salon, on live hair still attached to a sensitive human scalp. He had therefore to begin all over again. But by 1907 he had his formula; all that remained was to sell it.

How he summoned up the courage to go out and find clients he could never afterwards imagine. He was by nature rather shy, and a very bad salesman. But the product was excellent, and he soon got to know Paris's fifty top hairdressers, who formed a respectable core of clients. He made his products at night, took orders in the morning, and delivered in the afternoons. By 1909, he had the satisfaction, "which I think I deserved," of making a small profit. There were no margins. If he didn't sell, he didn't eat. Every bill, whether for raw materials or household necessities, was a nightmare. Nevertheless, L'Oréal was a going concern. On the strength of it he allowed himself to get married, and Mlle. Berthe Doncieux, whom everyone called Betsy, and of whom we know little save that she was musical and liked to play the piano and sing,[11] came to share his storage-room bed.

III

> In every town, there will be shops where the scalp will simply be massaged with lotions, each more wonderful than the last—liquids that will prevent hair from turning white in the first place.
>
> —Eugène Schueller, *Coiffure de Paris*, 1909

Although Eugène Schueller's public career is amply documented, the private man remains elusive. He makes a few cameo appearances in other people's memoirs. He gave two short accounts of his life, one in 1948, when he was tried for collaborating with the Germans, another in 1954, to Merry Bromberger. He produced a few treatises on politics and economics, and a good many articles and speeches. But in most of these writings he had one if not both eyes on his own or his country's future. He always remained committed to L'Oréal, but as the 1930s progressed it became more and more the means to an end—an inexhaustible source of money that would allow him to influence the economic and political scene.

There was little time for private life. The marital bed crowded out by laboratory and office requirements was as much metaphor as reality. And although later he surrounded himself with the trappings of luxury—big houses, a Rolls-Royce, specially commissioned furniture—his lifestyle remained ascetic. If you work, as he did, from five in the morning until nine at night, there is little time left for anything else.

We can glimpse his progress in a magazine called *Coiffure de Paris*, whose first issue, in October 1909, declared that it was "distributed free to Wholesale Buyers and to principal

Practitioners in the Five Corners of the World." A double-page photo-spread of founders' portraits showed a cluster of well-set-up gentlemen of a certain age, with neat gray beards. In this portly and expansive company, E. Schueller, listed as one of the magazine's "independent corporate publicists," was noticeable for his youth and his abundant black, curly locks. Confined to the bottom right-hand corner of the page, he was seemingly a sort of afterthought. But this placement was deceptive. He was one of the magazine's moving spirits. A hairdresser of his acquaintance had started it at the suggestion of a journalist, and co-opted Schueller because of his experience editing the *Grande Revue Scientifique*. Always publicity-hungry, he saw in it an excellent potential vehicle for his advertisements: L'Oréal occupied the whole of the back page, the space purchased at a cheap contributor's rate. Before long, in a foretaste of events to come, he had taken the magazine over entirely and become its proprietor, editor, manager, and publicist.

Coiffure de Paris, when it began, was largely about the now lost world of the postiche, the false hair piece every fashionable woman needed to achieve the bouffant hairstyles then in vogue (such as the one called "L'Auréole," the original inspiration for the new hair dye's name), necessary to support the vast hats of the period. Much of this hair came from Asia, though some was also harvested in the depths of *la France profonde*. A tragic photo in the magazine's first issue, "Cutting Hair in the Corrèze," showed one of the avuncular gents from the frontispiece, a large pair of scissors in one hand, triumphantly holding on high a thick mane of locks. Its erstwhile owner, shown in back view, sat crudely shorn on a bench, while to the right of the picture a second girl, still in possession of her hair, but about to lose it, and on the verge of tears, was being pushed forward by a grim-faced *maman*, intent on driving a hard bargain. But these were mere peasants, whose hair was wasted upon the Corrèze. Paris was its true home, where in studios such as "Postiches d'Art" "a buzzing hive of posticheuses" washed, colored, and otherwise prepared the raw material.

The art of the postiche consisted in blending it undetectably with the wearer's own hair—a complex and time-consuming business almost impossible to achieve at home. It had largely contributed to the spread of commercial hairdressing salons, as need overcame the traditional distrust of that immoral figure, the male hairdresser. And of course satisfactory matching necessitated a wide range of hair dyes.

Amid the magazine's fashionable hyperbole—"This season, *big* hats mean *big* hair"—the title of E. Schueller's article, "Practical Techniques for Dyeing Hair," struck a strictly down-to-earth note. Every month he supplied a piece on dyeing techniques and dangers, as well as answering readers' questions. How, for example, should one deal with accidents that left hair green or purple? "This happens because you don't know about hair dye, as you prove when you say 'I tried in vain to dye it again.' That's just what you mustn't do. When hair turns green, you don't dye it again, you remove the dye that's already there. What you're doing isn't colouring, it's interior decorating—applying coats of plaster."

Schueller's dynamism soon put him in charge of *Coiffure de Paris*. And that same year, 1909, L'Oréal, too, was financially transformed. One of Eugène's cousins gave him an introduction to an accountant by the name of Sperry who worked for the liqueur firm Cusenier in Epernay. Sperry had just come into a small inheritance of 25,000 francs which he was looking to invest. Impressed by Schueller's evident intelligence and excited certainty, he agreed to set up a joint venture, Schueller et Sperry. He insisted, however, on a special safety clause. At the end of each year Sperry was entitled to withdraw if he chose, and if he did, Schueller would repay his 25,000 francs. The clause was never invoked. On the contrary, when Sperry became ill some years later and had to retire, Schueller, grateful for the the help Sperry had given him when he needed it, suspended it and paid Sperry's full share of the annual profits (by then exceeding 25,000 francs) every year until he died.

This injection of funds allowed Schueller to set himself up more sustainably. He hired a delivery boy and splurged on some advertising. His first account books showed expenditures of 49 francs on salaries, 28 fr. 25c on publicity.[12] And he and his wife, Berthe, moved from their cramped quarters in rue d'Alger to a four-room apartment at 7bis rue du Louvre, at the eastern end of rue Saint-Honoré. As at rue d'Alger, this apartment housed not only living quarters but the firm's office, laboratory, and showroom. And as at rue d'Alger, the business expanded and expanded, until the Schuellers found themselves sleeping, as before, in a vacant maid's room at the top of the house.

For many years they remained childless. Perhaps this is hardly surprising. At first there was literally no room for children. And then war broke out, and Schueller enlisted. Whether by accident or design, it was not until 1922 that their only child, a daughter, Liliane, was born. Schueller was by then forty-one, and Berthe cannot have been a great deal younger. They had been married fourteen years; she did not become pregnant again. There are hints that this was not for want of trying. In the plan for an ideal world he set out in 1939, he insisted that women should marry young and conceive early, since after the age of twenty-five "children are conceived and born only with the greatest difficulty."[13]

The war interrupted the hair-dye business, along with everything else. Schueller was overage, and at first the army refused to take him. Later it agreed to admit him as a chemist, but he turned that down and was eventually inducted into the 31st Artillery at Le Mans, leaving L'Oréal in the hands of his wife. At the front he acted as a liaison officer, with spectacular success. The citations for his various decorations describe him as careless of personal danger, quick to grasp what was relevant, and precise in conveying necessary detail.[14] He was mentioned in dispatches at Verdun, the Aisne, the Chemin des Dames; in all, there were five citations. He was awarded the Légion d'Honneur in the trenches, and by the time he was demobilized, in 1919, he was a lieutenant of artillery and had been awarded the Croix de Guerre with several palms. He enjoyed the army's adventurous life, and its lessons in organization were useful to him later in business.

He returned to find that Berthe had done an excellent job of managing the business. L'Oréal was flourishing, and the rue du Louvre apartment was now far too small. They moved once again, just around the corner, to rue Jean-Jacques Rousseau, taking an entire floor at an annual rental of 16,000 francs—four times what they had previously been paying—and soon needed an additional floor for offices. Before long, revenue was running at 300,000 francs a month, and a large proportion of that was profit.

It all seemed too easy, and Schueller began to get bored. He diverted himself by embarking upon a voyage of industrial exploration, progressing from industry to industry as one led to another.

The first move arose through his prewar activities at *Coiffure de Paris*. In search of advertising, he had met some manufacturers of celluloid combs. The war, with its demand for nitrocellulose explosives, meant a large development of their chemical division. They asked Schueller if he might be interested in helping them expand it, and how much money he would want for doing so. He explained that money was not his principal concern—he was already making plenty of that. What did interest him was how big they expected the business to become. They would be happy, they replied, with a million francs a year profits. By the end of the first year, the profits stood at 4 million francs, of which Schueller was entitled to one-quarter. Five years later, he had become the company's principal shareholder.

At the same time he started a new company, Plavic Film, which took control of the Lumière film-manufacturing company of Lyon (run by Auguste Lumière, one of the two brothers who in 1895 had made the first true motion picture). Plavic manufactured movie and still photographic film. He bought into another company that made Bakelite, and yet another making cellulose acetate and artificial silk.

At this point, huge orders for celluloid began to arrive from Russia. Schueller had recently renewed acquaintance with Jacques Sadoul, his boyhood friend from the Lycée Condorcet. Capitaine Sadoul had been sent to Moscow in 1917 as part of a French military mission intended to make sure Russia remained on the Allied side. Excited by what he saw, he declared himself a Communist and declined to return to France. Having worked in various capacities for the Bolsheviks, he now returned to find that he had been accused of treason and sentenced to death *in absentia*, and took shelter with Schueller while gathering courage to give himself up. In the event, the charges were dropped. Sadoul returned to thank his old friend and, incidentally, put him in the Russian picture. The Russians, Sadoul said, were granting concessions to foreign businessmen to set up new industries in the U.S.S.R. Schueller, he insisted, should get himself in there.

The upshot was a concession to make celluloid and also photographic film stock. In reality this boiled down to a comb factory. But in 1928, Lenin's NEP (New Economic Policy), which had allowed small businesses to operate for private profit in an effort to rebuild Russian industry, was abandoned by Stalin in favor of a collectivization program of five-year plans, and the Russians bought Schueller out.

Meanwhile, in 1927, he became interested in the manufacture of cellulose paints, which shared many laboratory processes with celluloid, and was soon managing director of a paint firm, Valentine. As he put it, however, "it wasn't enough to manufacture paint—we also had to sell it"[15]; so he went to see André Citroën, whose company was the world's fourth-largest automobile manufacturer. Citroën gave him a contract for 23 million francs; there were also valuable contracts with Renault and Peugeot. But this arrangement, though lucrative, left the company at the mercy of just a few clients. Schueller decided to branch out and sell his quick-drying paints to the public—by radio.

Radio advertising was new. It had hit France courtesy of the young advertising genius Marcel Bleustein, who recognized its potential during a year's stay in America. Returning to Paris in 1926 at the age of nineteen, he opened his own advertising agency, Publicis. By Christmas of 1927, he had his first client, and in 1935 bought a private station, Radio LL, which he rechristened Radio Cité. It was the first station in France to broadcast uninterrupted from six a.m. till midnight, with talent contests, news reporting, singing stars such as Maurice Chevalier and Edith Piaf—and commercials interspersed amid the programming. Schueller persuaded Bleustein to let him advertise with a sung jingle, in the style of Maurice Chevalier:

Elle se vend en tout petits bidons,
Valentine, Valentine,
Elle se fait dans les plus jolis tons,
Valentine, Valentine. . .
(It's sold in little cans, / Valentine, Valentine, / And in such pretty tones, / Valentine, Valentine . . .)

At first Bleustein was reluctant—perhaps because he hadn't thought of this idea himself. But Schueller won him over, and the advertising jingle hit France.

After a while, Schueller decided to exchange his shares in plastic and celluloid for his partners' shares in Valentine, leaving him with just two business interests—Valentine and L'Oréal. But this comparative calm did not last long.

In 1928, following his Russian adventure, Schueller had got involved with yet another business: a brand of soap called Monsavon, created just after World War I by a M. Wisner. The brothers Henri and Philippe de Rothschild were persuaded to put 18 and 20 million francs, respectively, into the business, lost the lot, and wanted out. They were prepared to sell cheaply. Schueller bought it from them for nothing, paying only for existing stocks and such money as remained in the bank.

Monsavon went on losing money. It wasn't a bad product, but brands like Palmolive and Cadum were much better known—so much so that shoppers, especially in rural areas, would request "a cadum of Monsavon."[16] Schueller was losing 300,000 francs a month. He sold his cars and mortgaged the two houses he now owned, at L'Arcouest and at Franconville, just outside Paris.

With Valentine and L'Oréal both flourishing, the obvious answer was to cut his losses and close Monsavon down. But acknowledging defeat was something he could not bring himself to do. Business, for him, meant risk. "Difficult problems like Monsavon interest me more than easy successes," he said at the end of his life. "It's the way I'm made. . . . You can't argue with the way you're made."[17] He reduced production: the monthly loss fell to 30,000 francs, a level he could bear. He reformulated the product, reorganized the factory, publicized the improvements in the papers. Sales still did not rise.

The problem Schueller faced was the problem all cosmetics and toiletry manufacturers face—that their products are almost indistinguishable, and that brand loyalty must somehow be engineered despite this. Publicity is therefore all important. As Helena Rubinstein observed, "There's nothing like a clever stunt to get something off the ground." Her favorite campaign was the one for the fragrance "Heaven Sent," when in the late 1940s thousands of pale-blue balloons were released over Fifth Avenue, each one bearing a sample of the fragrance, with the tag: "A gift for you from heaven! Helena Rubinstein's new 'Heaven Sent.' "

Schueller, too, realized that he needed a really huge publicity campaign. He returned to Bleustein and Radio Cité, and this time he did not confine himself to mere jingles, but bought an entire program, the extremely popular *Crochet Radiophonique*, which he interspersed with catchy advertisements for Monsavon and sponsored singing contests, broadcast live from different locations. For six months nothing happened. Then sales suddenly took off. Monsavon took and retained first place in soap sales. Schueller was vindicated.

Sales of L'Oréal also rose during the 1920s, not because of any advertising campaign but because of a new hairstyle: the bob. The fashion for short hair began during World War I, when many women took jobs in factories. The popular film stars Clara Bow and Louise Brooks were famously bobbed, as was Coco Chanel, the up-and-coming fashion designer, who cut her hair off after singeing it one day. Just as Chanel's straight, comfortable clothes meant the end of corsets, padding, and petticoats, so her new short hair did away with laborious, long-drawn-out hair-washing and -drying sessions. Women everywhere began to cut their hair. Like lipstick a few years earlier, the bob became the symbol of a new freedom and independence. Men were horrified. "A bobbed woman is a disgraced woman!" thundered one in outrage. " . . . How strangely ill at ease our poor shorn sisters would have been had they been present in the Bethany home that day!"[18]

Schueller, too, was gloomy—not because of possible troubles in Bethany, but because L'Oréal's sales had always been predicated on women having lots of hair to dye. He anticipated a catastrophic drop in demand. He could not have been more wrong. Short hair needs frequent cutting, and only men's barbers had the appropriate skills. Faced with a female invasion, they were hesitant at first, but soon reinvented themselves as hairdressing salons, and flourished as never before. "Before the bob became the accepted style, there were less than 11,000 beauty shops in America. . . . Today there are more than 40,000 beauty shops in operation in America alone," wrote hairdresser George E. Darling in 1928.[19] And more hairdressers meant more hair-dyeing outlets.

Short hair did, however, present some difficulties when it came to coloring. The bob was about modernity, and hence youth: a gray bob looked anomalous. But a large proportion of short hair consists of roots, so that any coloring must be frequently retouched. And this meant frequent dyeing sessions, which were bad both for the hair and the pocket.

One easy answer was to bleach. Schueller set to work and produced L'Oréal Blanc. It quickly became the rage. Advertisements throughout Europe and America were overtaken by a blond invasion. He soon occupied the whole building in rue Jean-Jacques Rousseau, and opened, too, his first proper factory, in rue Clavel, out in Paris's 19th arrondissement. In 1929, for the first time, L'Oréal achieved revenues of more than a million francs a month.

Almost at once another problem presented itself: the permanent wave, or as it was more usually known, the "perm." The difficulty this time was that perms do not take on dyed hair if the dye forms an impermeable colored film on the outside of the hairs, as L'Oréal's existing dyes did. Permed hair needed a dye that would penetrate the hairs and color them from the inside. Some new British and American dyes did this, and threatened to sweep the market.

Schueller had in fact discovered and patented just such a dye during his early researches, in 1907. But he had never used it. As with the penetrating dyes his competitors were selling, its active ingredient was paraphenylenediamine. "Para" had a fatal flaw: as *Skin Deep* would reveal, some people were allergic to it. If they used it they would suffer from an itchy, flaky scalp, or in the worst cases a facial rash and swelling of the eyelids, face, and neck. Urged now by his colleagues to resuscitate this dye, Schueller hesitated. L'Oréal's reputation was built on its *not* provoking allergic reactions. "If one client starts to scratch, there go twenty years of confidence!" he objected. But without the new formula, sales would continue to fall.

Schueller decided the only remedy—and the only way to outflank his competitors—was to be frank. The new dye, called "Imédia," was launched with a warning: it might be dangerous. New users were advised to dab a drop behind an ear and wait forty-eight hours. If an inflammation appeared, the dye should not be used. At the same time he advised that should an allergic reaction declare itself, there was an antidote: a rinse of brine mixed with oxygenated water, which would remove the offending substance. The policy worked, and sales jumped.

By the mid-1930s, L'Oréal employed three hundred salesmen where once it had employed ten, and the company decamped once again, to the imposing building in rue Royale that remains its headquarters to this day. Like all L'Oréal's successive headquarters, as it outgrew one building after another, this building, too, was just a few steps from rue d'Alger. But by this time both L'Oréal and its founder had moved, definitively, into the other, brilliant world—the world of rue Saint-Honoré that in 1908, though physically close, had been at the same time so immeasurably distant.

IV

> What I always tried to do, in dealing with people, was to provide them with something they seemed cruelly to lack: a goal in life.
>
> —Eugène Schueller, 1957[20]

Like Helena Rubinstein's endless scurryings from one side of the world to the other, Eugène Schueller's zigzag path from industry to industry bore the mark of compulsion. They had to keep moving or they were lost. But these compulsions had diametrically opposite roots.

Rubinstein's career was chaotic, a progression of brilliantly executed extempore sallies. Just as her business was an extension of herself, peopled by the sisters, cousins, nephews, and nieces who were her pale imitations, so her constant journeyings reflected her emotional life. They might go under the name of business necessity, but the essence of Madame was that business and emotion were not separable. Every crisis—the row with her father when she turned down his choice of husband and left his house forever, Edward Titus's insistent desire that she marry him, the arrival of children, the outbreak of World War I, the sale of her American business to Lehman Brothers, the outbreak of World War II—was marked by physical flight, to another country, another continent, another beginning. Stuff happened, and she dealt with it somehow, and because she was clever and thought nothing of the world's opinion, simply following her instincts, which rarely led her astray, things turned out all right. And then there was more stuff, and she dealt with that. She ran on adrenaline: her chaotic, compulsive letters to Rosa Hollay, in which the worry of the moment was scribbled down whenever it might occur on whatever scrap of paper lay to hand, reveal the constant, jumbled panic beneath her assured exterior. "I haven't paid any bills the last three weeks, let me know again what must and should be paid now. I am frightfully short of money, it seems worse and worse. . . . I often don't know if I am on my feet or my head." "I am in such chaos, I am most thankful to have good constitution all the same I feel at times I will go mad, the worry and the responsibility is just eating me up. . . ." "I do actually nothing and work all the time."[21] However successful, however mountainously rich, hers was life as crisis management. "I have too much on my shoulders. I'm surrounded with people, but I can't get to them. . . . People . . . people . . . and I'm alone! With burdens . . . such burdens!" she told Patrick O'Higgins the day she offered him the indeterminate job that would keep him by her side for the rest of her life.[22]

Schueller, by contrast, was in control. In the world, as in the laboratory, he knew what he wanted to achieve and methodically set about achieving it. He was a scientist, and therefore saw the universe as a place of logic and patterns. Human life was no exception: without a pattern, all was chaos. Having abandoned the Catholic faith of his childhood, he spent the rest of his life constructing a substitute for it, a framework within which a modern industrial state might function fairly and efficiently for the benefit of its citizens.

This fascination with possible worlds surfaced in some unexpected places. The opening paragraphs of his earliest contribution to *Coiffure de Paris*, the October 1909 essay on "Technical and Practical Hints on Hair Dyes," plunged its readers into a world of scientific fantasy.

> *In four or five years from now, our bicycles will have become monoplanes weighing a hundred kilos, which will carry one or two people, and on which it will be possible to travel from here [Schueller evidently assumed all his readers lived in Paris] to Orléans in an hour.*
>
> *When that happens, there will probably be no more hair dyers. That delicate, difficult, and sometimes even dangerous profession will exist only in a few lost villages in Morocco or Calabria. Nor will there be any more dyeing of white hair. Instead, in every town, there will be shops where the scalp will simply be massaged with lotions, each more wonderful than the last—liquids that will prevent hair from turning white in the first place.*

Eagerly, Schueller outlined the chemistry by which this future would be achieved. The magic liquids would be "dilute solutions, in alcohol, tafia, or rum, of some di- or tri-ethylaminoparoxybenzene which will recolor any hair, whatever its original color, that will be harmless and that everyone will use each morning, like powder or toothpaste, but"—a bow here to the readers of *Coiffure de Paris*—"which many will prefer to have applied by a hair artist—the successor of today's hairdressers." Another miraculous invention would abolish the barbershop: men would simply rub their faces with an oil that stopped the hairs from growing.[23]

Here is the authentic voice of the times, of Jules Verne and H. G. Wells, of Fritz Lang's *Metropolis*. Like them, Schueller was enraptured by the new worlds science was opening up, convinced that it would transform the future in unimaginable ways, and eager to share this vision with a wondering public. There was, of course, an important difference between them and him. Where Verne, Lang, and Wells expressed themselves through stories, Schueller aimed to work his transformations in reality. But whatever its medium, one significant corollary of Schueller's visionary mind-set, with its scientifically argued blueprints for ideal worlds, was a deep impatience with the retrogressive dullards who refused to act on these excellent ideas. And this impatience would point the way to dark places.

Schueller was always conscious that had he not received the kind of education rarely available to bakers' sons, he would probably, despite all his abilities, have remained poor. He was aware, too, that that education had been largely a question of luck. Despite his parents' desire to give their son the best possible start in life, he would have had to make do with whatever the state could then provide had not the Collège Sainte-Croix, in an unusual access of imagination, accepted part payment of his school fees in pastries. He therefore directed his first social efforts towards education. He felt it was time to end the self-perpetuating mandarinate of the supercompetitive and expensive *grandes écoles* that excluded so much talent even when—as in his own case—a poor boy had demonstrated unusual intellectual potential. Intelligent working-class men seemed to him particularly disabled by their lack of math and science education,[24] and he wanted to remedy this personally, so far as he could. Before they were even twenty, he and his friend Jacques Sadoul, who shared his concerns, had founded a modest people's university at La Chapelle, a poor area to the north of Paris, where they taught in their free time.[25]

Soon enough, of course, there was no more free time, at least for Schueller, and the teaching lapsed. But despite his increasingly frenetic level of activity, first with L'Oréal, then in the army during World War I, then during his headlong progress through assorted chemical industries during the 1920s and thirties, his concern with the unsatisfactory state of the world, like Sadoul's, continued. Sadoul turned to communism and took refuge in the nascent Soviet Union; Schueller, the self-made man, set about designing a new, improved capitalism.

His sense that the old model was failing crystallized during the 1920s. In 1923, at the height of the great inflation, he made a trip to Germany, where L'Oréal had opened an agency, and "felt, for the first time, that the world had veered off-track." Three years later, in France, it veered off again, almost as catastrophically, though in the opposite direction, as the franc was revalued. "Factories full of orders were going day and night . . . and suddenly, customers stopped ordering. A month later they wouldn't even take delivery of stuff that was already in the pipeline, and I had to close two out of three factories."[26]

One day he realized that with modern machines he could double production using only half his existing workforce. But if only half the previous number of workers were earning salaries, who would be there to buy the goods? Then he had a revelation. *If salaries were doubled along with production, there would still be buyers.* "Capitalists had to realize that they should stop lowering prices while trying to maintain their profits by cutting salaries too. On the contrary, what they needed to do was not lower prices but raise salaries—not in an unplanned way, as when workers demanded and threatened [and employers gave in]—but mathematically, raising them as production increased. The trick was to raise buying power, not lower prices. Lowering prices would never absorb overproduction, because it was impossible ever to lower them enough."[27]

Over the next few years Schueller worked out his economic theories. He first expounded them in a speech to old Sainte-Croix pupils in 1934, later published as an article in the Sainte-Croix de Neuilly magazine. The article created such a stir that he was encouraged to spread the word wider, which he did at two meetings of industrialists. Later, in 1936, he published a journal, *L'Action patronale*, in which employers were exhorted to social reform. Finally he set out his programs in two books, *Le Deuxième salaire* (The Second Salary), written in 1938 and published in 1939, and *La Révolution de l'économie*, published in 1941.

What was needed, he was convinced, was a new formula for paying workers. They would receive their salaries as usual at the end of each month—but this basic pay would not be their only pay. In his own industry, he reckoned that salaries should amount to 30 percent of the product's factory-gate selling price. If, at the end of the month, 30 percent of total receipts amounted to more than the total of the workers' agreed-upon basic salaries, the difference would be paid out to the workers, apportioned according to their individual work records. Thus: the "second salary."[28]

This system would have several advantages, of which the first and most important was that workers, instead of spending the day watching the clock, would work hard because they would benefit personally if the business flourished. He himself, Schueller said, had spent a good deal of his youth performing boring manual tasks, and recognized that the reason this had never bothered him was because, unlike most workers, he had always, even when he was very young, been working for his own benefit rather than an employer's. Of course, few young men were as driven as he had been. Nevertheless, the second salary would make every worker a stakeholder in his own factory.

It would also, Schueller thought, solve the problem of impersonality, which inevitably increased as the business grew larger. While his own business had still been small, he had worked alongside his employees and transmitted his own enthusiasm to them. But when it grew larger, and personal contacts became rarer, he saw that most workers had no real interest in their job. It was then, he wrote, "that the problem of restoring some sense to the life of the men who worked in my businesses began to obsess me."[29]

These theories, dismissed by contemporaries as "Schueller's *dada*" (Schueller's hobbyhorse) were in fact extremely forward-looking. As he realized, in a recession nothing is more fatal than the deflationary spiral of ever-reduced prices, jobs, and wages. It was this problem he sought to tackle.

Schueller knew the second salary worked: he used the system in his own factories, and they, as everyone could see, flourished.* Others of his ideas—social security for the unemployed paid for through an automatically deducted national insurance (revolutionary, he admitted, "but we live in revolutionary times"[30]); a united Europe in which the mark and the franc would be one monetary unity in a European economy[31]—are now part of everyday life. In economics he was a visionary, and a benign one.

He did not stop at economics, however. Having lighted upon an idea that he felt would save the world, he felt impelled to design the world he would save. And that was altogether more problematic. For the second salary did not take the form of a simple monthly addition to the paycheck. Rather, it went to workers' wives and children, to the retired, the ill and the unemployed, in the form of grants. Only after these grants had permitted the wives, children, and old to live "properly" were surpluses passed on to the workers themselves, as bonuses.[32] But who was to define "properly"?

Not the workers, that was for sure. Schueller did not believe in consultation. To run an enterprise jointly was, he felt, "humanly impossible."[33] He saw egalitarianism, "the determination not to recognize any superiority, and never to admit the truth," as a sort of social gangrene. Trade unions and work councils were destructive rather than constructive; the noisiest propagandists always got elected, and then had to justify their election by making unreasonable demands. Concerned only with their short-term interests, they were part of the com-

---

* As it happens, one of the U.K.'s most consistently successful businesses, the John Lewis Partnership department-store chain, was, and still is, run in a similar way—in a "partenariat" (as opposed to a salariat), a scheme evolved by Schueller's almost exact contemporary, John Spedan Lewis, and begun in 1928. There is, however, a vital difference. Schueller would have viewed with horror the idea that a "partenariat" should make the workers actual partners, with shares in the enterprise, as John Lewis's scheme does.

pany, but not for it.[34] Everything about workers' lives precluded the visionary detachment essential if those lives were to be improved.

Schueller, on the other hand, felt himself uniquely well placed in this respect. France in the first half of the twentieth century was a very static society, and his rise from poverty to wealth and power had given him an unusually broad view of it. His scientific training and industrial experience meant that he had a wide personal experience of design, production, and publicity. Through his factories, he remained intimately acquainted with how the poor lived, and he devoted much of his business life to teaching them better habits, in the form of cleanliness. For him, advertising was not just a way to raise sales but a tool for improving people's living standards. "People are lazy," he told business journalist Merry Bromberger. "You have to push them to spend, to consume—to move on. When I advertise . . . I feel I'm working in the public interest, not just for myself."[35]

This evangelistic inclination was also evident in *Votre Beauté*, the magazine he published monthly. His original magazine, *Coiffure de Paris*, had become, by the 1920s, *Le Coiffure et la mode*. But despite carrying its articles in English, Spanish, and German, presumably to increase international sales, this was still of very limited interest compared to the general-interest women's magazines he saw on visits to England. So in 1933 *Le Coiffure et la mode* became *Votre Beauté*, complete with readers' letters seeking help for confidential problems (one of its most important sources of copy), as well as the latest from the couturiers, interviews with prominent society women and actresses, and assorted beauty hints. The result was a much wider readership and advertising base.

Although Schueller's name did not appear above any of the

articles, he wrote a great deal of *Votre Beauté* himself. And this gave it a particular flavor. In similar American and British magazines, beauty hints meant discussions of cosmetics, creams, and the best ways to apply them. But such things had little place in Schueller's world: he neither made nor used them. Instead, French women were exhorted to make themselves beautiful through strict routines of diet and exercise. From thinness and fitness, all else followed. "Do marrons glacés put on weight?" enquired "Rose d'Orléans" in the first selection of readers' letters. "Yes!" came the uncompromising answer—followed by a calorie breakdown showing that a single marron put you 100 calories to the bad (the recommended daily intake being no more than a meager 1,500 calories all told*).[36] Many readers wanted to grow taller: they were advised to stand up straight—and, above all, to exercise. "*It is a crime*," thundered an editorial in January 1934, "*not to make the most of such an easy and pleasant way of improving your physique, keeping young, and prolonging your life!*" Pages of detailed drawings and photographs introduced readers to winter sports (their skins protected, of course, by L'Oréal's *Ambre Solaire*), and every issue contained a new, health-giving diet. When Colette, whose love of good food was legendary and who in later life had become very plump, wrote a piece in her journal saying fat women were happier than thin ones, *Votre Beauté*'s disapproval was almost hysterical. "Colette, dear, wonderful Colette, we all know you're too fond of food. . . . But, for heaven's sake, don't try and make converts. . . . Go to all the banquets in the world, but don't put your genius at the service of big bottoms and fat thighs!"[37]

---

* The recommended daily intake for a woman between the ages of ten and fifty today is 1,940 calories.

In particular (a clue, here, as to the editor's particular predilection?) women were exhorted to take care of their breasts. How to stop them sagging? (Exercises.) How to prevent them getting too large? (Stimulate ovarian activity as soon as puberty sets in, as sluggish ovaries lead to oversize breasts.) How to make them bigger? (Exercise.) Every issue contained a page of before and after photographs, in which nipples, following the recommended treatment, migrated upwards as if by magic; every month Dr. Magnus Hirschfeld, a well-known pundit and "the uncontested master of sexology," recommended his special hormone treatment (also with before and after photographs). A despairing reader, writing in to ask if she should undergo breast reduction surgery, was, however, recommended not to do so immediately. Big breasts weren't necessarily a complete barrier to attraction; she shouldn't give up hope, and she should remember that surgery left scars.

Economics, health, beauty—who better than such a universally qualified man to propound the basic principles of utopia? The 1930s in France was a time of intense theorizing on both the left and the right, and everyone was eager to set out his own plan for national renewal. Schueller was no exception. In his book *Le Deuxième salaire*, published in 1939, he described his ideal world. To begin with, every family would have a house, ideally one designed by Schueller himself. In 1929 the American architect R. Buckminster Fuller had designed a house made of aluminum with premolded pipework, kitchen, and bathroom, and intended for low-cost mass production, that he called the Dymaxion House. Schueller made no mention of Fuller in his writings, but his own design incorporated many Dymaxion-type features—aluminum construction, industrial prefabrication, molded bathrooms. The Schueller house was prefabricated along the lines of an aircraft hangar, its triple-skinned aluminum frame providing heat and sound insulation, and its ogival shape giving a lofty sense of space. It was built from modules 85 centimeters long, 6 meters wide, and 5 meters high: house sizes would vary depending on the number of modules used. Large windows and skylights would make for light, airy spaces. Modern domestic necessities would be built in: piped water, washing machines, ironing machines, fridges, radios. The furniture would be of the latest wonder material, Bakelite, and designed by the best designers (Schueller was a connoisseur of fine furniture, commissioning his own from the great Art Deco designer Ruhlmann, whose clients also included Baron Henri de Rothschild, from whom he had bought Monsavon). Schueller's suburbs would be spacious and green, with widely spaced dwellings set among intensively cultivated vegetable gardens, along the lines of William Morris's 1890 utopian *News from Nowhere*, which advocated a bucolic lifestyle in harmony with the natural world.* Transport would consist of small family cars with an average ten-year life span. People would wear modern fabrics, crease-resistant and stretchy. Only young, strong men would work in industry, traveling to work in car pools. Women would stay home, devoting their lives to their families. Every working man, in Schueller's view, needed a wife waiting for him at home. Especially when work was scarce, he thought women had a duty not to compete with men: they should resign their jobs and look after their many children. "A home, for a man, means a wife at home, and if every member of the family over fourteen has to work for a living, it isn't a real home."[38] Older men would cultivate the gardens, and help the

---

* During the war, when food was scarce, he in fact did provide his workers with land to use as vegetable gardens, though by no means all of them actually cultivated the allotted plots.

women with household tasks and crafts. Artists and craftsmen were also accommodated in this worldview, their artifacts adding to the pleasure of life.

Under Schueller's system, poverty would be eliminated. So, too, would enormous wealth. Schueller admitted that getting rich was a not insignificant motivation in business, but in the end "we all have the same pen, the same telephone, the same radio, we'll all have more or less the same fridge, the same car, the same mattress, the same sheets—and anyway," he grumbled, like Helena Rubinstein indignant that such a large proportion of his rightful earnings should be confiscated by an ungrateful state, "there's not much left once you've paid your taxes."[39] Running a business was, rather, about reinvestment and development, and he had definite ideas about that.

First, it was important that employers personally own their concerns. They must be allowed to take risks and go broke from time to time—for Schueller, risk-taking was what being a successful industrialist was all about—and shareholders would always vote for income over investment, rejecting risk on the pretext that "it all works fine as it is." (L'Oréal remained a private company throughout its founder's lifetime, going public only in 1963, six years after Schueller's death.) Banks' money was especially to be avoided, since banks were particularly risk-averse.* So were those who owned a business through inheritance. Schueller thoroughly disapproved of businesses being inherited. The fact that so many of France's businesses were dynastic was, he thought, a great weakness. Not only did it entrench social immobility, it had left the country economically underdeveloped—to the point, indeed, where even Schueller

* An ironic observation, from the standpoint of 2010. But of course banks still don't like *lending* money to potentially risky enterprises.

felt France's most important resource was her land;* her industries relied for survival on tariffs and cartels.

Above all, Schueller felt that being an employer was about social responsibility. He offered his own experience as an example of the kind of management vision needed. In 1936, he had mechanized one of his factories, and two years later production had risen 34 percent, using 11 percent less in the way of manpower. Each sacked worker represented 12 francs a day saved, but 15 percent of those let go were unable to find another job, and to those he continued to pay 10 francs a day out of this saving. He also paid monthly supplements to his workers' families, 100 francs for the first child, 50 francs for the second, 200 francs to mothers who stayed home rather than going out to work. Motherhood was a social service: big families were essential if France was to be repopulated following the carnage of World War I.[40] He hoped such practices would become widespread. All that was needed to achieve the revolution was a handful of strong-minded men like himself. If they persevered, they would prevail.

To connoisseurs of twentieth-century self-made men, all this will sound oddly familiar. A dynamic employer who rises from poverty to create a new industry through his own outstanding technical and commercial abilities, and who then uses part of his profits to create a kind of self-contained mini-state in which to impose his idea of how things should be—such a man already, and famously, existed. Schueller's trajectory, so rare in France, would have raised no eyebrows in America. And his hero was indeed American—the automobile magnate

---

* Painting his ideal society in *La Révolution de l'économie,* he said that France, with her rich land, should concentrate on food production, leaving other trades to countries less naturally blessed and with more mechanical skills.

Henry Ford. Ford, like Schueller, directed some of his profits into social services—housing, schooling, hospitals—for the families of his workers. Like Schueller, he was concerned that these subventions should be used properly—that is, used as Ford thought best. Like Schueller he was a political idealist, the idealism, in his case, taking the form of pacifism. (In 1915, his Peace Ship initiative tried vainly to bring World War I to an end.) And, like Schueller, he had an economic *dada*—in Ford's case, the five-dollar day, his aim being to ensure that every one of his workers could afford to buy one of his cars.

When Ford instituted the five-dollar day in 1914, it seemed like an act of reckless generosity. In fact it paid for itself handsomely as higher wages led to better health and morale, and hence increased production. But it was not, in practice, as straightforward as it sounded. You *could* earn five dollars a day, if you worked uncomplainingly on the production lines Ford had built and led the kind of life he thought you should lead: not smoking or drinking (Ford did neither), and putting some of your money into savings. Ford created a Sociological Department to educate and inspect his workers, and decide how much each man should be awarded. You didn't have to be a respectably married nonsmoking teetotaller to work at Ford's. But you wouldn't earn five dollars a day unless you were, any more than Schueller's workers would see their share of profits until their families were certified as living "properly."

Schueller was a great admirer of Ford, and his economic and social theories were heavily influenced by Fordism.[41] And Fordism led to a particular kind of politics. Unlike most businessmen, whose interest in their workers ceased once they had left the plant, Ford and Schueller's form of extended paternalism effectively turned their businesses into mini–welfare states. And in the chaotic world of the 1920s and thirties, it seemed logical that what worked for their businesses might also work in the wider political arena.

Ford first dipped his toes into political waters in 1918. He ran for the United States Senate, as a Democrat, but was defeated in a viciously corrupt campaign. In 1923 there was talk of drafting him to run for president. But he hated public speaking so much, and was so bad at it, that after his one and only failed attempt at a political rally, he determined never again to risk a comparable humiliation. "I can hire someone to talk for me that knows how," he said. "That talking thing is a gift. I'm glad I never acquired it, and I'll never try again."[42] Nor did he need to. Why humiliate himself at the hustings when he could practice his theories upon a captive audience and a captive population?

Untrammeled by the need to accommodate public opinion, what had begun as a benign dictatorship soon changed into something altogether unpleasant. Ford's Sociological Department, begun in a genuine spirit of philanthropy, was after a few years replaced by a Service Department, which sounded equally altruistic but whose function was very different. Set up to coordinate the protection of the plant, the Service Department soon transmuted into a network of spies, informers, and enforcers who terrorized the Ford factories and suppressed all dissent. Labor organizers were beaten, strikes were broken brutally, protesters were sacked: one ex-member of the Service Department referred to it as "our Gestapo."*[43] Indeed, Hitler was a fervent admirer of Ford. *Mein Kampf* was written with Ford's autobiography, *My Life and Times*, and philosophy—"an

---

* Ironically, through all this, Ford's public image remained that of an enlightened humanitarian. In 1937, the year his thugs broke the back of one union organizer and severely injured several others, 59 percent of Americans still believed the Ford Motor Company treated its labor better than any other firm.

absence of fear of the future and of veneration of the past"—much in mind.*

Schueller, too, was an unashamed authoritarian: as he put it, "An elected leader is already less of a leader."[44] He thought democracy should mean government *for* all, but not *by* all. Running a modern state was too difficult to be left to anyone the masses might choose.[45] However, when it came down to picking actual men, he showed himself to be somewhat uncertain. The list of leaders he admired included Stalin, Mussolini, Franco, Hitler, Horthy, Atatürk, Pilsudski, Roosevelt, Chamberlain, and Daladier—that is, pretty much every available one, elected or otherwise. From which we can only conclude that the mere fact of making it to the top was evidence, as far as he was concerned, of the right stuff. Similarly, although he did not at this stage think France should ally herself with Germany—on the contrary, his great concern was the unpreparedness of the French army—as a committed authoritarian he could not help admiring Hitler's style. Hitler hadn't pandered to the trade unions with a New Deal like Roosevelt in the United States, or with a forty-hour week and unemployment pay like Léon Blum in France. Instead, he had taken all the men he could get hold of and put them to work, creating a formidable military power. France, Schueller felt, should do likewise. Nevertheless, despite his dislike and distrust of the unions (a dislike wholeheartedly reciprocated), he continued to employ union men, and did not persecute them as Ford did.

Of course Schueller and Ford were not alone in being attracted by the idea of dictatorship. They were probably unique,

---

* Hitler took more than philosophy and money from Ford. He saw how the auto industry, led by the Model T Ford, had transformed the American economy, and applied those lessons to the Third Reich, with impressive results that Schueller and many others came to envy and admire.

outside the ranks of politicians, in actually running, to a greater or lesser extent, their own state; but as the broke and dithering thirties limped on, many idealists with no personal experience of power were attracted by the capacity for unimpeded action that dictatorship seemed to offer. "I am asking for a Liberal Fascisti, for enlightened Nazis," declared H. G. Wells, addressing the Oxford Union in 1932, still, despite all the evidence, apparently believing that a benign dictatorship was not an oxymoron. "The world is sick of parliamentary democracy. The fascist party is Italy. The Communist is Russia. The Fascists of liberation must carry out a parallel ambition on a far grander scale."

With hindsight, Wells's call seems extraordinarily naive. But it was a true expression of his personal creed, which managed to combine socialism with unambiguous elitism. Many of his novels—*The Time Machine, A Modern Utopia, The New Machiavelli, Anticipations*—envisaged worlds ruled by a special governing order of the best and the brightest. And Wells was not alone in this seemingly incompatible combination of beliefs: this was the generation of socialists who embraced the new "science" of eugenics—but who were appalled when those theories were actually translated into action.

It is tempting—though probably false—to wonder whether eugenic considerations partly explain the fascist sympathies of Europe's beauty tycoons. The perfumier François Coty famously backed the far-right Faisceau and Croix de Feu movements during the 1930s, and a little later founded the infamous paramilitary group Solidarité Française; Coco Chanel was a renowned horizontal collaborator. Eugenics, after all, did identify physical beauty—which, for these Europeans, naturally meant Caucasian beauty—as a prerequisite for most other desirable qualities. As the then-celebrated American psychologist Knight Dunlap put it in 1920, "All dark races prefer white skin."[46]

In his book *Personal Beauty and Racial Betterment*, Dunlap, who, *inter alia*, saw baldness as a sign of physical degeneration—"It is difficult to conceive of a baldheaded musical genius or artist"[47]—pointed the way, twenty years before the event, to notions of the Untermensch and the Final Solution. "Perhaps there are limits beyond which the preservation of the individual is undesirable. It seems not only useless but dangerous to preserve the incurably insane and the lower grades of the feeble-minded."[48]

Dunlap was not alone in these thoughts. Similar theories were commonplace among psychologists at the time, some of whom had little hesitation in acting upon them when they could with impunity. Their use of inmates in American state hospitals as fodder for experimentation during the 1920s and thirties has become notorious. If fascism is the absolute subjection of the individual to the needs of the state, as defined by the ruling dictatorship, then those psychologists—absolute dictators in their own realm—were undoubtedly fascists. And if—as after World War II—culpability is graded along a scale of readiness to eradicate undesirable individuals, with Hitler at one end and, say, H. G. Wells at the other, then Dunlap and his ilk would probably not have survived a Nuremberg.

Most of those who held these views, however, lay at some point between these two extremes. In those cases, the matter of gradation could become a question of crucial personal concern. And one of these cases would be Eugène Schueller.

CHAPTER THREE

What Did You Do in the War, Daddy?

I

> Our readers are true Frenchwomen. They are worried and sad. That's only natural. But sadness is not the same as losing heart. No one, in France, should lose heart. . . . Not to care about your appearance shows a lack of courage. Beauty is a discipline, and it's cowardly to reject it.
>
> —*Votre Beauté*, NOVEMBER 1940

In 1939, the year World War II broke out, Eugène Schueller was fifty-eight. Small, shy, rotund, full of a disarming nervous enthusiasm, his words tripping over each other in a vain attempt to keep up with his ideas, he had, Merry Bromberger remarked, "the candid eyes and hesitant manner of Charlie Chaplin. . . . [His] curls, whether permed or natural, have survived fifty years of experiments. . . . When people say chemicals are not good for the hair, the great hair chemist need only show his own froth of little waves."[1] Those waves were now an odd violet tint that suggested frequent use of his own products.

Those products had bought him the grandest possible lifestyle. He had built himself two houses, the villa at L'Arcouest, where he relaxed, and an imposing pile at Franconville, just northwest of Paris, surrounded by elaborate terraced gardens—a highly impractical venture, he observed ruefully: seven servants and seven gardeners were needed to keep it up properly, and he liked to complain, somewhat hyperbolically, that the taxes he so bitterly resented paying meant he would never be left with enough to run it as it should be run. There was also a luxurious Paris apartment, on avenue Suchet, overlooking the Bois de Boulogne. And now a new war threatened, and who knew where he, and France, would be left at the end of it?

Unlike Henry Ford, whose enthusiasm for Hitler (including generous financial support) was rewarded in 1938 by the Grand Cross of the German Eagle, Schueller spent the prewar years warning his countrymen against the German "wolf" and the dangers it threatened. General mobilization and the ramping-up of war industries had at least averted the open civil war that had threatened France earlier in the decade, getting the economy moving and solving the problem of mass unemployment. But he saw that France was no match for Germany. Unless Britain sent 300,000 men and 5,000 aircraft, and the United States the same, all would be lost.[2]

The Ministry of Defense was more sanguine, or more fatalistic. Its response to the impending threat was to extend the so-called Maginot Line of concrete fortifications and tank traps built after World War I to prevent any new German incursion (and to provide its defenders with munitions that in many cases were the wrong size for the guns).[3] Few people thought it would work. As a gamekeeper on his father's land near the Belgian border observed to the young François Dalle (later to become L'Oréal's managing director), "You know as well as I do, Franchot, that the Maginot line won't stop the Germans. They'll go through Holland like they did last time."[4]

They did just that, in a furious attack launched on May 10, 1940, through Holland and Belgium. By May 26 the French were in retreat and the British Expeditionary Force, sent to support them, had been driven back to Dunkirk beach. During the following week over 338,000 British, French, and Canadian troops were evacuated across the Channel, under constant German fire. On June 14 the Germans entered Paris, declared an open city to avoid bombardment; on June 17 Marshal Pétain, whose troops had triumphed over the Germans at Verdun twenty-five years before, ordered the French army to stop fighting; and on June 22 he signed the armistice, under the terms of which two-thirds of France would be occupied by Germany.

Although in the immediate aftermath of the invasion ten million panicked French citizens took to the roads, eventually most of them trickled back home and tried to take up the threads of their lives. Many put their faith in Pétain, who at least offered the promise of a French rather than a German government, and made themselves inconspicuous in hopes that the occupying authorities would leave them alone. The more defiant retreated into sullen noncooperation or more active resistance. A core of diehard nationalists and furious young men joined de Gaulle in London. And at the other end of the political spectrum, some actively welcomed the new German rulers:

among them, prompted by a mix of practical necessity, economic evangelism, and political ambition, Eugène Schueller.

A good many French businessmen of the time were, like Schueller, interested in social reform. Several thought, as he did, that a benign dictatorship—the equivalent of H. G. Wells's "enlightened Nazis"—was the only efficient mode of government. One of these, Ariste Potton, wrote a novel on this subject in 1937 in which he set out his countrymen's (and his own) psychological position: "The Frenchman wants to be free," he declared, "but he's happy to accept discipline, if he has confidence in the person in charge."[5] Potton's fictional businessman, clearly a wishful self-portrait, is loved by his workers, whom he's always treated well—something on which Schueller, too, prided himself. Unlike Potton, however, who left the question of his leader's actual political standpoint unelaborated (he simply brings "social progress and economic revival" to France and peace to Europe) Schueller did not mince his words. "Need I say, I believe in an authoritarian state, properly led, and that I consider it impossible to build a representative state based on universal liberty and equality? . . . Everyone must realize that many are his superiors and deserve more than he. Life is about opportunity. Everyone must have his chance, and not try to deprive others of what he hasn't got himself."[6]

In this state of inferiors and superiors, Schueller was in no doubt as to his own position. The merest handful of men, so long as they were true revolutionaries, would be enough, he thought, to change a nation's fate.[7] Postwar France would badly need such men—"what these days are called 'Führers of the professions' "[8]—and Eugène Schueller would be one of them, hopefully as finance minister in whatever French government would replace the Germans when they left. He therefore set himself to acquire the skills without which success in politics is impossible. He was not a natural orator and was determined not to repeat the experience of Henry Ford. He engaged a private speech tutor to visit him every morning, and fitted out one of the rue Royale rooms as a small auditorium, where he could try out speeches on a few friends before risking himself in front of a wider public. And at the same time he looked around for a political group that would make a suitable vehicle for his ideas.

Schueller's decision to throw in his lot with the Germans was governed more by pragmatism than doctrine. An engineer hired by him during the war, and who made it clear he did not wish to work even indirectly for the Germans, reported that Schueller "saw my point of view." But "he said he thought the Germans were very strong, and better organized, while the other side seemed completely without organization. It was just a social conversation . . . and I have to say, I think M. Schueller is too much of an opportunist to risk engaging himself absolutely in favor of anyone."[9]

In fact, there was more than mere opportunism to Schueller's vocal welcome of the invaders. The Occupation solved a dilemma that had long frustrated him: that although Hitler's new order corresponded remarkably closely to his own long-held visions, Hitler himself was unfortunately the enemy. Had that not been so, France would now be in a far better state. "We haven't been as lucky as the Nazis, who came to power in 1933," he would write in *La Révolution de l'économie*, published in 1941 by Guillemot et Delamotte, whose list was headed by the collected speeches of Adolf Hitler. But now, at last, the years of stasis were over. Finally, the French people would realize that only a complete transformation could save them; and then all the suffering—"the war, the defeat, the destruction of our armies, an entire nation in flight"[10]—would not have been in vain.

Although almost all enthusiastic collaborators would have agreed, most had arrived there by a very different route. Schueller was a pragmatist. But for his future allies, fascism's attraction lay in doctrine rather than practicalities. By no means all were pro-German. But the Germans had achieved something they had long hoped for: the destruction of the hated Republic—*la gueuse* (the beggarwoman), as they disdainfully referred to it.

Nor did they find any problem with other aspects of Nazi philosophy, such as anti-Semitism. Most had begun political life as followers of Action Française, the right-wing nationalist pressure group that had arisen out of the Dreyfus affair, and which advocated that the unfortunate Captain Dreyfus should not be pardoned even though he had been proven innocent, and that his accusers should not be charged with perjury. That would tarnish the honor of the French army—something rather more important than an injustice meted out to a mere Jew. For them, Jews and Freemasons not only represented the sinister forces of international capital and secularism that had imposed themselves on France at the time of the Revolution, but threatened, by their alien culture, everything that made France special.

This toxic mix of xenophobic nationalism, Catholic fundamentalism, and fascinated envy was summed up by Henry Charbonneau, who would for a while become one of Schueller's political colleagues:

> *In every walk of life—political, economic, artistic, intellectual—the Jews were disproportionately prominent. Some professions were effectively under their control. It was truly a state within a state. . . . Personally, I've always felt defensive about this tentacular Jewish influence. Not that I've actually known many Jews, but they've always interested me. I*

> *was one of the first to see The Dybbuk when it was put on at the Théâtre Montparnasse in 1931. And later, when I was studying the culture of Andalusia, I really loved digging into the writings of the great Jewish savants of the Caliphate and Cordoba. . . . So it isn't that I had anything against Judaism as such, but what always got under my skin was the notion that . . . you couldn't really be talented, intelligent, witty, or even courageous unless you were a Jew or had Jewish friends. How could I bear to see intellectual and political life taken over by a minority many of whom weren't even properly assimilated yet?*[11]

For Schueller, who had once been a Freemason and who had many Jewish colleagues, these obsessions played little if any part in his thinking. He disliked the Republic not because he looked back nostalgically to the days of a Catholic monarchy but because, as he never tired of repeating, he was an authoritarian. For a man convinced that "Everyone's first duty, whether boss, employee, or civil servant, is to obey,"[12] the wave of strikes that paralyzed France in 1936 had been a glimpse into a terrifying future. His main objection to Léon Blum, who ended this situation by caving in to many of the unions' demands, was his socialism, not his Judaism. The formulaic phrase, compulsory for all right-wing orators, about freeing France from "la franc-maçonnerie et la juiverie," appeared only once in Schueller's speeches and writings, when he used it to underline the need to make a complete break with the failed Third Republic—an institution with which, in the circles he was addressing, that phrase was conventionally associated.[13]

For Schueller, as for many industrialists, the new Europe essentially meant a new economic order, neither French nor German but "mixte." They had long hoped for a breaking down of economic boundaries—as Schueller put it in *La Révolution de l'économie,* "a day when the mark and the franc would be one monetary unity in a European economy."[14] For years that had been a pipe dream: but if the Germans won, it would be the future. And if one thought this way, collaboration was a logical way forward.

And this was not just a question of theory. At the most fundamental level, it was the only way to stay in business. The war years were very profitable for those who could keep manufacturing—anything that could be made could be sold, the occupiers would pay any price for luxuries, and there was a flourishing black market in scarce necessities. But only collaboration ensured access to raw materials.[15] Later, Schueller would argue that he did only the minimum business with the enemy, but L'Oréal's profits quadrupled between 1940 and 1944, and Monsavon's doubled. He must have been selling something, in quantity; and it hadn't been manufactured out of air.

Part of this may be put down to ingenuity. Most industrialists, Schueller scornfully pointed out, were not good at making do. Despite a law making it compulsory to recycle scarce substances, they found it impossible to operate without their usual quantities of basic materials. Schueller, by contrast, tried wherever possible to use substitutes. Before the war, Monsavon soaps had contained 72 percent fats; during it, only 20 percent. The quality, admittedly, was less good—but people didn't complain: anything was better than nothing.[16] Even inferior materials had nonetheless to be sourced somewhere. And there was inevitably a price to pay. The Germans demanded not just that French manufacturers supply them, but that shares in French companies be transferred to German hands.

For manufacturers commited to the idea of a Franco-German community, however, this transfer of assets presented no problem. Rather it made sound economic sense. A *mixte* economy required *mixte* management. An investigative commission set up in the Lyon region in 1945 found "no trace of forcing" by Vichy or the Germans in this respect. On the contrary, when, as happened from time to time, Vichy tried to prevent such moves, the businessmen generally managed to get around the prohibition. "They say now that resistance, in 1940 and 1941, would have been premature and useless," the commission reported. "But the question . . . never really arose for the bosses of finance and industry. . . . It simply didn't concern them. . . . Resistance seemed absurd and pointless—a fight against themselves."[17]

Naturally, little if any of this was ever stated in so many words. When the occupation ended, and Schueller was tried for industrial collaboration, he was asked about his paint firm Valentine, whose product was of course of considerable interest to the occupiers, and which appeared to have sold them a good proportion of what it made. Schueller simply replied that he was no longer in charge there at the time. He had relinquished his majority holding, along with his position as Valentine's CEO, in October 1940. What he did not say was that Valentine was closely involved with the German firm Druckfarben, and helped it take control of another French paint firm, Neochrome, in which Valentine had a 50-percent holding. Valentine (and thus Schueller) ceded 15 perent of its Neochrome holdings to the Germans, and as a "participation française" was necessary, retained the remaining 35 percent. . . .[18] The German in charge of this transaction was a Dr. Schmilinsky. He valued his acquaintance with Schueller and went out of his way to introduce this "eminent industrial chemist and an eminent and ardent partisan of the Franco-German accord," to his superiors in the German embassy.[19]

Dr. Schmilinsky also described Schueller as being head of the economic section of a political party. For he had now made his choice. He would offer his services—and his money—to the Mouvement Sociale Révolutionnaire (MSR—which, in the French pronunciation, emerges as "Aime et Sers," or Love and Serve—an acronym we shall encounter frequently in the following pages).

MSR were the most extreme of the extreme. They were led by Eugène Deloncle, a clever and charismatic naval engineer whose hypnotic personal charm nullified his somewhat absurd appearance—short, plump, invariably bowler-hatted—and kept his inner circle spellbound. Deloncle, who operated under the nom-de-guerre of "Monsieur Marie," was a plotter and intriguer; his favorite reading was Malaparte's *Technique of the Coup-d'état.* Ultranationalist and deeply anti-German, he was nevertheless convinced that, given the fait accompli of the Occupation, collaboration was a "biological necessity" if France was to become, as he hoped, an independent fascist state.[20] "The first priority for France is to collaborate. Why is she wasting so much time?" he demanded in a radio broadcast in January 1941.[21]

Deloncle had been spurred into independent political action by the failure of the great antigovernment demonstration of February 6, 1934. Ever since 1789, French politics had been dominated by the never-resolved conflict between those who supported the Revolution and those who were against everything it stood for. For the antis, who included many if not most of the governing and officer class, this February day represented the last best chance of overturning the hated Republic. Forty thousand supporters of the royalist right—Charles Maurras's Action Française and its youth wing, the Camelots du Roy; Colonel de la Rocque's ultra-Catholic Croix de Feu; the fascist

Solidarité Française; and the Jeunes Patriotes—gathered in the Place de la Concorde to march on the Chamber of Deputies in the Palais-Bourbon, on the other side of the Seine. For more than a month the rhetoric had been building. The climate of insurrection had reached the boiling point; the time had come for action.

By the end of the day, sixteen were dead and a thousand wounded, including four hundred police. But at the crucial moment La Rocque, whose Croix de Feu were massed in a vital passage from where they could have overwhelmed the *garde républicaine,* called off his troops. He had decided that as a serving officer he could not march on the Chamber of Deputies. None of the other factions had either the men or the arms to act without him. The Republic was saved, and in the 1936 elections, a huge left-wing majority swept Léon Blum and his Popular Front to power.

There was general gnashing of right-wing teeth, but for some, gnashing was not enough. In February 1936, Blum was attacked by Jean Filliol, the little killer who would become Deloncle's hit man. On his way back from a meeting, Blum's car had got caught up in the funeral cortege of a popular royalist historian. Filliol, who was attending the funeral, noticed it and seized his opportunity. He broke the car's window, sank a bayonet into its backseat, and was preparing to sink it into Blum himself when workers from a nearby building site rescued the prime minister, who eventually found refuge in the nearby headquarters of the League of Catholic Women. Blum was bloodied and terrified but still alive. That June, he dissolved the right-wing ligues, making them illegal.

Deloncle, always attracted by the clandestine, thereupon decided to set up his own secret army: the *Organisme spécial de l'action régulatrice nationale,* or OSARN. It was more commonly known as La Cagoule, "the hood"—an epithet referring to the Klan-type red hoods supposedly worn when members were inducted, and soon generally adopted. These chosen shock troops would be a French fascist party in embryo, and would counter what Deloncle dubbed "inaction française." He organized them along the lines of the secret societies that perennially fascinated him, even when (as with the Freemasons) he hated them. Potential members were vetted. They needed a reliable "godfather" to vouch for them, and were allotted to separate cells that knew only their own members and doings, and that operated under names with anodyne and vaguely patriotic associations, different in every region. Connections between the center and the regions were kept indirect. Army officers received what was in effect a contract, promising protection in exchange for their support. And "traitors" were pitilessly executed. "*Nous sommes méchants*," Deloncle liked to say—something Filliol made sure was no idle boast.

The proper equipment of this organization would require funds. Deloncle obtained signed letters of endorsement from the aged Marshal Franchet d'Espèrey, France's most senior soldier, and set about raising them. Many of France's biggest businessmen—Lafarge cement, the Byrrh and Cointreau liqueur interests, Ripolin paints, several of the big Protestant banks, the Lesieur cooking-oils magnate Lemaigre-Dubreuil—were sufficiently terrified by the looming specter of communism to fill his coffers. Louis Renault donated two million francs; Pierre Michelin gave a million, and sent another three and a half million in cash, in a briefcase. The Michelin tire empire was based in Clermont-Ferrand, in the Auvergne; the local branch of La Cagoule was composed entirely of Michelin engineers, placed by their employer at Deloncle's disposal. Soon Deloncle's organization had ten thousand members, among them many senior army officers.

They at once set about their business. When Franchet d'Espèrey demanded a "blood proof" before raising any more money, it was provided in the shape of Dmitri Navachine, the Soviet representative in Paris, who in addition to being a Communist was a Jew and a Freemason, thus ticking all the hate boxes of the right. Filliol murdered Navachine in his trademark way—shot, then finished off with a dagger—while the diplomat was out walking his dogs in the Bois de Boulogne on January 24, 1937.

Other murders followed. On March 16, 1937, a La Cagoule commando fired missiles into a socialist demonstration in Clichy, a working-class district of Paris. In June, in exchange for machine guns from Mussolini, the Italian socialist Carlo Rosselli was assassinated, along with his brother, Nello, in the quiet Normandy spa of Bagnoles de l'Orne: "the sad death in exile that seems almost inevitable for the best sons of Italy," as Rosselli himself wrote of another Italian socialist (Filippo Turati) who had suffered a similar fate. The police solved none of these crimes: the details did not emerge until La Cagoule was finally brought to trial after the Liberation.

On September 11, 1937, Deloncle overreached himself. At ten that evening, in a coup organized by Filliol and a team that included a Michelin engineer, two bombs exploded in Paris near the Arc de Triomphe. One destroyed the façade of the rue de Presbourg offices of the Confédération Générale du Patronat Français (the general confederation of French employers), raising a cloud a hundred meters high and blowing over a nearby taxi. The second destroyed the building of the iron and steel manufacturers' association at 45, rue Boissière. Two people were killed and many more injured. Deloncle spread rumors, propagated by the right-wing press, that this attack was the work of Communist plotters. The police had infiltrated La Cagoule and soon began to unravel what had happened, but Deloncle's numerous supporters in the army all believed in the Communist plot, their fears further fanned by a new Deloncle rumor, this time that a Communist takeover had been planned and was imminent. It was agreed that they would descend on Paris, avert the danger, and take over. The night of November 15–16 was fixed for the operation and assembly points arranged at four addresses where La Cagoule had established arms dumps: in a *pension de famille* for elderly ladies, an antiques shop, a radiography center, and a villa in the suburb of Rueil where the basement had been fitted up as a torture chamber. Unfortunately for the plotters, the police were waiting, arrested those cagoulards unable to escape in time, and confiscated the arms. Deloncle and his brother were picked up, as were a number of others, including, sensationally, a general—Duseigneur—and a duke, who held the Corsican title of Pozzo di Borgo. They were held in prison awaiting trial. When war was declared, however, the cagoulards were provisionally freed to join—or rejoin—the armed forces. And after the German triumph, they went their different ways.

Supporting La Cagoule did not mean that you automatically supported the occupying Germans. On the contrary, many, especially among army officers, were proud nationalists. They had been unable to bear the spectacle of their beloved France mismanaged by a leftist rabble, and now found the thought of a teutonic hegemony equally intolerable. Some followed de Gaulle to London; others supported General Giraud, who had been an active cagoulard while governor of Metz, and who became a rival focus for resistance. Several joined Pétain in Vichy, where an increasingly vain pretense of independence was maintained. But a hard core, including Filliol, chose out-and-out collaboration. They followed Deloncle to Paris, becoming the MSR.

For Deloncle, the debacle offered the prospect of a dazzling revenge as the hated Republic was destroyed, along with its "puppets." "I witnessed their agony," he wrote to his wife. "If you could have seen their faces, masks of terror, sweating dishonor, you'd have hugged yourself with joy."[22] Now he, whom they had forced into hiding and imprisoned, would prepare to take power. But to do so he would need money, and Schueller offered it.

SCHUELLER SAID HE FIRST MET Deloncle at the end of 1940, "when he came to find me and said he was utterly converted to my social and economic ideas, which he wanted to include in his party's program."[23] In fact, many historians claim he was the secret financier behind La Cagoule, in which case they would have met much earlier. But there seems to be no evidence—other than the historians' assertions—to support that. La Cagoule's finances were not secret, at least within cagoulard circles; nor did Schueller's name appear on the carelessly uncoded list of members kept by La Cagoule's archivist, Aristide Corre, and found by the police when they searched his rooms five days after the Arc de Triomphe bombs. The list was sketchy regarding the provinces, but was clear and full as far as Paris membership was concerned, giving all members' names and addresses.

When the new party was born, on September 15, 1940, describing itself as "European, racist, revolutionary, communitarian [i.e., Franco-German in outlook], authoritarian," Schueller was the first member to sign up (the second was Filliol).[24] On the new party's letterhead, where his name appeared just below that of Eugène Deloncle, he was named as "president and director of technical commissions and study committees." As well as money, he gave the MSR a meeting room adjacent to his own luxurious offices in the L'Oréal building on rue Royale.[25] In return, a nod to the proportional salary was included in the MSR manifesto of aims. Alongside the standard racist and nationalist clichés that Deloncle took so chillingly literally ("We want to construct the new Europe in co-operation with National Socialist Germany and all the other European nations liberated, as she has been, from liberal capitalism, Judaism, Bolshevism, and Freemasonry. . . . The racial regeneration of France and the French . . . Severe racial laws to prevent such Jews as remain in France from polluting the French race . . . We want to create a united, virile and strong youth . . .") there was a promise "To create a socialist economy that will assure a fair distribution of goods by raising salaries along with production."[26]

What all this meant varied according to one's point of view. When the young engineer Georges Soulès (later to become known as Raymond Abellio, a writer on the occult) visited MSR headquarters for the first time, he noticed with some amusement that Deloncle, "so warm, voluble, full of charm and Gascon verve," and who spoke so spontaneously and enthusiastically when he was discussing his militias and their doings, only mentioned Schueller—whom he referred to as "our future minister of the national economy, the most important man in the movement"—at the end of their conversation, as an afterthought.[27]

The truth, of course, was that what mattered to Deloncle was Schueller's money. Indulgence of his economic ideas was the price that had to be paid for it. But if Schueller recognized this (later he said, "No doubt Deloncle knew how passionate I felt, and how easy it would be to use me as a front man in certain industrial circles if he flattered me"[28]), it was of little importance. All that mattered was that his ideas be propagated and, eventually, implemented. And why not through the charismatic and energetic Deloncle?

Other right-wing politicians could see plenty of reasons why not. The prospect of Schueller's money being made available to this crazed fanatic terrified them—so much so that in 1940, General de La Laurencie, Pétain's then representative in the Occupied Zone, sent his nephew to try to persuade Schueller to moderate his support for the MSR.[29] But Schueller stuck with Deloncle. Part of the attraction, Soulès said, was that Deloncle was an engineer, not a professional politician. Like Schueller himself, he was a new and energetic force amid the professors, lawyers, and old soldiers who generally cluttered the political scene.

Schueller's defense, when he later had to try to justify his actions, was that he had been misunderstood and misled—that, in the words of his daughter, Liliane, "He was a pathological optimist who hadn't the first idea about politics, and who always managed to be in the wrong place."[30] That, though, was not convincing. It was hard to believe that a person who had made such a huge success in the cutthroat world of business could be quite such an innocent. On the other hand, his decision to associate himself with a murderous fantasist like Deloncle threw serious doubts on his political judgment. No one familiar with Deloncle's cagoulard past, with its melodramatic plots and bloody assassinations, could have imagined the MSR would ever form a government.

Perhaps the explanation is that the past, even the recent past, had no interest for Schueller. A true Fordist in this respect, his sole concern was to select the most efficient route to the desired future. Having picked the MSR as his route, and with his blind faith in the power of his economic ideas, perhaps he truly thought he could promote a coherent political program within it—that, in Soulès' words, it "would take on new colors, and an intelligent game would become possible, Deloncle's personal game reduced, channeled, made wise, by the application of systems and ideas."[31] If he did think this way, however, he had misread his man. Deloncle was happy to tolerate intellectuals, but only so long as they confined themselves strictly to cultural activities.[32] He, and only he, would dictate the action.

In February 1941, Otto Abetz, the German ambassador to Paris, pressed the MSR to combine with Marcel Déat's far larger Rassemblement Nationale Populaire (RNP) to maximize their power and influence. As Abetz perhaps foresaw, it was not a natural meeting of minds. Déat was an old pacifist and socialist who had been part of the Front Populaire. He had bitterly opposed France's entry into this war, which he saw as a British plot to further its imperial interests, and had worked his way across the political spectrum to become a pro-German national-socialist. He thus embodied everything that the anti-German, right-wing, bellicose Deloncle most loathed. At the RNP, Soulès noted, "one was received in a quiet, discreetly elegant salon that might have belonged to a studious professor who had suddenly become famous; at the MSR the anteroom was a closed guardroom, entirely military, with no trace of politics."[33] Indeed, the MSR had acquired smart new paramilitary uniforms, with khaki shirts, cross-belts, breeches, and black boots and gloves, in which they continued to stalk their enemies just as in the glory days of La Cagoule.

Deloncle agreed to Abetz's arrangement—he could hardly

have done otherwise. But, as always, there was a plot. He would take over the RNP from within, *à la Cagoule*, beginning, in the classic manner, by assassinating several Déatists. When these assassinations happened, Déat himself was in the hospital. A former secretary of Deloncle's, a Mme. Massé, went to visit him there. A few days later, she too was killed and her body found in the Seine. She may have shown Déat some documents proving that Deloncle, his supposed ally, had been behind the assassinations, or perhaps simply wanted to warn him that Deloncle planned to use his absence in the hospital to take over the RNP. Either way, the visit proved fatal. An attempt was made, some time later, on Déat himself. It failed. But Marx Dormoy, who had once been Déat's colleague in the Front Populaire, and who was now under house arrest in Montélimar, was blown up in his bed that July. Dormoy had been minister of the interior at the time of the Arc de Triomphe bombs and had overseen the arrest and imprisonment of the cagoulards. They had not forgotten—"*nous sommes méchants*'"—and this was their revenge.

Not surprisingly, morale in the wider RNP plummeted. Its membership had expanded during the early weeks of the enforced cohabitation, but soon fell into an irreversible decline. For Schueller, so accustomed to success, this was his first real experience of failure. "I've never known a man able to inspire so much confidence in a movement, so long as he was in charge," Soulès observed.[34] But now he was not in charge, and MSR no longer inspired confidence. Was it a good idea to associate so closely with a man as shady as Deloncle, and to throw good money after bad into a product as unsatisfactory as the RNP's dreadful magazine, the *Révolution Nationale*? It was clearly time to distance himself. In late 1941, Schueller severed his connection with Deloncle and the MSR. This prompt dissociation was one of the main planks of his defense during his postwar trials for collaboration. Whatever his dealings with MSR, it was to his credit, the judges decided, that he had quit it in good time.

II

> It is the opinion of German men and women that women who pluck their eyebrows, use cosmetics, color their hair, and try to draw attention to themselves through eccentric behavior (for example smoking, face powder, etc.) belong to an older generation whose time has passed. The younger generation is against all these things, and youth has to be counted not by years but by strength of feeling. The women who are doing such things should be ashamed. . . . To be young means to be natural, and to understand the admonitions and demands of a great era.
>
> —Dr. Krummacher, leader of the National Socialist Women's Organization, writing in *Koralle* (a German general-interest magazine), 1936

Schueller could not deny that throughout the war years he had been one of the voices of the Occupation. The radio broadcasts and newspaper articles, the public lectures and the pep talks to his workforce spoke for themselves. But politics, he assured the court, had played no part in those talks: they had been concerned purely with economics. "If, like me, you're convinced that you've found the answers to the world's economic and social problems, you obviously can't stop talking about them just because the wrong people listen."[35]

The burden of his broadcasts, speeches, and articles was indeed economic, the same ideas—about the proportional salary and bosses' responsibilities—that he had been preaching for years. Thus, a radio talk on May 8, 1941, entitled "How Not to Die of Hunger This Winter," was about the efficiency, or otherwise, of workers' allotments and the importance of making the most of small parcels of land. And a public lecture titled "The Revolution of the Economy Is the Economy of a Revolution" (given at the Salle Pleyel, the concert hall on rue du Faubourg Saint-Honoré) was about the proportional salary and new ways to calculate taxes. But there were other ideas, too. In June 1941, he promised, to a standing ovation, that "We are going to become the first state of a new Community. We shall issue twenty decrees in twenty days, one a day following the Rassemblement Nationale Populaire's assumption of power. Then, in spite of her defeat—because of that defeat—France will once again take her rightful place in the world."[36] A talk on taxes was more problematic, culminating as it did with the phrase: "There can be no patriotism without a mystique of blood and soil." Since ignorance of that mystique's associations was unlikely for one so well acquainted with Hitler's writings, this implies extreme innocence, Nazi leanings, or amoral opportunism. After the war he pleaded ignorance and innocence; and since that was what people preferred to believe, they did not question it, or him, too closely.

These broadcasts and lectures were often published as articles, in propaganda newspapers such as *L'Oeuvre* or *La Gerbe*, or periodicals such as *Révolution Nationale* (which Schueller financed himself). But there was also another, and much more popular, vehicle for his ideas—his beauty magazine, *Votre Beauté*. For cosmetics were still, as they had always been, acutely political.

In Britain and America, where women worked alongside men as a vital part of the war effort, glamor was recognized as being of the greatest psychological importance. When Helena Rubinstein asked President Roosevelt what she could do to help the war effort, FDR told her the story of a woman in London being stretchered out of a blitzed building. Offered a sedative, she insisted, first, on touching up her lipstick. "It just does something for me," she said.

It certainly did something for Helena Rubinstein, Inc. The company's range that year included 629 items: 62 creams, 78 powders, 46 perfumes, colognes, and eaux de toilette, 69 lotions, 115 lipsticks, plus soaps, rouges, and eye shadows. In 1941, its profits were $484,575; by 1942 they had almost doubled, to $823,529. That year every woman in the United States spent an average of twelve dollars on cosmetics.[37] "You have got to look right down into their pocketbook and *get that last nickel*," Madame remarked.

The war was good for business in other ways, too. In a development that she could never, at her most optimistic, have imagined—and one that would transform the postwar beauty industry—Helena Rubinstein became an official supplier to the U.S. Army. A few years earlier, Madame had tried to introduce a line of men's toiletries, House of Gourielli, opening a lavish salon on Fifth Avenue she hoped would induce a new habit of male pampering. It failed to take off, however. The salon closed, and the men's toiletries line faded away. But the war succeeded where all her efforts and advertising had failed, and moved men's toiletries into the mainstream. When the Allies invaded North Africa in 1942, every GI was issued a kitbox containing sunburn cream, camouflage makeup, and cleanser, discreetly lettered on the inside "Helena Rubinstein Inc" and including instructions on how to apply cosmetics in desert conditions. Army PX stores routinely stocked a range of aftershave lotions, skin creams, deodorants, talcum powder, sunburn lotions, lip cream, and cut-price cologne, for use where no bathing facilities were available.[38] A lucrative new market beckoned. "Men could be a lot more beautiful," Madame observed hopefully in 1943,[39] and if she had anything to do with it, they would be.

In Britain, too, glamor was taken seriously. It was becoming increasingly hard to source raw materials for the manufacture of cosmetics, which were classed as a nonessential industry. Even so, recruitment posters for Britain's all-women Auxiliary Territorial Service, which provided drivers and ran army camps—a laborious and often drab life of catering, cleaning, and general maintenance—emphasized the importance of looking good. The most famous of these posters, Abram Games's profile of a beautiful, poutingly lipsticked girl, her ATS cap set becomingly amid blond curls, caused something of a furor—for a poster, the ultimate compliment. People complained it was too sexy—and indeed, the girl might have stepped straight off a film set, perhaps one of those Powell and Pressburger wartime fables in which immaculately coiffed telephonists with cut-glass vowels inspire crashed airmen to cling to life. Games, however, stuck by his poster. It was, he insisted, drawn from life—a genuine ATS girl he had met in a train. British *Vogue* set out a detailed regime by which its readers might achieve comparable perfection, setting out a timetable for rising, washing, dressing, breakfasting, and making-up in one hour. Twenty of those sixty minutes were devoted to makeup. Lipstick, properly applied—color, blot, powder; color, blot, powder—would last all day without retouching. Helena Rubinstein had begun her career turning evening dresses into curtains. Now *Vogue* urged its readers to defeat rationing by turning their curtains into dresses—"Toile de Jouy curtains are ideal for pretty housecoats."

The Nazis, with their embrace of naturism, sport, and motherhood, officially abhorred such degeneracy. Hitler stopped short of closing beauty parlors and hairdressers, allowing them to remain open throughout the war because, as he remarked to Goebbels in 1943, "women after all constitute a tremendous power and as soon as you dare to touch their beauty parlors they are your enemies."[40] But as always when women were offically relegated to the kitchen and the nursery, cosmetics were frowned upon. As early as 1933, it was decreed in Breslau that "painted" women could not attend Party meetings. The single women chosen to breed for Germany in the "Lebensborn" project, in which Aryan maidens were put at the disposal of SS officers, were not permitted to use lipstick, paint their nails, or pluck their eyebrows. Reddened lips and cheeks might suit the "Oriental" or "southern" woman, the sort of woman destined for Auschwitz or Belsen, but Aryan beauties supposedly preferred the purity of a suntanned skin, with its natural sheen of perspiration. "Though our weapon is but the wooden spoon, its impact must be no less than that of other weapons!" declaimed *Reichsfrauenführerin* Gertrud Scholtz-Klink.[41]

This stern philosophy was alien to France, where feminine beauty was an important part of the culture, and where devotion to style was epitomized by the *haute couture* for which Paris was renowned. Schueller's own taste, however—oddly, it might be thought, for one whose business was so bound up with feminine beauty—tended, if his *Révolution de l'économie* is to be believed, rather toward the Nazi *Kinder, Kirche, Küche* (children, church, kitchen) model of womanhood. *Votre Beauté* reflected this. Its stern emphasis on fitness, sport, and diet, not to say the commercial imperative of selling more bottles of Ambre Solaire, had always inclined it to promote a healthy tan rather than lipstick and face powder, which were not L'Oréal products. Now it bracingly reflected the new hardship. Reappearing in a half-size format in November 1940, its first issue began with several pages of exercises as prescribed by Jean Borotra, the aging tennis star who had become the new regime's General Commissioner for Sports. "Beauty," the magazine declared, "is a discipline: it's cowardly to let yourself go." Naturally, wartime imposed certain difficulties when it came to grooming. But they could—must—be overcome. "No hot water? Tell yourself it's all for the good! Cold water is far better for your health than hot. Hot water is a luxury for people made soft by carelessness. No more hot water, *vive l'eau froide!*" The magazine urged readers not to be nostalgic for the old days of culinary plenty: pictures of lamb chops were sternly crossed out, while plates of potatoes received a nod of approval with the exhortation: "Accept the restrictions bravely and with good grace—rationing will help you live longer."* Feeling the winter cold? Exercise was the thing! As for cosmetics, they were quite simply a relic of a discredited past age. "Women used to use far too much makeup—now we're finding our true nature again," readers were assured in the April 1941 issue.

When it came to product placement, however, the demands of commerce won out over propaganda. "For a woman used to looking after her body, soap is as necessary as bread!" urged an ad for Monsavon. A neighboring ad for L'Oréal was equally forthright. "Dyeing your hair is no longer a matter of coquetry,

* This may well have been true. At least in Britain, people ate more healthfully in wartime, when food was rationed, than they have ever done since.

it's a gesture of defiance, a social necessity." But the tone remained stern. Frivolity and flirtation in the dancehall belonged to a past age. In wartime, survival was what mattered—and the race went to the fittest. "Jobs are scarce, competition's hot—you have to look young! However capable and experienced you may be, gray hair will mean you don't get hired."

Strangely, *Votre Beauté* continued to feature the couture collections, some of which—Lanvin, Gres, Balenciaga—continued throughout the war years. Few of the magazine's readers would have been able to afford these creations, but they had always been featured, and perhaps provided a comforting sense that life as it had once been was not wholly extinct. The most enthusiastic wartime clientele, however, was German. There was even a plan (soon abandoned) to remove the Paris couture houses wholesale to Berlin, a strangely schizophrenic notion given the official Nazi attitude toward chic, but one accurately reflecting the invaders' taste for luxury.

Whether *Votre Beauté*'s readers shared its stern outlook was doubtful. Most wartime photos of young Frenchwomen show no sign of a retreat into scrubbed dowdiness. On the contrary, they tried their best to stay seductive against the odds. One urban legend told how a smart hairdresser employed young men to generate electricity for the dryers by cycling on stationary tandems in the cellars. And perhaps it was true: similar tandems can still be seen in the catacombs beneath the 15th arrondissement.

In those days of scarcity, when only approved publications were allotted paper and ink, *Votre Beauté*'s continued appearance confirmed that its owner toed the official line. It would form part of the case against him when, after the Liberation, Schueller had to face trial. In fact he was tried twice: once in 1946 for industrial collaboration as the owner of L'Oréal and Valentine—when he was all but convicted, scraping out an acquittal on the second hearing—and once in 1948 in his personal capacity as one of the leaders of MSR, when he was acquitted. Had he been found guilty on either count his businesses would have been nationalized, and he would have been banned from ever running a business in France again.

Fortunately for him, little of the evidence brought against him was as clear and undeniable as the volumes of *Votre Beauté*. As usual when alleged collaborators were brought before the courts, there was a jumble of conflicting testimony, leaving gaps and ambiguities that could be interpreted more or less according to taste. The transcripts of the evidence given in Schueller's trials show how hard it was to be certain either of witnesses' motivations or of their veracity.

For example, an item of evidence in both trials concerned a van requisitioned from L'Oréal by the Germans in 1944, when the Occupation was ending and they needed transport to evacuate both themselves and their loot. Everyone agreed that a van had indeed been handed over. But the courts heard three different versions of this story. In one, a late-model van was unquestioningly provided; in another, a van was provided, but it was a *gazogène*, a vehicle developed for use when petrol was unavailable and that ran on methane gas; in the third, a smart new van was promised, but the German in charge omitted to make a final check, and a broken-down old *gazogène* was substituted—one so decrepit that it had to be towed to within a few meters of the factory gate on a trailer, as it would never have made the entire journey unaided. Which story was true?

At least vans were visible objects. Either they were or were not there, had or had not been provided. Less tangible, and so that much harder to pin down, were policies and attitudes. The detested Service du Travail Obligatoire, or STO, under which Frenchmen were compelled to go and work in Germany, was one example.

At first the Germans had tried to raise a volunteer workforce by promising that for each volunteer who went to Germany, a French POW would be released. This arrangement was known as the Relève, and many of Schueller's employees attested that he had addressed his workforce urging those unmarried and without family responsibilities to volunteer in this way. He offered substantial sums to any who did so volunteer, and explained that no one should hesitate to leave because they were worried about the living conditions they might expect: they would sleep in good beds and eat well. This was very far from the general horrific experience, though L'Oréal employees returning from Germany testified that they had received regular food parcels.

Schueller admitted that he had indeed encouraged men to volunteer for the Relève, but insisted that he had been motivated purely by the desire to repatriate prisoners. When it became evident that the Germans were not in fact fulfilling this promise, he ceased to support it. In any case, the program soon ceased to be voluntary, and the Relève was replaced by the compulsory STO.

But was Schueller's real motivation as innocent as he tried to make it appear? One man testified that when he and his group left, "M.Schueller gave us lunch and a little pep talk, saying we didn't need to be afraid, he had always felt more at home in Germany than in England."[42] The man was shocked to hear this overt enthusiasm for the invaders, though perhaps it was not entirely surprising given Schueller's Alsatian parentage. Alsace borders Germany, its dialect is a form of German, and many Alsatians (though not Schueller) felt more German than French—so much so that some of the SS troops who perpetrated the massacre at Oradour-sur-Glâne in 1944 were Alsatian.*

There is no doubt that Schueller, like all employers, tried to minimize the number of workers obliged to undertake this hated journey, as much for his own sake as for theirs. Experienced men were hard to replace. His line was that the reason he had agreed to fulfill some German business orders was in order to keep his workers in France, which may have been true but of course was also a handy way of justifying collaboration. He pointed out that his products had no military value, produced figures showing that the profits derived from German sales were zero in 1940 and 1941, less than 3 percent of profits in 1942, just over 5 percent in 1943, and zero in 1944[43]—and reiterated that he thought taking a few German orders would reduce the number of his workers forced to go to Germany. Schueller's loyal manager at L'Oréal, Georges Mangeot, confirmed this story. He said they began to deal with the Germans in 1942 because they thought that otherwise, with no German business and in a nonvital industry, they would be disadvantaged with regard to STO.

The STO numbers did indeed come down—from 200 to 93 for L'Oréal, and from 75 to 5 for Monsavon. But Mangeot also described how, after discussing the matter with Schueller, he got the numbers reduced in quite another way—by bribing a German member of staff at the Bureau Allemand, who was

---

* The person who selected Oradour as a suitable site for German reprisals was none other than Jean Filliol, Schueller's colleague in MSR. In 1943 he joined the Milice, the dreaded Vichy paramilitary police, and in 1944 was put in charge of the Limoges region, in which Oradour is situated.

later shot, having been caught taking similar bribes.[44] And at Monsavon, the reduction was achieved by the young François Dalle, who persuaded a friendly *commissaire de police* to mislay, at considerable risk to himself, the factory's list of eligible men (which included Dalle himself).[45]

Necessary collaboration, or bribes, or a bit of both? In the complex and shadowy world of occupied France, survival, even for those as well-placed as Schueller, was an endless balancing act, this morsel of disobedience bought at the price of that obeisance to authority. And this balancing act was inevitably reflected in the postwar trials that came to be known as the *épuration*, or purge. Evidence depends on record, and the record reflected at best only a small part of the reality. The judging panels had to reconstitute what was missing as well as they could.

Notoriously, people's motive for testifying in these cases was, more often than not, revenge. Schueller's case was no exception. His chief accuser, in both his trials, was a man called Georges Digeon who had once managed the L'Oréal canteen. It was Digeon who, in 1944, first drew the authorities' attention to Schueller, in an affidavit accusing him of giving the MSR more than 20 million francs; of providing a room for it at rue Royale; and of being a member of the executive committee of Déat's party. Digeon also raised the question of two vans: the one mentioned earlier, requisitioned by the Germans in 1944, and another allegedly given by Schueller to the MSR. This van had all its windows darkened except one at the back, enabling people to be photographed without their knowledge. Schueller, Digeon said, had provided these vehicles without question when asked. But others raised questions about Digeon himself. He was loathed throughout L'Oréal, was known by all as a collaborator who had done regular business with the Germans, and had been sacked in September 1944 "on the demand of the factory" for making baseless accusations. He had then gone straight to the local *mairie*, and had laid the accusations against Schueller that formed the basis of both the personal and industrial *épuration* trials.[46] It could hardly be clearer that he was motivated by fury—and also, as with many such accusers, by an urgent need to divert attention from what he himself had done. On the other hand, that did not mean his accusations were groundless.

Another piece of evidence presented at Schueller's trials was an anonymous letter from some members of the CGT trade union at Valentine, denouncing Schueller for his support of the STO, and for employing known collaborators.

> *If the few workers who are still there can bring themselves to tell the truth, they'll confirm all this. We swear on the heads of our wives and children that we're telling the truth, and we hope you'll arrest that whole nest of collaborators, whether they're millionaires or just working for a boss. . . . We promise to tell you who we are as soon as you start your enquiries, but you can't trust these bastards, and as we need to eat we can't sign our names yet because we'd be thrown out. . . . We swear on our honor that there's no question of vengeance in all this, we're just good Frenchmen who want to see the wicked punished.*[47]

But of course they were a bit more than that. As everyone knew, the trade unions had obvious reasons for hating Schueller, who publicly despised the workers' democracy they stood for.

Another difficulty was that, as the war progressed, people's behavior changed with their expectations. In June 1940, a Nazi victory seemed imminent and inevitable. But in June 1941, Hitler invaded Russia, extending his fighting front by 1,800 miles and bringing the Red Army into the war on the Allies' side. And in December 1941, the Japanese bombing of Pearl Harbor finally brought America, too, into the war. The German victory, which had seemed so certain, now seemed far less assured. Behavior that had seemed most ill-advised yesterday suddenly began to make sense, as prudent persons hedged their bets—among them, Schueller. On December, 10, 1942, he sent a note to L'Oréal representatives:

> *Competitors are spreading lies about me. They come to clients with their order book and my book The Economic Revolution with passages underlined in red pencil, and use them to present me as a bad person who shouldn't be dealt with.*
>
> *They accuse me of being German. I'm not.*
>
> *They accuse me of being Jewish. I'm Catholic. My father was a seminarist for a time. . . .*
>
> *I'm not interested in politics, but in political economy. . . . I was almost made a minister or an undersecretary but I refused because it would have been impossible to do what I would have wanted.*
>
> *I belonged to the Economic Commission of MSR—but only so long as MSR was approved by Marshal Pétain. When that was withdrawn, I resigned. . . .*
>
> *I think it my duty, in the present circumstances, to do all I can to help in what I consider to be the revival of my country. . . .*[48]

He did so by quietly extending his support to the Resistance as well as the occupiers. On the one hand, L'Oréal set aside a room for MSR meetings; on the other, Schueller also organized a weekly mail and parcel drop across the boundary between the *zone occupée* and the *zone libre*, using a L'Oréal van driven by an employee who happened to have an American passport (accredited with a forged German stamp). On the one hand, he continued to finance *La Révolution Nationale*; on the other, he gave 700,000 francs to the underground in the maquis in the Puy de Dôme and sent 2 million francs to de Gaulle. He joined a network that helped more than two hundred people escape into the *zone libre* in the Cher, near Saint-Aignan; he helped others escape from Paris. At the beginning of 1944, his paint firm, Valentine, gave over 100,000 francs to help *réfractaires*—workers who went underground to escape the STO. And all the time, while publicly supporting the official line, he maintained, within occupied Paris, amicable contacts with friends from earlier days.

One such was Fred Joliot-Curie. The two had moved far apart since the early days at L'Arcouest. Joliot-Curie had remained in academic research, which, far from being "dusty," had won him, together with his wife, Irène Curie, the 1935 Nobel Prize in chemistry. Like Schueller, he had always been socially conscious, but there, too, they had moved in opposite directions. Joliot-Curie was now a Communist and active in the Resistance, and had sent his papers on atomic research to London as soon as war broke out, keeping them out of Hitler's grasp.

The contrast between Joliot-Curie's wartime life and that of Schueller illustrated the material advantages of collaboration. Both men were now famous and distinguished. But despite his eminence, Joliot-Curie was not sheltered from the general hardship, while for Schueller, life in wartime was far from austere.

Schueller's only real wartime inconvenience occurred in 1941, when he was forced to move out of his luxurious apartment on boulevard Suchet, in the smart 16th arrondissement, as all the apartment buildings in that street had been requisitioned by the Germans. The owner of the buildings wrote a pleading letter on behalf of his lessees to the sinister Fernand de Brinon, then Vichy's "Ambassador to Paris." None of the foreigners living in the apartment buildings had had to move; couldn't at least the Aryan French be spared? These were important people: Madame Roederer of the champagne family; the president of Cinzano; M. Guerlain the perfumier; bankers; industrialists.[49] No, they all had to go, even though Schueller's name was included on a list of important industrial collaborators who, on the strict and express instruction of Reichsmarschall Göring, were to be allowed to keep their apartments in otherwise requisitioned districts. He moved to avenue Paul Doumer, a short walk away, but preferred to spend his time at his grand house, the Villa Bianca, at Franconville. Joliot-Curie, by contrast, could not even obtain a new tire for the motorbike on which he relied to commute between the Collège de France, where he held a chair, his lab at Ivry, and his temporary home outside Paris. His request was turned down, and a little later he registered the acquisition of a bicycle, with gears.

Despite this disparity, the two remained on surprisingly amicable terms. For Joliot-Curie, Schueller presumably represented that invaluable wartime necessity—one of the enemy who could be trusted on a personal level. Despite what he must have felt about Schueller's politics, he still felt able to request help for a Jewish chemical engineer languishing in a prisoner-of-war camp and who might be a useful employee in Schueller's businesses. Schueller replied to his "cher ami," from a spa where he was taking the cure for rheumatism, that to his great regret he could not help—he had "approached M. Scapini many times, and we got a few people out at first, but there's been nothing doing on that front for a while now. You can imagine, I'm really sorry about this."[50] Georges Scapini was the man deputed by Pétain to negotiate with the German authorities regarding prisoners of war. If he couldn't help, no one could.

In return, Schueller requested a favor of his own—one that throws a rare light on his personal life. In 1927 his first wife, Berthe, had died, and in 1932 he had married again. The second Madame Schueller was Liliane's English governess, Miss Annie Burrows from Fulham (a genteelly run-down part of southwest London), a choice that may reflect her charm, or simply Schueller's own loneliness and lack of social life. He felt that a wife at home was something every man needed. It was one of the social rules set out in the *Révolution de l'économie*. And his work-centered life afforded him few opportunities to meet suitable ladies.

At the time, Miss Burrows (generally known as Nita) must have been overwhelmed by her good luck. Although governesses in novels frequently married their wealthy employers, they rarely did so in real life. But when war broke out, her position, as an Englishwoman married to a leading collaborator, became equivocal, to say the least. She was by no means the only wife to find herself in a similarly awkward fix. The chief Vichy Jew-hunter, the odious Darquier de Pellepoix, was married to an Australian, while Fernand de Brinon, an arch-anti-Semite, had a Jewish wife. How Madame de Brinon felt we do not know. Madame Darquier drowned her troubles in drink. As for Madame Schueller, she seems to have taken refuge in nervous ill health. "The doctor who used to advise Madame Schueller, Dr. Layani, is a non-Aryan, and has escaped to the *zone libre*," Schueller wrote. "I'm looking for a replacement, someone really good on women's illnesses . . . and who can put up with my wife's short temper. Would the director of the

Hôpital Curie know anyone?" Joliot-Curie gave a name, and undertook to write a letter of recommendation. He enclosed, along with his note, two flasks of rabbit urine, one irradiated, the other a control.[51] Between the politics and the business maneuvers, Schueller still kept up his interest in chemistry.

Obviously, when forced to account for himself by the *épuration*, he did his best to emphasize his Resistance-friendly activities and draw a veil over the others. It was not an easy task, given that those others had been so very public. But although Schueller's was an extreme case, so many businessmen were prosecuted for collaboration following the Liberation that at least one employers' federation, that of the ironmasters, circulated a questionnaire to its members to help them prepare dossiers in their own defense. Two main defense planks were recommended: one, that they had kept the largest possible proportion of their production for the use of the French civilian economy and had done as little as possible for the Germans; two, that they had obstructed the deportation of their workers for the STO.[52]

Schueller, like everyone else, stressed these. And like everyone else, he showed how he had helped Jews escape the Nazi horrors. All those he had helped in their hour of need now repaid the debt by writing letters in his support. Two brothers named Freudiger, neighbors in Brittany, had told him they were thinking of joining de Gaulle in London. Schueller warmly encouraged them to do so. Professor Levy of the École Normale, a consultant chemist to L'Oréal, fled to Lyon in the *zone libre* and received money while he was there, paid through L'Oréal's Lyon branch. Another professor of chemistry, M. Meyer, who taught at Lyon University, was sacked from the faculty by Vichy and left without work. Schueller offered a loan to be repaid after the war, as well as other unspecified help. Every time the two met, Meyer testified, Schueller repeated his hatred of the Germans, of the Nazis, of racism. A L'Oréal chemist, M. Chain, first continued to work under a false name, but then had to vanish. He continued to be paid. Mlle. Huffner, a secretary, was paid under a false name, and money was sent to her when she left for the *zone libre*. M. Kogan, the factory manager at Valentine, was a Russian émigré, naturalized only recently, and was therefore caught by the Nazi laws that declared all Jews in this situation to be noncitizens, liable to deportation. Schueller bought him false papers to escape to Portugal; when they failed, and he was stuck in Spain, Schueller arranged a job with L'Oréal's Spanish subsidiary. M. Schatzkes, L'Oréal's commercial director, was sent to Lyon; when competitors complained that the Lyon branch had a Jewish manager, he was sent to Marseille; and when that became dangerous, he stayed in a villa at St. Jean Cap-Ferrat until Marseille became safe again. When the Germans finally arrived there, he and his wife were enabled to escape to Switzerland.

Almost everyone hauled up before the courts in the postwar purges could offer similar examples. Admiral Darlan himself, who for some time was Pétain's deputy (and, thus, effectively head of the Vichy government), and who negotiated a political alliance between French Vichy forces and Nazi Germany, pleaded for Jews who had married into his own family—all belonging to "good old French Jewish families"—to be spared deportation. Perhaps helping a few individuals made it easier not to think about the rest—or perhaps, conversely, the thought of people one knew and liked being subjected to some terrible fate made the awful reality too uncomfortably clear.

The few contemporary documents that survive from the Jewish community show just how difficult it was to persuade people to confront that reality. Hélène Berr, the daughter of a prominent Jewish industrialist,* kept a journal giving a day-by-day account of life as a Jew in occupied Paris. In entry after entry, she records her helpless horror as one after another of her friends and acquaintances is deported. In November 1943, the Berrs' neighbor, Mme. Agache,

> *came rushing in because she had just heard that young Mme. Bokanowski, who had been sent to the Hôpital Rothschild with her two infants when her husband was in Drancy, had been taken back to Drancy. She asked Maman: "You mean to say they are deporting children?" She was horrified.*
>
> *It's impossible to express the pain that I felt on seeing that she had taken all this time to understand, and that she had only understood because it concerned someone she knew. Maman . . . replied: "We have been telling you so for a whole year, but you would not believe us."*
>
> *Not knowing, not understanding even when you do know, because you have a closed door inside you, and you only can realize what you merely know if you open it. That is the enormous drama of our age. Everyone is blind to those being tortured.*[53]

Schueller, of course, had invested everything in *not* confronting these realities. While he comforted his conscience by helping his own Jewish acquaintances, his new friends and colleagues from MSR were dividing the spoils of abandoned Jewish property—that property whose "administration" was such a valued perk of collaborationist life. "I didn't much enjoy the

---

* Raymond Berr was managing director of the chemicals firm Kuhlmann, and was killed in Auschwitz. Hélène died in Bergen-Belsen five days before it was liberated. She was twenty-three.

Friday policy meetings [of MSR at the L'Oréal offices] because they went on too long," Henry Charbonneau remembered. "I was only too happy to leave L'Oréal's fancy panelling for my office in rue Paradis (where we had taken over the LICA building) and get on with working on propaganda."[54] LICA was the Ligue Contre Antisémitisme.

Schueller's *épuration* hearing for personal offenses took place in 1948. He was acquitted with little trouble. In the end what seems to have weighed with the judge was less the evidence, which could be read so many different ways, than the character references given by two witnesses. One was his old friend Jacques Sadoul, who was still a Communist—an important recommendation, since the Communists had been the only political party to support the Resistance officially—and had now also become mayor of Ste. Maxime in the Var. And the other, whose evidence tipped the scales in Schueller's favor, was Pierre de Bénouville, a garlanded Resistance hero, founder in 1942 of the Mouvements Unis de la Résistance, organizer of the Free French forces in Algeria, and who had been named a general on the Italian front—one of only three *résistants* to end the war with this rank.

Bénouville's testimony concerned one of those incidents that now reads like something out of an action movie, but which were quite commonplace during the dark and dramatic days of the Occupation. One of Schueller's Resistance contacts, a man named Max Brusset, notified him that a delegate of the Provisional Government in Algiers wanted to meet him. The meeting was to take place at Brusset's apartment at 28, boulevard Raspail. It was agreed that Schueller would prepare a report concerning certain questions, and deliver it Saturday morning. Needing a little longer, he asked to delay the delivery until Monday morning at eleven. But at nine o'clock Monday, there was a phone call from Brusset: he had the flu, Schueller shouldn't come. In fact, at seven that morning the Gestapo had arrived at the apartment. Brusset's sixth-floor bedroom gave onto a terrace, from which he had been able to jump onto another terrace on the fifth floor and enter the apartment from which he was now phoning. He was able to contact all save one of the people who had been due to meet that morning; that one arrived as arranged, carrying incriminating papers, was arrested, and almost certainly shot. Bénouville knew Brusset, and had promised him that he would provide an authenticating certificate for this story when he returned to Paris.[55] The panel accepted Benouville's evidence and recommended a *relaxe*.

The hearings for industrial collaboration, however, which began in 1946 and were not resolved until two years later, had been more problematic. The panel found that Schueller's Resistance activities were not enough to outweigh the evidence that he had collaborated with the Germans. He had organized lectures in his factories, promised help to men who volunteered to fight alongside the Germans, funded the MSR, published *La Révolution de l'économie* with its anti-union tirades, devised the economic policy of the RNP and encouraged the Relève. The panel did not feel that the various Resistance activities he had brought to their notice counterbalanced this, and found him guilty. In addition to disqualifying him from business, the panel also threatened to forward the evidence to the Court of Justice, which might have confiscated his assets, sentenced him to national disgrace, to a prison term, or even to death.

And if Schueller was not guilty of collaboration, who was? Not only did his name appear in RNP and MSR literature alongside those of Marcel Déat, who was sentenced to death, and Eugène Deloncle, whom only assassination saved from a comparable fate, but he had left an indelible trail in numerous articles, pamphlets, and broadcasts, all urging collaboration; his book *La Révolution de l'économie* had been published on the same list as the works of Hitler himself. Acts or motives might remain cloudy, but the published word was one thing that could not be denied.

Once again, however, Bénouville saved him. Twice—at the first hearing, and again after the guilty verdict—he sent urgent letters, stressing his desire to testify on behalf of the accused, visiting the judge and the Préfet, apologizing when business took him away from Paris at the crucial moment. Schueller, he insisted, was a victim of his fixation on proportional salaries, which had led him into various imprudent actions. But he had been of inestimable help to Bénouville.[56] Bénouville got his way, and Schueller was let off.

Such solidarity between resisters and collaborators was not unusual during the *épuration*. As Schueller's own activities demonstrated, channels of communication between the two sides had always remained open. During the Occupation, collaborators often put in a word for a Resistance figure in trouble. Now those who had been helped, helped in their turn. Bénouville testified in this way on behalf of many old friends. What was interesting about his efforts for Schueller, however, was that the two had met only once, and then briefly (when Schueller, anxious to buy himself onto the winning side, had promised financial aid when Bénouville needed it). Indeed, Bénouville insisted that Schueller had never approached him personally for help. What he had done, he had done for Max Brusset. Even so, it seems surprising that he should have put quite so much effort into getting Schueller cleared. Why had he done so?

The answer, like everything else about Schueller, could

be traced back to the life rules he had evolved. The way both Schueller and Rubinstein conducted their family affairs would be decisive in the intermingling of their stories. And Bénouville, for Schueller, was family—albeit that family was a surrogate one, and Bénouville only a tangential member.

CHAPTER FOUR

Family Affairs

I

> The sons and grandsons of an industry's creators won't take risks. Sons should inherit money, but not management. If a son wants to work, he should take a job elsewhere and work his way up.
>
> —Eugène Schueller, *La Révolution de l'économie*

Among the most strongly held of Eugène Schueller's many strongly held beliefs was the conviction that businesses (as opposed to money) should not be passed on as a family inheritance. When Helena Rubinstein's first grandchildren were born, she declared, "Now the business will last for three hundred years!"[1] But such a thought would have been anathema to Schueller. On the contrary, he thought entrepreneurship required very particular skills, and that "being a general's son doesn't automatically make you a good general." (This was a pet expression of Schueller's, and he used these same words in article after article, lecture after lecture.)

Of course, it was easy for him to say this. His only child was a daughter, which (given his view of woman's place in the world) ruled her out as a possible candidate. And since he had no siblings, he had no aspiring nephews. But it also left him with a problem. Building up L'Oréal had been his life's work. It would have been less than human, not to say irresponsible, to give no thought to his eventual successor. Schueller, of all people, knew that his day-to-day decisions affected the lives of hundreds, possibly thousands, of people. Since he was not immortal, perhaps the most important decision of all concerned the man who would take his place when he died or retired. But who would that be? And how would Schueller identify him? As the thirties drew on and he moved into his middle fifties, he began, consciously or subconsciously, to look around for the young man who would become, in effect, his surrogate son.

As it turned out there would be two such people, each playing a different filial role.

The first, André Bettencourt, was introduced to Schueller in 1938 by a journalist friend, who invited Bettencourt to lunch with "a man you really ought to meet, he's extraordinary."[2] Bettencourt was then nineteen, Schueller fifty-seven. The meeting took place in Schueller's boulevard Suchet apartment, where Bettencourt also met Schueller's daughter, Liliane. The friendship flourished. In December 1941, Bettencourt referred in an article to "a remarkable book by a friend, M. E. Schueller, called 'La Révolution de l'Economie' . . . that all businessmen ought to read."[3]

In that same year, 1941, Bettencourt drew Schueller's attention to another promising young man: his friend François

Dalle. The two had met as students in 1936, when both lived at a university residence for young men such as themselves—Catholic, provincial, well-connected—run by the Marist Fathers at 104, rue de Vaugirard. In 1941, Dalle needed a job, and Bettencourt thought Schueller might have one for him.

Although Bettencourt and Dalle were both members of the Catholic bourgeoisie, they had grown up in very disparate milieux. The Bettencourts were traditional Normandy landowners, conservative and rooted in their village, St. Maurice d'Ételan, of which André's father was the mayor, of which he would in time become mayor himself, and where they were intricately intermarried with the surrounding seigneurial families. They were pious, and M. Bettencourt *père* went on frequent religious retreats, although meditation did not prevent him writing home to remind his gardeners, when planting new apple trees, to "if possible put some fresh soil in the holes."[4] These two preoccupations—religious and agricultural—were passed on to André, and were reflected in his wartime activities.

By contrast, the Dalles were industrialists from France's gritty Nord. François's father was a brewer in Wervicq-Sud, near the Belgian border. The family lived beside the brewery, and their neighbors were mostly working families. François grew up in an austere and socially conscious household, aware from his earliest youth of industrial conflict and the ravages of war. He realized, too, that the main source of unrest in the local textile industry—the workers' continuing and justified complaints about their low level of pay, the factory owners' riposte that as their profits were so low, they could not afford to pay more—arose because of outdated attitudes and machinery. Capitalism, he concluded, could be justified only insofar as it brought material abundance. [5]

By the time the two young men arrived in Paris, toward the end of 1936, it was clear that Europe was sliding toward another general conflict, and that France, if involved, would almost certainly be defeated. In 1937 and again in 1938, Dalle, Bettencourt, and some other friends from the old university lodgings at 104, rue de Vaugirard, including France's future president François Mitterrand, whose family was in the vinegar business in the Charente, visited Luxembourg, Belgium, and Germany during their vacations. They saw tanks rolling at full speed through villages while the villagers cheered and girls threw flowers. On one memorable day, on a riverbank near the German-Luxembourg border, they watched as a thousand soldiers in swimming-gear stood at attention while a hundred-piece orchestra played Beethoven, and then, at the sound of a bugle, threw themselves, as one man, into the river. It was an impressive show of fitness and discipline, and the young Frenchmen were left wondering how their ragtag conscript army could ever stand up to a force composed of men such as that.[6]

In this charged and uncertain atmosphere, the young men from 104 inclined to the right. The left seemed to offer only chaos. Fascism—not as practiced by Hitler, but of the Mussolini and Salazar Catholic variety—at least held out the possibility of order. "We didn't think Mussolini would go in with Hitler," Dalle said. "We were bourgeois students, Catholics. . . . We knew the war was lost before it began, because our arms were as hopeless as our high command. We were just cannon fodder. . . ."[7] They were mostly studying law, and preferred to use the faculty library, which was recognized as the province of the far-right Camelots du Roi, rather than the Sorbonne library, where, Dalle said, "less than 5 percent were non-Marxists, and not a single girl ever caught your eye."[8]

When the war came, Dalle, Mitterrand, and Bettencourt, like all young Frenchmen, were called up. Following the debacle of France's capitulation, Mitterrand was captured and sent to a prisoner-of-war camp inside Germany, an experience that would shape his future political career, while Bettencourt and Dalle returned to Paris, and looked around for something to do. Bettencourt found a job in journalism, writing a youth-interest column under the heading *Ohé les jeunes!* for a magazine called *La Terre Française*, directed at agriculturists. Dalle thought of resuming his studies. But his preferred professors were no longer teaching their courses, and besides, having just married, he needed to earn some money. Going through the want ads one day he noticed that the Society of French Soapmakers, working through Monsavon, was looking for trainees. He knew that Schueller owned Monsavon, and knew and liked his economic theories. He knew, too, that his friend André was acquainted with the Schuellers. Bettencourt encouraged him to apply for the job.

Schueller, who always took a personal interest in trainees, met Dalle, agreed to hire him, and asked where he came from. The Nord, Dalle replied. "That's good," Schueller said. "In this country there are only two sets of people who really work, the ones from Alsace, and the ones from the Nord." A few days later, Dalle presented himself for work at the Monsavon factory in Clichy, a dank place in what he described as "the miserabilist style of the Paris suburbs." He was twenty-four. His job was to help the sales director's secretary—"a radical change of direction," as he observed, "for someone who had always dreamed of teaching law."[9]

His first job, which he hated, consisted of multiplying the number of soaps sold by their price, to calculate turnover. But at the end of 1943 the sales director fell ill, and the managing director mysteriously vanished: suddenly, at the age of twenty-five, Dalle found himself the de facto boss of a large factory. Schueller liked to divide his colleagues into two categories: people men and things men. Dalle certainly wasn't a "things man," though there were two in the factory: they had just devised an innovative continuous soap-making process that would prove valuable in the immediate postwar years. However, they couldn't try it out on Monsavon's wartime product, which consisted almost wholly of bentonite and kaolin and contained virtually no fat. It could hardly be called soap at all. And there were problems with morale. Keeping Monsavon's little community going in those desperate days, when food of any kind was short, good food almost unobtainable, and nobody trusted anyone else, was an invaluable experience for the "people man" François Dalle would become.

Monsavon survived the war. But it then faced the problem of surviving the peace, which had its own difficulties. In wartime the buying public had grabbed anything put before it, including Monsavon's ersatz soap; but now the presence of American troops and American products reminded battered Europeans of a long-forgotten abundance. American competition meant hard times for indigenous companies facing huge shortages of raw materials. Dalle thought for a while about returning to the law, but he had lost the habit of study, and soon realized that the subject no longer interested him. So he returned joyfully to Monsavon and the entrepreneurial life he found so exhilarating, and was put in charge.

During these years, Schueller let Dalle get on with the job without interference. One summer Sunday in 1948, however, an indication came that Schueller had plans for him. Summoned to the Franconville house, Dalle was informed that, starting the next day, he was to work at L'Oréal as well as Monsavon. He had done well with Monsavon and, hopefully, would continue to do so. But now it was time to find his place within the company as a whole. "I was flattered, but terribly embarrassed," Dalle remembered. "It hadn't ever crossed my mind that women's hair grew white as they got older, let alone that they might dye it—the notion that one might want to change the natural order of things would have seemed odd to me, actually almost shocking. Where I came from women didn't use cosmetics."[10]

This uncertainty was soon buried, however, beneath the whirlwind of his new life. He was given an office at rue Royale and began the long task of getting to know a new business and gaining the trust of longstanding lieutenants over whose heads he was all too evidently being promoted. He soon became Schueller's chief confidant, which meant adopting his chief's frenetic pace. From six till eight a.m. he read notes dictated by Schueller the previous evening, then walked for an hour around the park at Bagatelle, near where he lived, before dictating his responses. He spent the morning at Monsavon and the afternoon at L'Oréal, staying there until nine—the hour when Schueller left the office.

After a few months of this pace he became tired, and Schueller offered him and his family the L'Arcouest house for a couple of weeks of relaxation and enjoyment. It rained solidly; when the offer was renewed the following year, Dalle's wife and children refused to accompany him. It rained again; cooped up all alone in the big house, Dalle thought longingly of Paris and all the work awaiting his return. He called for his secretary and resumed his Parisian work schedule, wondering later if this had not been a deliberate ploy on the part of Schueller, who did the same thing during *his* vacations.

It was soon clear to them both that Dalle would be L'Oréal's next chief executive. But it was not until 1957, when Schueller's health began to fail, that this was said in so many words. That July, Dalle was summoned to L'Arcouest. He found Schueller tanned and apparently well, but appearances were deceptive: he was dying. He was L'Oréal's present, the old man said, but Dalle would be its future. The speech left both of them in tears. Not long after it, Schueller died, and Dalle became managing director of L'Oréal. Where, politically and commercially, Schueller had remained essentially a man of the 1930s, Dalle would move L'Oréal into the post-war world.[11]

WHILE DALLE WAS TAKING HIS place as Schueller's industrial heir, André Bettencourt had maintained their friendship on a more personal level: in 1950, he would marry Schueller's daughter, Liliane. The file of papers concerning Schueller's *épuration* trial contains two letters from Bettencourt, one written in January 1944, the other in September of the same year. They make it clear that the two had become close enough for Schueller to trust the younger man with both money and personal confidences.

By 1944, the course of the war had turned in the Allies' favor, and those who had positioned themselves three years earlier in expectation of a German victory now found themselves somewhat awkwardly placed. Bettencourt had spent the first years of the war as a journalist, writing for collaborationist and Pétainist publications, and had later spent some time at Vichy, working for the Pétain administration there. It is clear from his January letter to Schueller that both of them anticipated difficulties if, as seemed increasingly likely, the Germans were defeated.

> *You told me about your fears, and various conversations I had before I left Paris seem unfortunately to justify them. Do be very careful. You're so terribly impulsive about everything, but I think you should be very cautious about revealing too much regarding the way you've helped some of us, and some friendships should also be kept quiet; if you're publicly compromised, those who have been close to you might find themselves in a delicate position.*
>
> *I think, and I hope you'll agree, that the essential thing for you is to get social matters organized. . . .*

This prophecy of trouble ahead was soon fulfilled. When the war ended, Schueller was hauled in front of the courts on a charge of collaboration, where, as we have seen, he was liberated largely because of the efforts of Pierre de Bénouville, whom he had barely met. And here, at last, is the explanation for this surprising intervention: Bénouville had been a contemporary of Dalle and Bettencourt at 104 rue de Vaugirard, and it was largely to oblige these friends that he agreed to testify for Schueller. Bettencourt, if not Schueller, had social matters highly organized, and Schueller now benefited from his excellent connections.

Bénouville was not in any way put out by Schueller's links with the cagoulards and MSR—rather the opposite: he had himself been an enthusiastic cagoulard. His name appears in the Corre list of members, and although when questioned in old age he refused to admit directly that he had belonged to La Cagoule, he reaffirmed that he thought Filliol and Deloncle had been "good chaps who refused to give in" (*Des gens très sympas* *qui ne voulaient pas céder*). On the same occasion he said that he quite understood why it had been necessary to assassinate the Soviet diplomat Dmitri Navachine—he had been trying to infiltrate the royalist journal *Le Courrier Royal*, something Bénouville seems to have felt merited a death sentence.[12] His nationalism was so extreme that it was impossible for him to countenance any form of collaboration with the German occupation. But his gut loathing of the left remained undimmed, even when they were his fellow *résistants*. As Pierre Péan's *Vie et morts de Jean Moulin* shows, he was almost certainly part of the complex machinations that betrayed the Communist Resistance leader Jean Moulin to the Germans. Moulin, a man Bénouville saw as standing "on the very left of the left," was an associate of Pierre Cot, who had been interior minister at the time of the great demonstration of February 6, 1934, and who had ordered the police to fire on the crowd: "That was something about Moulin that I didn't like at all."[13] Bénouville preferred to deal with characters like Georges Soulès, who had belonged to MSR but who in 1943 switched over to the Resistance, and who was close enough to Bénouville to have a special postbox arrangement to communicate with him.[14] Indeed, Bénouville was, if anything, to the right of Schueller politically—certainly in his anti-Semitism. In 1937 he had been a regular contributor to *Le Pays Libre*, a violently anti-Semitic publication.*

It was the 104 network, too, that steered Bettencourt clear of the anticipated post-Liberation hazards. By the summer of 1944 it was obvious that anyone who wanted to enter public life after the war would need to show they had been a *résistant*,

* It is ironic to note that after the war Bénouville became a director of Dassault-Breguet, the aircraft company run by Marcel Dassault, *né* Marcel Bloch, who had been deported to Buchenwald in 1944 with his wife and children.

and Mitterrand and Bénouville, who both had starry Resistance credentials, had worked together to ensure, while there was still time, that their old friend Bettencourt would come out of the war with the correct reputation. They did so by arranging to send him to Geneva on Resistance business.

> *I'm just back from Geneva [Bettencourt wrote Schueller that September]. I can't come to rue Royale immediately, but I can tell you that your Swiss affairs are in good shape. . . . As it turned out I didn't need the money you so kindly made available to me there. There was enough credit available from the Resistance delegation. . . .*[15]

The Geneva trip did what it was intended to do, and in the years following the war, Bettencourt swiftly climbed the political ladder. Meanwhile, his intimacy with the Schuellers grew. Liliane Schueller was tubercular, and spent the winter of 1947–48 in the Swiss resort of Leysin; André joined her there, at the chic Hotel Belvedere. Soon the two were engaged, and on January 9, 1950, André Bettencourt and Liliane Schueller were married. The ceremony took place at Vallauris, the home of a family friend, rather than at Franconville or L'Arcouest. Evidently Liliane did not regard the second Madame Schueller as part of the family—or not enough to host her wedding reception. Nor, it seemed, did Schueller himself. Interviewed in 1954, he told journalist Merry Bromberger that he had "lost his wife, who had been such a support to him [and that] his daughter, Madame Bettencourt, the wife of a young deputy for Seine-Infèrieure, looks after the house at Franconville."[16] Of the former Miss Burrows there was no mention.*

---

* She outlived him and is buried at Ploubazlanec, near L'Arcouest.

By this time the 104-L'Oréal connection had widened to include François Mitterrand. Mitterrand had had a busy and productive war. After escaping from his prisoner-of-war camp he had become caught up in Vichy politics, receiving the Francisque medal from Pétain himself, at the same time using his position at the head of the prisoners-of-war organization to run an important Resistance network. He had also fallen in love and got married. It was a varied, thrilling, and risky double and treble life, and one he hugely enjoyed. When the Liberation brought it to an end, he felt restless and dissatisfied. He wanted to enter politics, but was unable to locate a suitable political niche. Meanwhile his wife was pregnant, and he urgently needed to earn some money. So he turned to his friends for help—and, as always, 104 did not disappoint. Dalle, supported by André Bettencourt, used his influence with Schueller, and for a while, before returning to politics and getting elected as deputy for the Nièvre, Mitterrand edited *Votre Beauté*.

He hated it. Editing a women's magazine for a beauty-products company was not the future the ambitious François had envisaged. Every evening when he came home he grumbled to his wife about how he was wasting his life. For Schueller, L'Oréal represented first a scientific challenge, and then a bottomless fountain of cash. For Dalle, it would be a fascinating and lucrative career following in the footsteps of a man he revered. But although Mitterrand was grateful for the comfortable salary, he felt his association with *Votre Beauté* made him look ridiculous. Although his actual name never appeared, his alter ego Frédérique Marnais was much in evidence, writing articles and responding to readers' letters. Why was François Mitterrand, of all people, advising women on their emotional problems and beauty routines? He made a few feeble attempts to turn *Votre Beauté* into a literary magazine, but met with no encouragement—there were, Danielle Mitterrand remembered, "constant battles with the editorial board."[17] And at home, things were also not going well. The Mitterrands' first baby died at the age of three months, an event from which both he and his wife struggled to recover.

Frédérique Marnais welcomed in the new year of 1946 with a touching and heartfelt piece entitled "A Woman's Most Beautiful Necklace: The Arms of a Little Child."[18] But by then the association was clearly doomed. "I don't exactly see this job as a religious calling,"[19] he wrote irritably to his L'Oréal superiors—a fatal admission in a company where this was precisely the kind of dedication required from senior staff. As was inevitable, Mitterrand left L'Oréal soon after, and spent the summer of 1946 looking for a winnable seat in the Chamber of Deputies. In November he found it, in the department of the Nièvre, and by 1947 he was minister for war veterans.

It was Mitterrand who brought Pierre de Bénouville onto the Schueller scene. Hauled up before the courts in 1946 on a charge of industrial collaboration, Schueller was in real danger of being convicted. And he knew—none better—the damning evidence that might be brought against him, even though a lot of what had been most compromising had not been recorded. In the end it was the quality of the witnesses that mattered—who testified against you, and who supported you. He needed to find people who would testify in his favor and whom the court could not dismiss—in other words, people with good Resistance credentials and political connections. The obvious person was Mitterrand, but he was taken up by political campaigning. So Pierre de Bénouville was called in—Mitterrand being an even older friend of his than Bettencourt, since the two of them had not only been students together, but had attended the same school in Angoulême.

Bénouville did not disappoint. It was thanks to him that Eugène Schueller survived. He, who for the whole of his life had stood quite outside the family, business, and educational networks whose members controlled France, became caught up, through the boys from 104, at the very center of one such network. From this moment on, Schueller, his family, friends, and associates, would be part of the establishment—with all the potential for scandal and embarrassment that entailed.

II

FOR HELENA RUBINSTEIN, TOO, THE war changed everything.

The buyback from Lehman Brothers had marked, as Titus feared, the end of their marriage. They divorced in 1937, and by 1938 Madame had married again.

She met her new husband, the Georgian prince Artchil Gourielli-Tchkonia, at a bridge party given by her old friend Marie-Blanche de Polignac (the daughter of her even older friend, Jeanne Lanvin). His title was a little dubious—gossip had it that when he presented his intended bride with a copy of the *Almanach de Gotha*, the page detailing his heritage had been specially printed and inserted. But no one was about to travel to Georgia to check it out. And in the meantime he was handsome, charming, and he made her laugh. They met again, several times, before she left Paris for New York. "Where do you like to dine in New York?" Artchil artlessly enquired. At the Colony, Helena replied. "Two weeks later he telephoned me, in New York. He had just arrived and meant to hold me to my promise, he said. Within an hour he called for me at my home, and that evening we dined at the Colony. How could I resist such a man? Our courtship was brief. In his usual direct way he said, 'We are neither of us children, Helena, and you need me.' "[20] He was forty-three, she, sixty-six. They understood each other perfectly.

It was an excellent marriage. Unlike Titus, Artchil was only too happy to be Mr. Helena Rubinstein. He appreciated the opulent living and material peace of mind this title bestowed, and the price was not excessive: "I only had to sleep with her once," he is reported to have said.[21] After that he looked, with tactful discretion, elsewhere—an arrangement which suited them both perfectly. At sixty-six, an ardent sex life was not one of Helena's requirements, if indeed it ever had been. She had married Artchil for other reasons. He was presentable, sweet-tempered, funny, and affectionate; her family, who mostly regarded each other with suspicion and dislike, all loved Artchil. And—he made his wife a princess! That little Chaja Rubinstein would become Princess Gourielli was a fate even her most extravagant imaginings could not have anticipated.

It was also indirectly because of Artchil that she had to acknowledge something that had not concerned her since she left Kazimierz: the fact of her Jewishness.

Helena's idea of relaxation had hitherto been limited to bridge or the theater. But Artchil wanted to give parties, so she found a suitable apartment: a twenty-six-room triplex on Park Avenue at Sixty-fifth Street. When she tried to buy it, however, her offer was turned down: the building had a no-Jews policy. Enraged, Madame bought the building. The apartment was hers. But for the first time in her life, anti-Semitism had become something she could not ignore.

Since leaving Krakow she had not lived among Jews; neither, until the problem with the Park Avenue apartment building, had discrimination brought her Jewishness home to her. It was true that her Jewishness enforced certain business imperatives. When she set up her first American branches they were in cities where Jews were accepted, such as San Francisco, Philadelphia, New Orleans, Atlantic City; she left strongholds of anti-Semitism such as Boston, Washington, Palm Beach, and Newport to her goyishe rival Elizabeth Arden, whose business was distinctly WASP-oriented. But she felt no personal affinity with Jews—rather the contrary. She had refused to live on New York's Upper West Side because it was "too Jewish," and disliked the French Riviera, the preferred playground of her rival Estée Lauder, for the same reason.

It looked, for a while, as though this distancing would survive even World War II. When, toward the end of the thirties, Marc Chagall asked her for some money to help relatives escape from Germany, she told him to try elsewhere. And when war broke out she followed her usual practice and left for distant parts, taking an extended cruise with Artchil to Central and South America. Everything, including real estate, was wonderfully cheap there, and she took the opportunity to establish branches in Buenos Aires, Rio de Janeiro, and Panama. She was soon, she happily told the *New York Times*, doing "astounding" business.[22] Over the following four years she went back twice, eventually, as always, placing relatives in charge of the new offices.

But as the war dragged on, even Madame had to recognize that being Jewish enforced perspectives and priorities rather different from those she had hitherto preferred. She urged all those members of her family who still remained within Hitler's reach to leave while they could, with the promise of jobs wherever they might choose to settle. Her sister Stella went to Argentina, and a great-niece named Regina was sent to Australia. But the sister after whom that Regina had been named, the only one of Helena's generation not to have left Krakow, refused to budge and was killed in the death camps.

Regina's death was a turning point for Helena. She threw herself wholeheartedly into the war effort, becoming a booster for War Bonds and organizing concerts on behalf of the Polish Red Cross. She had always been unenthusiastic about the Germans, furious during World War I when her German-sounding name had led people to accuse her of being pro-German herself. "Poles hated always the Germans. . . . I am really upset. I got a letter . . . which mentioned that some letters were received from England re my pro-German feelings and so on. Fancy I wish them going to hell, excuse the expression, I hate the sight of them. . . ."[23] Returning now from one of her trips to South America, where so many Nazi war criminals would soon find shelter, she assured the *New York Times* that among all the people she met, the Germans were universally unpopular, "and even when it was hard to get servants many people would not engage a German cook." She "estimated that 90 percent of the Argentine people were 'really our allies.' "[24]

When the war ended, she became a keen supporter of the new State of Israel (which she always called Palestine). "I'm going to build a museum and a factory in . . . in? Not Jerusalem but the other town," she told Patrick O'Higgins in 1958.

"Tel Aviv?"

"Yes, that's the place."

Feted as a big donor, she sat through any number of tedious receptions, and finally met Israel's then foreign minister, Golda Meir. Surveying Mrs. Meir's craggy features, she remarked disapprovingly on the minister's lack of makeup. Then the two formidable ladies got down to business—in English, although Yiddish was in both cases their mother tongue.

"Madame Rubinstein, what do you think of our country?" Mrs. Meir asked.

"If I plan to build a factory *and* a museum, I must think highly of it."

"Which do you think is the more important?"

"The factory!"

"I agree!"[25]

And with that simple exchange, the stage was set for the drama to come.

CHAPTER FIVE

A Takeover and Three Scandals

I regret having done . . . for a noble cause, things that may have inconvenienced other human beings.

—Jacques Corrèze, June 20, 1991

It is true that I hired Jacques Corrèze although he had been condemned twice . . . but he had just been released from jail. I don't regret having hired him, he was everything I hoped he might be. And I'm not going to take lessons in patriotism from anybody!

—François Dalle, June 19, 1991

A weak man will always be more of a coward than a man in his prime; a Jew will always be more avaricious than a Christian.

—André Bettencourt, *L'Élan*, December 13, 1941

I've led a useful life, after all.

—André Bettencourt, March 9, 1995

I

On April 1, 1965, Helena Rubinstein relinquished her avid grip on life. In a memoir published the previous year she had for the first time admitted her real birthdate. She was ninety-two years old.

Until a year before her death, Madame had remained in active, some thought hyperactive, charge of her business. But on the morning of May 21, 1964, she was surprised by thieves in her New York triplex. They gained entry by pretending to deliver a flower arrangement, then tied up the butler at gunpoint and made for the main bedroom, which they expected to find empty. Madame, however, was no longer an early riser. On the contrary, she liked to conduct much of her business from her bed. At eight thirty a.m. she was eating her breakfast toast, prior to conferring with her secretary and publicity adviser.

Presented with the traditional choice—her money or her life—she retorted that at her age she didn't care if they killed her, but she was damned if they were going to rob her. At which point she realized that her keys—including the keys to her safe and the filing cabinet in which she kept her jewels—were in her purse on the bed, under the intruders' noses.

Fortunately the purse was buried deep in papers, and the thieves were by then busy emptying drawers and disconnecting phones. Madame silently extracted the keys and with characteristic presence of mind dropped them in the one place she could be sure no one would ever look: down her ample bosom. By the time the thieves noticed the purse it contained only some handfuls of paper, a powder compact, five twenty-dollar bills, and a pair of diamond earrings worth around forty thousand dollars. The earrings rolled away as they upended it, and Madame covered them with a Kleenex. One of the thieves grabbed the money. "Your friend took a hundred dollars out of my purse. See that you get your share," she admonished his friends. Furious and frustrated, aware that time was passing and that other household members would soon arrive, they ripped off her bedcovers, tore the sheets in strips and tied her to a chair, before fleeing with their negligible loot. And there, screaming at the top of her still-considerable lungs, she was found by the butler, who had managed to break free of his own bonds. After he freed her, Madame instructed him to put the thieves' roses in the icebox, in case there should be company for lunch. She calculated that after paying $40 for the roses, they had made just $60 profit on their morning.[1]

Madame was justifiably proud of her sangfroid. But the shock drained her, and she never recovered either her confidence or her health. As always when faced with a crisis, she took refuge in motion, traveling from New York to Paris, on to Tangiers and evenings of bridge with such of the ancient International Set as still survived ("If you add up the combined ages round this table we're back in the sixteenth century," quipped one of the players, at which Madame snapped "Don't—until you've paid the ten francs you owe me!"), back to Paris, on to Normandy, which held sentimental memories of her romance with Edward Titus, a stop at Saint-Cloud, where she had established her first French factory ("It's where I was always happiest," she sighed, "in my kitchen, my laboratory"). Then she returned to New York, suffered a stroke, and died.[2]

Helena Rubinstein's death liberated a small mountain of possessions. Her estate was variously estimated at between $1 million and $100 million, depending on what was counted in. The American business alone grossed over $22 million a year.[3] Officially, it was publicly owned, but in fact Madame personally held 52 percent of the shares—worth around $30 million—as she had done ever since the Lehman Brothers maneuver. The Park Avenue triplex was rented, in a move that would surely have appalled her, to Charles Revson of Revlon, an upstart whose name she had always refused to utter, referring to him only as "the nail man." Her will, when it was read, contained 121 individual bequests.[4] But that was just the property: gowns, jewels, pictures, real estate. The business was not so easily disposed of. The industry that she had founded in one room and a "kitchen" was by the time of her death the tenth-most important in the United States, just behind rubber. Helena Rubinstein, Inc., had become an empire. Where would it end up?

For her American competitors, the problem was easily solved. The business would be sold, and one of them would buy. Particularly keen was a firm called Cosmair. Set up in 1953, Cosmair, although nominally independent, was part-owned and effectively controlled by L'Oréal, and was L'Oréal's sole U.S. licensee. The person appointed to run it by Schueller, John Seemuller, was half-American—he was the person who had performed those risky missions for the firm in France during the war, using his American passport to run forbidden items across the border between the occupied and nonoccupied zones. The Cosmair job may have been Schueller's way of showing his appreciation. But Seemuller did not appreciate how tricky it might be to penetrate the American market, and made little headway.

Seemuller's incompetence frustrated François Dalle, who was keen to extend L'Oréal's reach into the huge market of the United States. He was also anxious to broaden L'Oréal's range to include cosmetics, whose sales, as women cast off housewifery and flooded into the workplace during the 1960s and early seventies, were rising at an average of 10 percent a year. One

HR aged sixteen, before she left Krakow.

Photo: Helena Rubinstein Foundation

Helena Rubinstein milling parsley in her Saint Cloud "kitchen," 1932. Here was where she always felt happiest. Fresh flowers and herbs were favorite ingredients for beauty creams.

Photo: Helena Rubinstein Foundation

Madame Rubinstein the scientist: as she liked to see herself and project herself to the world.
PHOTO: HELENA RUBINSTEIN FOUNDATION

Helena Rubinstein by Marie Laurencin, 1934. She was sixty-two years old, but you would never guess it from this portrait, which showed her as an "Indian Maharanee."
PHOTO: HELENA RUBINSTEIN FOUNDATION

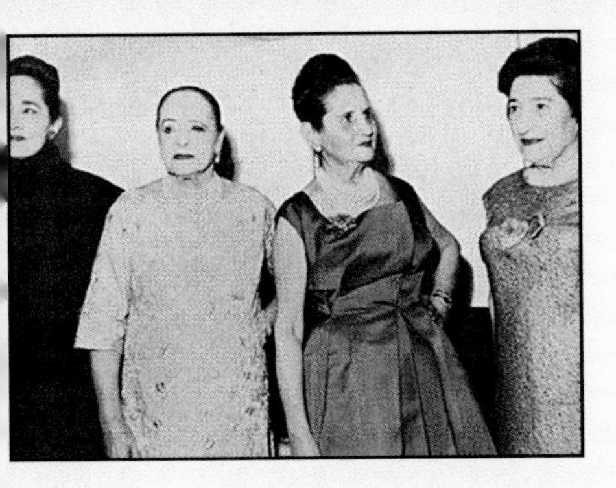

Helena Rubinstein with her surviving sisters, *l to r:* Manka, Helena, Stella, and Ceska, 1963.

PHOTO: JEAN-PAUL CADÉ/HELENA RUBINSTEIN FOUNDATION

Edward Titus, the first Mr. Helena Rubinstein.

PHOTO: HELENA RUBINSTEIN FOUNDATION

Prince Artchil Gourielli, Rubinstein's second husband, on holiday in St. Moritz, 1949. Pleasures like this were one of the many advantages of being Mr. Helena Rubinstein.

PHOTO: HELENA RUBINSTEIN FOUNDATION

Helena Rubinstein at eighty-six, by Graham Sutherland. When she first saw this picture, Rubinstein hated it, commenting, "I never imagined I looked like this." But after the painting was exhibited and admired in the Tate Gallery, she changed her opinion: "I had to admit, it's a masterpiece."

PHOTO: HELENA RUBINSTEIN FOUNDATION

Patrick O'Higgins, Helena Rubinstein's goy, leaving Australia at the end of his and Rubinstein's 1958 visit.

Eugène Schueller in 1909, the young chemist making his way in the world. From an insert in the first issue of *Coiffure de Paris.*

L'Auréole–the 1905 hairstyle that gave its name to L'Oréal.

Coiffure de Paris: October 1909

Eugène Schueller giving a lecture, Paris, 1941.

Archive, Mémorial de la Shoah, Paris

chueller's design for an ideal home, gothically arched for aximum light, and complete with an ideal family, including dog, a car, and three children. Note that it is the wife who olds the baby. From *Le Deuxième salaire*, popular illustrated dition, 1940.

Eugène Deloncle, founder of La Cagoule and Schueller's colleague in the Mouvement Sociale Révolutionnaire, 1940.

Jacques Corrèze aged thirty-three, at the time of the Cagoule trial, 1945.

"The young are life's favorites. . . . And youth lasts longer for those who use L'Oréal."
L'Oréal ad, 1923

Les "jeunes" sont les favorisés de la vie...
Paraître jeune... c'est attirer toujours vers soi les regards admirateurs, qui se détournent des têtes grisonnantes. Et l'âge heureux de la jeunesse dure longuement pour ceux qui emploient :

an Frydman in 1944, at the time of the Liberation.

The stolen Rosenfelder house in Karlsruhe.
COURTESY MONICA WAITZFELDER

André Bettencourt in 1973 when he was acting Minister for Foreign Affairs.
OFFICIAL PHOTO, ARCHIVES DIPLOMATIQUES

André and Liliane Bettencourt: the wealthiest couple in France, on the occasion of André Bettencourt's election to the Académie des Beaux-Arts, March 23, 1988. Bettencourt's sword was specially designed by the sculptor Yves Tremois.
JAMES ANDANSON/SYGMA/CORBIS

Liliane Bettencourt and François-Mari
Banier at an exhibition of Banier's photographs at the Museum Haus Lange, Krefeld, Germany, in June 2004 before their friendship became a matt
of scandal.

Horst Ossinger/Corbis

Helena Rubinstein's New York drawin
room, 1950s. "Quality is nice, but quantity makes a show."

Photo: Helena Rubinstein Foundation

Liliane Bettencourt's salon in her Neuilly mansion, a model of tastefulness.

Photo: *Architectural Digest*/Condé Nast

of Dalle's first acts on taking over as CEO was therefore to appoint his own man to head Cosmair: the suave and charming Jacques Corrèze, who had been vice president of L'Oréal's Spanish subsidiary, Procasa. Corrèze was good at both administration and business, and was particularly good with money. Seemuller had quickly run through all the cash Paris allowed him, to little effect; Corrèze, Dalle remembered, was "close with his—which was to say, our—pennies."[5]

In 1965, when Helena Rubinstein died, Cosmair was still small. It had only twenty employees, producing and distributing L'Oréal's hair-care preparations to beauty parlors. But Corrèze had made a point of getting to know Madame—he was just the sort of man she liked, smooth, cultivated, and full of Old World charm—and when she died, he was determined that if anyone took over Helena Rubinstein, Inc., it would be Cosmair. At the end of the war, French manufacturers, who since 1940 had enjoyed a market in which anything they produced was snatched from the shelves, had been rocked by the sudden influx of unaccustomed competition from America. Now it was L'Oréal's turn to extend its reach into America.

Helena Rubinstein, however, was not for sale. Although the American branch was publicly quoted, all its other branches (except the English business and its South African and Far East subsidiaries, which were the property of a foundation set up to avoid inheritance taxes) remained privately owned. The company was now managed by Madame's son, Roy Titus, and her nephew and niece, Regina's son and daughter Oskar Kolin and Mala Rubinstein, who were reported to have metamorphosed "from depression to a vibrant pragmatism."[6] Released from Madame's beady eye and unsettling tendency to descend unannounced and bawl out all those present, they were enjoying the unaccustomed pleasures of self-rule.

But those pleasures did not last, for they did not get on. Indeed, the experience of Helena Rubinstein, Inc., as it declined after its founder's death (in marked contrast to L'Oréal, which continued from strength to strength under Dalle) might have been designed to prove Eugène Schueller's theory that business and family were best kept separate. Although Madame had always assumed that "the family" would carry on the business after her death, she had never trained a successor. That would not only have meant admitting her own mortality, but would have run the risk of transferring too much of her own power to someone else, something quite alien to her autocratic character.

Instead, she had encouraged rivalries. Although Roy was her firstborn, she had never taken him seriously, preferring his younger brother, Horace, whose only real interest in the firm while he was alive (he predeceased his mother, much to her anguish) had been as a source of cash. Her real business partners had been Oskar, a sharp accountant who did any necessary dirty work and was known to all as the Lord High Executioner, and his sister Mala, of whom she had been fond, and whom Roy bitterly resented. "She enjoys it," her long-time secretary, Ruth Hopkins, said, she "plays one against the other."[7] But all this was secondary—for Madame, and nobody else, made the decisions: as she had liked to say, "I *am* the business." The inevitable upshot was that her death left an unfillable void at the business's center. Once the firm's living trademark and main motive power had vanished, all that remained was a disunited boardroom with no clear strategy.

By 1972, the family had had enough and decided to sell. The buyer, Colgate-Palmolive, paid $146 million: more than twenty times earnings. But Colgate soon regretted its purchase. The overseas businesses, which continued to operate much as before, remained profitable. But the American arm soon began to lose money. Colgate's idea had been to integrate the Rubinstein product range into its existing marketing operation. But as Madame could have told them had she still been around to do so, high-end beauty products require special sales techniques, different from those that sell everyday necessities like soap and toothpaste. By 1978, Helena Rubinstein's losses were estimated at $22 million, and its debts at $50 million. Colgate had had enough, and Helena Rubinstein was once more for sale.

In early 1979, KAO, a Japanese toothpaste business, was reported to have offered $75 million for it. Later that same year, L'Oréal was again in the picture, the price now having dropped to $35 million. But neither sale materialized. In 1980, however, Colgate finally offloaded its unwise acquisition. The buyer was a privately owned concern, Albi Enterprises, the price $20 million, plus a Colgate guarantee for up to $43 million in bank loans.[8] Albi quickly recouped its outlay by selling off Helena Rubinstein's mass-market lines and its American headquarters. By 1985 the company's only American employees were a dozen people in a New York office. They spent their days consolidating international financial statements, and no longer had any idea who they worked for.

Cosmair, by contrast, was doing very well. During the 1970s, Dalle had pushed L'Oréal's U.S. subsidiary into high gear, investing heavily in research and identifying profitable niches in what the industry jargon called a "maturing" market. Some of this success was down to deep pockets: L'Oréal, and hence Cosmair, was now part-owned by the Swiss foods giant Nestlé. But Cosmair also had a dynamic new managing director of its own. Dalle, like Schueller before him, was looking out for a suitable successor, and had recently identified him in the person of Lindsay Owen-Jones. In 1985, Dalle planned to retire. There would follow a short interregnum, when the firm would be run by its head of research, Charles Zviak, after which, in the autumn of 1988, "O-J" would become L'Oréal's CEO. In the meantime he was put in charge of Cosmair.

Arriving in New York in 1981, Owen-Jones won a reputation as a ruthless and aggressive player in an increasingly tough market. In 1983, Cosmair staged a brilliant coup, buying up the entire European stock of aerosol cans in preparation for the introduction of its Free Hold hair-styling mousse. The mousse became terrifically popular, and since Cosmair owned all the aerosol cans, no one could compete until they had found another source, which did not happen for several crucial months. Magazines that failed to place Cosmair's ads in what O-J considered the best spots had the company's advertising withdrawn. And the company ferociously, and successfully, jockeyed for counter space in department stores and other outlets. By 1984, Cosmair's sales had tripled, to $600 million.

Meanwhile, L'Oréal had not given up its ambitions regarding Helena Rubinstein, which was becoming weaker by the day. In 1983, following a Rubinstein family quarrel, a L'Oréal subsidiary had quietly acquired Helena Rubinstein's Japanese and South American branches. And in October 1988, HR's U.S. employees discovered, when they read the papers, that they had a new owner. Cosmair had bought Helena Rubinstein, Inc., including the European branches, for "several hundred million francs" (the franc was then valued at about ten to the pound sterling, and about seven to the dollar) in what the business press described as "a shrouded deal."[9] It made L'Oréal the biggest cosmetics business in the world, and put Jacques Corrèze where he had long wanted to be—in the chair of Helena Rubinstein.

"Nothing ever happens at L'Oréal—it's really boring, nothing but bigger and bigger profits," a financial analyst told *Le Monde* in June 1988.[10]

It would not stay boring long.

II

IN FEBRUARY OF 1988, EIGHT months before the purchase of Helena Rubinstein was completed, L'Oréal learned, to its "utter astonishment,"[11] that it had been placed on the blacklist of the Arab League's anti-Israel boycott committee. The committee, whose offices were located in Damascus, had been set up in 1948, when the State of Israel was established, in an attempt to strangle the new state by cutting off all Arab trade with companies linked to Israel, or doing business with it. This proved rather an empty threat at first, but took on new force after oil prices quadrupled in 1973, leaving oil-producing countries with huge surpluses of petrodollars that made them highly desirable trading partners.

L'Oréal had for many years maintained subsidiaries in Egypt, Syria, and Palestine. But although no company likes to face the prospect of losing an entire segment of the world market, it might in principle have ignored the boycott committee. Indeed, in principle it had no option but to do so, since complying with the boycott had been outlawed in France in 1981, at the start of President Mitterrand's first term. L'Oréal, however, was not the only company involved. In 1974, Liliane Bettencourt had exchanged a large block of her L'Oréal shares for shares in the Swiss food conglomerate Nestlé—a company of which Dalle, when he retired in 1984, had become vice president. All these shares were now owned by a holding company, Gesparal, of which Liliane Bettencourt owned 51 percent and Nestlé 49 percent, and which itself owned 53.65 percent of L'Oréal. And if Nestlé, as part owner of L'Oréal, were to become involved in the boycott, that would be serious indeed: Arab markets accounted for 15 percent of its milk products exports.[12]

On the face of it, L'Oréal's astonishment at being singled out by the boycott committee was logical. Helena Rubinstein did have an Israeli subsidiary—but L'Oréal had, as yet, no official ties with HR. In reality, however, the committee's announcement came as no surprise at all, nor had the boycott committee suddenly acquired the gift of prophecy. This affair had been rumbling on ever since L'Oréal's 1983 acquisition, through a subsidiary, of Helena Rubinstein's Japanese and South American businesses. The boycott committee had told L'Oréal then that it was taking a risk, since the Rubinstein parent company had strong Zionist ties, but L'Oréal had set its sights on Helena Rubinstein and refused to be put off. On the contrary, the following year, 1984, they discreetly, and via another subsidiary, bought 45 percent of Helena Rubinstein, Inc., from Albi; and that same year, they sold off HR Inc.'s Israeli subsidiary to Israeli nationals in an attempt to head off the boycott threat. In 1985, however, the boycott committee announced that it was still not satisfied. L'Oréal indignantly riposted that it was not the owner of Helena Rubinstein—which indeed it was not. And there matters rested—until 1988.

L'Oréal had two problems. The first was that French law forbade it to deal with the Arab boycott committee. The second was that its ties to Israel, far from being cut, had recently been strengthened.

The first problem was annoying but not insurmountable. L'Oréal had for years been conducting discreet negotiations with the boycott committee. Now it dispatched France's one-time ambassador to the United Nations, Claude de Kémoularia, to represent it in Damascus. M. de Kémoularia was a particularly apt choice, as he knew the people concerned: when President Mitterrand first outlawed all dealings with the boycott, it was Kémoularia who had been deputed to convince the Arab leaders that they would have to accept this new stance. Now he returned with a (to them) much more acceptable message, and was soon back in Paris with the boycott committee's conditions. Among them was a stipulation that L'Oréal must either buy the whole of Helena Rubinstein or drop all links with the company; that all Israeli manufacture of Helena Rubinstein products must be stopped, along with all Helena Rubinstein activity in that country; and that all existing directors of Helena Rubinstein be removed and replaced (it was understood, by non-Jews: this was when Jacques Corrèze became HR's chairman).

Since L'Oréal was anyway about to finalize the total purchase of Helena Rubinstein, Inc., Corrèze, who was in charge of the Israeli end of these negotiations, was dispatched to offer the Israeli buyer of the business in that country a manufacturing deal in Germany that would be far cheaper than maintaining an Israeli factory. The Israelis were happy to accept this offer, and were also persuaded to drop the name "Helena Rubinstein" for the preposterous reason that if the firm was to be L'Oréal's Israeli agent, there was no reason to use this particular brand name. It was agreed that HR Israel would henceforth be known as Interbeauty. Only the paperwork remained to be finalized.

But just as the Helena Rubinstein problem seemed to have been settled, a new one arose. Although François Dalle was no longer CEO of L'Oréal, he still maintained ties with the firm, heading its strategy committee. L'Oréal had money to invest—in 1987 its net profits had for the first time topped the billion-franc mark—and in 1988 Dalle, looking for profitable ways to invest it, had done a deal with an old friend, Jean Frydman. Frydman, the son of Polish-Jewish parents who had emigrated to Paris when he was five, had known Dalle for thirty years. They had met soon after the war, in which Frydman had been a daring *résistant*, and had been good friends ever since. One of Frydman's enterprises, CDG, owned a valuable catalogue of film rights, including the non-U.S. rights to *High Noon*, *Citizen Kane*, and other movie classics. It was agreed that L'Oréal would form a joint venture with CDG called Paravision, and that Frydman would sit on its board.

The Paravision deal was only a few weeks old when Dalle realized that it might raise problems for L'Oréal. Dalle had thought Frydman lived in Canada, where he owned a ranch, but in fact he now spent most of his time in Israel, and was domiciled in that country. And although the boycott committee's conditions regarding Helena Rubinstein had been met, the final removal of L'Oréal from the blacklist had not yet been signed and sealed. That would not happen until the end of 1989. Meanwhile, in Damascus and Paris, multiple copies of questionnaires and affidavits languished on bureaucrats' desks or got lost in embassies awaiting signature, and more and more generous sub rosa sweeteners to intermediaries were required, and envoys expensively shuttled back and forth, and nothing was settled. In the spring of 1989, therefore, Dalle suggested to Frydman that it might be a good thing if he temporarily stepped down from the joint venture's board.

Thus far, both Dalle and Frydman agreed that this was the way things were. As to what happened next, however, they disagreed bitterly.

Dalle said Frydman had not objected to resigning temporarily from the Paravision board, and had even had a letter of resignation prepared by one of his aides. Frydman, on the contrary, insisted that he had objected, and strongly: he had no wish whatever to accommodate the Arab boycott committee. Despite this, however, his resignation was offered and accepted—without his knowledge—at a board meeting held, also without his knowledge, in April of 1989.

That he had known nothing about the meeting was not surprising, since investigations revealed that it had never taken place. L'Oréal at first tried to deny any such maneuver, then admitted that that was indeed what had happened. But such proceedings were apparently not unusual. Notional board meetings, fleshed out later on paper, were, Dalle insisted, quite normal in France.

However, Frydman was in no mood to listen to feeble excuses. For he had made another disturbing discovery. It concerned Cosmair's Jacques Corrèze, who as the original instigator of the Helena Rubinstein deal was deeply involved in the boycott negotiations. Frydman knew Jacques Corrèze—or *a* Jacques Corrèze—only too well. While the fifteen-year-old Frydman had been escaping deportation and risking his life with the Resistance, Jacques Corrèze had been Eugène Deloncle's loyal lieutenant in MSR—not merely propagating its hateful doctrines but actually leading the gangs who took possession of properties once owned by Jewish families like the Frydmans. After the war he had been disgraced and condemned to ten years' hard labor. Could this Corrèze be the same person?

He could, and he was. This one-time Jew-baiter not only held an important position in a leading French company but was now engaged in the ethnic cleansing of an American Jewish firm whose takeover he had engineered. He had even had the chutzpah to visit Israel, several times, to negotiate the sale of Helena Rubinstein's Israeli branch and the closure of its manufacturing operation there. It was Corrèze, Frydman declared, who had wanted him removed from the Paravision board. He was determined to expose L'Oréal's fascist and racist connections, and show the world how it conducted its affairs.

Dalle was apoplectic. He insisted that not only had he never been an anti-Semite, but that Frydman's real aim in raising these irrelevant, if embarrassing, matters, was financial: to blackmail L'Oréal into conceding a better settlement regarding Paravision than they were prepared to offer. "Frydman's using the Shoah to make himself some money, and that's the beginning and end of it," Dalle declared,[13] a remark he later regretted, but did not retract. At L'Oréal's 1991 annual general meeting, its new CEO, Lindsay Owen-Jones, gave shareholders a long explanation of its antiracist principles. His speech was met with "ringing applause,"[14] and the company's unions, including one that was Communist-led, issued a statement confirming that in all their dealings with L'Oréal and Dalle they had never been aware of any racism.

Frydman admitted that the Paravision affair had done him no harm financially. On the contrary, he emerged 200 million francs to the good—by no means negligible, though far less than he had asked and less than he had hoped for.[15] But he was infuriated by Dalle's insinuations (repeated by L'Oréal's vice president, André Bettencourt) that money was his real concern in this affair. "There are three things he regards as sacred," his brother, David, said, "his family, Israel, and the Resistance."[16] And L'Oréal, by employing Jacques Corrèze, had insulted two of them.

III

Just as the boycott committee's interest in L'Oréal had not exactly been a total surprise, so Jean Frydman's revelations regarding Jacques Corrèze's previous life were not news to L'Oréal's senior management.

Corrèze's last public appearance in France had been in October 1948, when he had been chief defendant in the Cagoule trial, which had been postponed when war broke out but not canceled. For a while it had seemed as though the trial would be postponed indefinitely, for the enormous dossier of relevant papers—more than two tons of them—had vanished. There was a rumor that just before the Germans arrived in Paris in 1940 the papers had been sent for safekeeping to Lesparre in the Gironde, the constituency of Georges Mandel, then minister of the interior. But after the Liberation, when the examining magistrate traveled there from Paris to find them so that the prosecution could proceed, no one at the Lesparre Palais de Justice could help him.

The magistrate was about to return to Paris empty-handed when someone suggested that the concierge, who had been there throughout the war, might know something. As it turned out, she did. One night in June 1940, a party of men had arrived with a load of boxes which they hid in the washrooms. The boxes had been stacked up at one end, a wooden partition erected to conceal them, and the concierge sworn to silence. Then the men left. She had never said a word, but as far as she knew, everything was still where they had put it. Sure enough, there, behind a heap of assorted odds and ends, was the partition—and there, behind it, were the Cagoule papers: damp and stained, but still legible. In October 1945, those of the seventy-one accused who could be located were politely requested to present themselves at police stations. Fifteen obliged, and forty were eventually tried: amongst them, Jacques Corrèze.

CORRÈZE'S STORY, AS HE TOLD it to the court, was a bizarre mix of thuggery, courtly love, and melodrama. He was, a reporter noted, "dark and romantic-looking, extremely courteous and remarkably intelligent"; he affected "a hand-on-heart frankness"[17]—but did not, in the end, reveal much. He told the court that before the war his father had been an interior decorator in Auxerre, where the Deloncles had a country house. In 1932 they decided to do the place up: Jacques went to look it over—and fell under their spell. "I was nineteen, and I fell deeply in love with Mme. Deloncle," he testified. He insisted, however, that their relations had remained platonic. He joined the household as a sort of additional son, and lived with them from then on. But although Deloncle inducted him into La Cagoule, and later the MSR, he insisted that he had played little part in their policymaking. "I was just a soldier, they weren't going to share the secrets of the gods with a boy like me!"[18]

The truth, as it emerged from the documents, was rather different. Corrèze had been no minor figure in "Monsieur Marie's" clandestine universe, but had been his chief aide and confidant in both La Cagoule and MSR. His dossier contained an envelope with all the keys of the Ministry of Post and Telecommunications, and maps of how to get to the minister's private office, for use during the planned coup d'état of 1937. During the Occupation, "Colonel" Corrèze, whose group marched the streets of Paris in high boots, tunics, and cross-belts, oversaw expropriation operations, received reports from concierges and neighbors when the buildings were taken over, and made inventories of their contents. Among these was the building in the rue du Paradis that had housed the Ligue Contre Antisémitisme, where, subsequent to Corrèze's "liberation" of it, the fascist Charbonneau so enjoyed returning to his cozy office after MSR meetings chez L'Oréal in rue Royale. Its filing cabinets, desks, chairs, safes, stepladders, were all carefully listed.[19] And alongside the highly profitable expropriation business, rumors held that Deloncle had set up a "parallel" police to extort money from Jewish entrepreneurs, with Corrèze as its chief enforcer.[20]

However, in the middle of 1941, when the Germans abandoned the Nazi-Soviet pact and marched on Moscow, Deloncle lost interest in expropriations. The most important task as he now saw it was to join the fight against the Bolsheviks. He therefore set about raising a French volunteer force to fight in Russia alongside the Germans. The Légion de Volontaires Françaises (or LVF) was perhaps the extreme point of the collaboration. Of little consequence militarily (only 3,205 volunteers signed up), it had considerable psychological importance, allowing French fascists to feel that the Germans really valued them as partners. Corrèze, Deloncle's loyal protégé, was one of the first to sign up. He spent the hellish winter of 1941–42 on the Russian front, failing to take Moscow, and returned in April 1942.

By then, however, the MSR was in disarray. For now that German victory seemed less certain, Deloncle was rethinking his position vis-à-vis collaboration. Unseated in a putsch by the assassin Jean Filliol, he opened contacts with the Americans, hinting that he was working with the *résistant* (and ex-cagoulard) General Giraud. The German army was already less than enthusiastic about him on account of a mini-Kristallnacht he organized in October 1941, when his men blew up seven Paris synagogues using explosives supplied by the Gestapo—a gesture that may have pleased the Berlin high command but appalled the Wehrmacht because it needlessly antagonized the French, without whose cooperation, or at least indifference, the Occupation would become much harder to sustain. Deloncle was becoming a liability.

On January 7, 1944, he was dealt with. At seven thirty that morning, the concierge of his apartment building in the fashionable 16th arrondissement was awakened by repeated knocking on the door. She opened it to find fifteen civilians armed with machine guns, some speaking perfect French, others with heavy German accents. They ordered her to go up to Deloncle's apartment via the service stairs. They would follow. She was to ring Deloncle's bell and say it was the gas meter reader. On the stairs, however, the party met Lucienne, the Deloncles' maid. She opened their door with her key, and the armed men found themselves face-to-face with the Deloncles' son Louis and a manservant holding a breakfast tray. Louis shouted, "*Papa! Papa! Des terroristes!*" and Deloncle appeared, wearing only his pyjama jacket. He left the room to get his pistol; the armed men followed. There were a number of shots. When the men left, Deloncle was dead, and Louis had a bullet in his head, leaving him permanently disabled.

Corrèze, who still lived with the Deloncles as one of the family, and who was standing naked in the hallway when the posse burst in, threw himself to the ground as soon as the shooting started, and escaped unharmed. He and Mercédès Deloncle, with whom he was still in love, were arrested and imprisoned, but released after a few days. Mercédès then vanished, not reappearing until more than a year later, when her daughter Claude married Guy Servant, an LVF stalwart and the son of a pro-Nazi friend, Patrice Servant.

Corrèze, for his part, abandoned politics following the assassination and went underground to join a Resistance network. This volte-face counted in his favor when it came to the *épuration*: he was sentenced only to ten years' hard labor. At the end of the Cagoule trial he received a further ten years, to run concurrently with the first sentence.

He was freed in 1949, when an amnesty was announced: the three years he had already served before the Cagoule trial were judged to count as part of his sentence, making him eligible for freedom as this meant he had served five years in all, 50 percent of his sentence. However, prison was not his only punishment. Like many collaborators, including Mercédès Deloncle, whom he married as soon as he was freed, he had also been sentenced to *dégradation nationale* (public disgrace) and confiscation of all his property in France, past, present, and future. He turned to the man at once most likely to sympathize with him and most able to help: his old friend from the MSR, Eugène Schueller. Schueller had, after all, employed François Mitterrand, whose brother was married to Mercédès' niece. And Schueller did not disappoint him.

In fact, it was not Schueller who officially hired Corrèze, but François Dalle. Dalle insisted he did so without any input from Schueller. He thought Corrèze had paid his debt to society, his sentence was "not amongst the most serious," and "as a participant in the Resistance, I thought it was important to demonstrate tolerance at a time of reconciliation in France."[21] But like so many of the pronouncements emanating from L'Oréal after Frydman's revelations, this left much unsaid. For Corrèze was by no means the only cagoulard to find salvation at L'Oréal after the war. It was rumored that even Jean Filliol, who had been sentenced to death in absentia on three separate counts and had lived the rest of his life on the lam, was among them (though one scandal sheet hinted that Filliol didn't actually have a L'Oréal job but was living on blackmail money extorted during a clandestine trip to Paris in 1946).[22] Indeed, it was common knowledge in certain circles that Schueller "looked after his own" and "could be relied on to fish out people who were going under."[23]

Of course this was hardly surprising. Schueller had only by the narrowest of margins, and by a concerted effort on the part of influential friends, escaped the punishments meted out to so many of his wartime colleagues. The least he could do was to help the less fortunate as he himself had been helped. Just as Helena Rubinstein's business success had allowed her to provide a refuge from the Jew-hunters, in the shape of far-flung employment, for her nieces, nephews, sisters, and brothers-in-law, L'Oréal allowed Schueller to do the same for Deloncle's band of brothers. Jean Filliol's son and daughter, using their mother's name of Lamy, took a job with L'Oréal's Spanish subsidiary, Procasa, as did the son of Michel Harispe, Corrèze's confederate in Jewish expropriation, and Deloncle's brother and son.*

Corrèze, like the other ex-cagoulards, followed the well-trodden route to Franco's Spain, where a sympathetic regime allowed them to start life afresh. But unlike most of them, for whom this exile was little more than an afterlife, he took his work seriously and put all his considerable energy and charm into making a success of it. Sent to the United States in 1953, "he visited all the New York hairdressers with his little bag of samples, selling our hair dyes."[24] Within a few years Corrèze was heading a sizable organization, had become an important figure in L'Oréal, and was considering the purchase of Helena Rubinstein, Inc. His subsequent negotiations in Israel were

---

* For some of these, L'Oréal remained a family firm. In 2005, a questioner on a website was asking for news of "Mr. Patrice Servant Deloncle who when I knew him worked for L'Oréal in Chile" (elsassexpat.blogs.com/weblog/2005/10/loreal_le_vautil.html). The full name indicates that this was the son of Claude Deloncle and Guy Servant.

congenial on both sides. "They knew all about my past," Corrèze said (somewhat of an exaggeration: what he told the Israelis was that he was not proud of his past during World War II, and that they should not bruit his name about because "then he wouldn't be able to help anymore"[25]). He found them "delightful people."[26] And this liking was wholly reciprocated. "He was a big man, very warm and charismatic. You really wanted to please him," said Gad Propper, the Israeli businessman who dealt with him.[27]

In 1959, Corrèze was officially amnestied, and in 1966 he was rehabilitated. He could once more participate in French life and own property there. From then on he lived between the Bahamas and Paris, where his apartment overlooking the Seine was described by those who knew it as "palatial."

But although his past was now officially expiated, it lived on in the minds of those Corrèze and his friends had hunted. Deeds that the perpetrators recalled only with great difficulty remained vivid in their victims' memories. Serge Klarsfeld, the indefatigable French lawyer and Nazi-hunter, had amassed a large collection of papers pertaining to the Nazi persecution of the Jews in France, among them several documents attesting to Corrèze's anti-Semitic wartime activities. In the wake of Frydman's accusations, Klarsfeld passed these papers on to the American Office of Special Investigations, so that the Justice Department could decide whether or not to place Corrèze on its special watch list of foreigners believed to have participated in religious or racial persecution.

The affair was now getting seriously embarrassing for L'Oréal, and on June 25, 1991, Jacques Corrèze resigned from the company. He was seventy-nine years old and suffering from cancer of the pancreas: on June 26, the day after his resignation, he died. A short statement was issued in his name. "I cannot change what has been. Allow me simply to express my most heart-felt and sincere regrets for the acts that I may have committed 40 years ago, and their consequences, however indirect."[28]

IV

At the same L'Oréal annual meeting, in 1991, where Lindsay Owen-Jones had been cheered when he rejected any taint of racism, André Bettencourt, L'Oréal's vice president, had reiterated Dalle's contention that Jean Frydman's real concern was financial.[29] Infuriated, Frydman vowed he would not rest until Bettencourt had been forced to retract and, hopefully, was hounded out of L'Oréal.

His task was not, on the face of it, easy. Since the war, Eugène Schueller's group of young friends from 104 had done spectacularly well—and become spectacularly influential. By 1991, when the Corrèze scandal broke, François Dalle had become one of France's industrial elder statesmen; Pierre de Bénouville was (among other things) second-in-command to Marcel Dassault, *né* Bloch, the aviation magnate; François Mitterrand was well into his second term as president of France. As for André Bettencourt, he had become not only a powerful political figure but immensely rich. He had been a valiant *résistant*, with the Resistance Medal and the Croix de Guerre 1939–45, with palms, to prove it. He was a senator, and had been many times a minister under presidents of both the right and the left—in the Foreign Ministry during the presidency of Pierre Mendès-France, a minister under General de Gaulle, and a cabinet minister under Georges Pompidou, who had been not just president but a close friend, as was François Mitterrand, the current holder of that office. And he was one-half of France's wealthiest couple: the fortune inherited by his wife on her father's death had grown. She was now France's richest woman.

Frydman was undeterred. In 1994, after reading Pierre Péan's book *Une Jeunesse française*, which revealed the far-right connections and dubious youth of Bettencourt's friend Mitterrand, he thought he would do some basic research himself—starting with the weekly columns Bettencourt had written for *La Terre Française* between December 1940 and July 1942. On the rare occasions Bettencourt had been confronted with his authorship of these pieces he had played them down as being harmless, unimportant contributions to an obscure farming magazine. But was that true? It should be easy enough to find out: the Bibliothèque de Documentation Internationale Contemporaine at the Nanterre campus of the University of Paris had a set of copies. Frydman's brother David went to have a look at them.

His first finding was that *La Terre Française* was by no means as innocuous as Bettencourt implied. It might have been, once, but during the Occupation it had been taken over by the Germans, acting through a small company called "Le Comptoir financier français." This was wholly financed by the Nazi Propagandastaffel and in 1949 suffered the fate narrowly avoided by Eugène Schueller, of having its assets confiscated as punishment for aiding the enemy. The magazine's contents were a careful mix of agricultural articles and general-interest hearts-and-minds pieces designed to appeal to a deeply conservative and distrustful section of the population.

Bettencourt's column *Ohé les jeunes!* was a mix of religious and political uplift geared to the Church calendar and the changing seasons. The pieces appeared between December 1940 and June 1942, and were featured prominently, sometimes taking up the entire front page. And what they contained was dynamite. Bettencourt's public image was founded on his being an old *résistant* and a pillar of the Republic. But his wartime writings promoted a down-the-line antidemocratic pro-Nazi agenda. "All the old formulas of excessive liberty" must be abandoned: "the words democracy, dictatorship, republic, universal suffrage, organized proletariat, liberty, equality, have had their day."[30] Denunciations of suspect neighbors were a duty "insofar as they truly serve the community."[31] As for the Jews, "rubbing their hands [after the crucifixion, they] cried, 'Let his blood fall on us and our children!' You know exactly how it fell, and still falls. The edicts of the eternal Scriptures must and will be accomplished."[32] And, if this material were not graphic enough, "Their race is forever stained with the blood of the just. They will be universally accursed. . . . Today's Jews . . . will be spat out [*seront vomis*]. It's already happening."[*33]

All these prejudices had long been familiar to the devotees of *Action Française*, and it was no surprise to find them voiced by an ambitious young man of Bettencourt's religious and conservative background. His generation had never seen the Republic as anything but enfeebled and corrupt; for the circles in which he moved, the Jews embodied everything—liberalism, secularism, cultural dilution—that was destroying their beloved France. For forty years these same prejudices had been brandished in an ongoing and increasingly bitter war of words. Bettencourt was simply repeating what he had heard all his life.

---

* This horrible and violent language was common currency. It occurs, for example, in the anthem of the Vichy Milice:

Faisons la France pure:
Bolcheviks, francs-maçons ennemis,
Israël, ignoble pourriture
Ecoeurée, la France vous vomit.

However, it could hardly have escaped this highly intelligent young man that by the time he wrote his pieces the war was no longer a war of mere words. On the contrary, in the context of the Nazi Occupation, the familiar phrases had become lethal weapons. The extolling of denunciation was particularly sinister—not just repellent in itself, but because it laid a duty on readers to impose what was probably a death sentence upon anyone who did not conform to the ruling ideology.* And to denigrate the Jews in an era of deportations, expropriations, and extermination camps, was direct incitement to persecution.

Bettencourt's first intimation that Frydman had disinterred his articles and was preparing to publish them was at a symposium on museum management he was moderating. When questions were invited, David Frydman stood up and said he was proposing to fund a museum of the collaboration. He had a set of Bettencourt's articles for *La Terre Française*. Would Bettencourt agree to donate the manuscripts to Frydman's museum?

Later, Bettencourt would try to pretend that he could not remember what he had written all those years ago, and that in any case, his articles had been anodyne and unimportant. But his reaction to Frydman's intervention indicated that, on the contrary, he remembered only too well, and knew the effect disclosure might have on his current image. The shock was palpable. He turned pale and left the room. When he returned, he was urged by a member of the panel not to answer, but rejected this suggestion with the words "I am a public figure, I must answer." He went on: "It is true that I had the misfortune

---

* There are 55 million letters of denunciation in French and German archives: an astonishing statistic. (Lucy Wadham, *The Secret Life of France*, p. 153.)

to write for *La Terre Française*, but I redeemed myself. I was in the Resistance. I even represented the National Council of Liberation at Geneva."[34]

Bettencourt at once used his powerful position as a senator to try to prevent the matter going any further. When Frydman returned to the library to make sure he had photographed everything, he found that all copies of *La Terre Française* had vanished. He looked elsewhere, in vain: the magazine had been removed from every library in France—except the Bibliothèque Nationale's Versailles site, where he finally tracked it down. It had recently been moved there from the library's then main building in rue Richelieu, probably escaping Bettencourt's sweep because at the crucial moment it was in transit between locations.*

In the autumn of 1994, Jean Frydman set out his findings in a pamphlet, *Pour servir la mémoire*, giving the names and details of the old fascists "recycled" by Schueller and reproducing the more explosive of Bettencourt's *Terre Française* articles. The result was all he had hoped, and all Bettencourt had dreaded. Not only was there a renewed focus of attention on L'Oréal's dark history, both in the French press and in other countries, but Serge Klarsfeld requested the U.S. Department of Justice to put Bettencourt on its watch list of undesirable aliens. That listing in turn prompted New York congressman Eliot L. Engel to write Bettencourt a letter demanding clarification on three counts. How had he been able to obtain an American visa, given that applicants were required to state whether they had been implicated in any Nazi persecutions? What about those

* Similarly (though perhaps coincidentally), the otherwise uninterrupted run of *Votre Beauté* in the Bibliothèque Nationale contains no numbers for 1945, the year it was edited, to his extreme embarrassment, by François Mitterrand.

articles, now republished by Frydman, from *La Terre Française*—in particular one containing the phrase "Today's Jews will be spat out. It's already happening"? And had Bettencourt, during the war, been a collaborator or a *résistant*?

Bettencourt declined to respond to Frydman's allegations, on the grounds that the conflict between Frydman and L'Oréal was still before the courts, and that as vice president of L'Oréal he was debarred from commenting. But he did reply to Congressman Engel's letter. He had no memory of filling in a visa application form, as he normally used a diplomatic passport; in any case, he would not fill in such a form himself—tasks like that were the job of his staff. As a *résistant*, he had been imprisoned in Nancy and had met Allen Dulles, head of the American OSS, while on a mission to Switzerland. He had been asked to write for *La Terre Française* because he had previously been active in the Catholic young farmers association (Jeunesse Agricole Catholique), and this was a farming magazine. He had been France's official representative at the funeral of Israel's David Ben-Gurion, when he had been received by Golda Meir and Abba Eban, hardly a mission for an anti-Semite. Nor would anyone with a record of collaboration have been tolerated by de Gaulle or Mendès-France, who had not only been a staunch *résistant* but was himself Jewish. He held the Resistance Medal. His son-in-law was a Jew. He rested his case. As for Mr. Engel's citation of a phrase about the Jews being "spat out," supposedly published in the Christmas 1940 edition of *La Terre Française*, he assured him that no such phrase appeared in that article. Indeed, it did not: it turned out that Frydman's notes were in error. The phrase had appeared the following Easter, in a piece, also by Bettencourt, entitled "Carillon pascale."

Frydman's pamphlet, and its repercussions, prompted investigations into other aspects of André Bettencourt's wartime life—in particular, his claim to have been active in the Resistance. He had undeniably been awarded the Resistance Medal, but for what, exactly?

In his letter to Congressman Engel, Bettencourt wrote that in 1944 he had been sent to Geneva to represent the Conseil National de la Résistance. There, under the assumed name of Grainville, he had contacted many members of the Resistance and also members of the English and American intelligence services, in particular Allen Dulles and Max Shoop of the OSS, on behalf of the Ministry for Prisoners of War. He returned to France with Dulles at the time of the Allied landings in the south of France.

But these claims did not stand up to examination. It was true that Bettencourt did go to Switzerland in the summer of that year. Mitterrand had tasked him with contacting American agents in Switzerland in order to obtain funds on behalf of the Ministry for Prisoners of War, which was trying to foment unrest in German prisoner-of-war camps. Once he had the money he was to pass it on to Mitterrand.

It was not a hard task, and he accomplished it easily enough, making the requisite contacts and forwarding the money—$2,500,000 in all,[35] though what became of it is unclear. No POW insurrections of the type it was supposed to fund were recorded. However, he certainly did not, as he claimed, represent the Conseil National de la Résistance. That organization was headed by Jean Moulin and General de Gaulle, who were convinced that America's ultimate intention was to turn France into an American client state, and forbade all contact with the American secret services in Switzerland, particularly in financial matters. When confronted with this faux pas by the satirical weekly *Le Canard Enchaîné*, Bettencourt backtracked: he had made a mistake, he had actually been part of the delegation of the Mouvements Unifiés de la Résistance—a different and much less significant body, headed by his old friend (and Jean Moulin's mortal enemy) Pierre de Bénouville. But it transpired that this position, too, was impossible: the MUR had ceased to exist on December 31, 1943,[36] nine months before Bettencourt visited Switzerland.

Nor did he meet Allen Dulles: Bettencourt's dealings were with Dulles's deputy, Max Shoop.[37] And even had Dulles and Bettencourt been acquainted, they could not have journeyed to France together. Dulles did not leave Switzerland until the night of August 29–30, while Bettencourt told Pierre Péan in an interview that from August 21 he was in Paris, where he and Dalle were helping Mitterrand with post-Liberation policy regarding prisoners of war.*[38]

Bettencourt's first line of defense was to insist that everything about his past was known and had long been dealt with and dismissed. "I answered the questions about *La Terre Française* in my very first electoral campaign," he told New York's Congressman Engel. And some years later, interviewed for a book, he said, "Everyone knew perfectly well what my position was during the war."[39] When this tack failed to impress, he declared that although he regretted what he had written, it was insignificant: "I mentioned the Jews two or three times and the freemasons once. . . ."[40] And finally he pleaded ignorance. He had not known what was happening to the Jews: "I would

* Though even this turned out to be cloudy: a telegram exists sent by Bettencourt from Berne in mid-August, saying that "Because of the insurrection in Paris, I've been completely cut off from all contact. . . . I expect to leave here [Berne] in a fortnight, as my mission is now accomplished and I shall leave others to follow it up." (A.N. 72AJ47, quoted in Frydman, *L'Affaire Bettencourt*, p. 25.) And another source, Jacques Benet, also one of the 104 group, says that André Bettencourt "returned to Paris with him at the end of August. . . ." (A.N. 72AJ2174.)

never have written those words if I'd had any idea of what the Jews were going through. . . . No one knew anything about Jews being arrested and deported to extermination camps," he complained to an interviewer.[41] Nor had he had any idea who the real owners of *La Terre Française* were: "I knew absolutely nothing about that. . . . For me it was just a magazine with a large circulation among agriculturalists."[42] And when all these excuses failed, he simply went into denial. When confronted with yet another outrageously anti-Semitic, antidemocratic article written for yet another Pétainist youth publication (*L'Élan*, published in Bordeaux), "I don't remember," he flatly replied.[43]

None of it worked. The Frydmans' revelations ended Bettencourt's public career. On December 13, 1994, he quietly resigned from L'Oréal (where he was replaced as vice president by his son-in-law, Jean-Pierre Meyers, by a supreme irony a Jew whose grandfather had died in Auschwitz) and declared he would not be standing in the Senate elections due to take place the following year. He insisted that these decisions had nothing to do with the Frydmans' investigations or Congressman Engel's letter, which he made a point of not having received until December 16, three days after his resignation. On the contrary, he said, L'Oréal's CEO, Lindsay Owen-Jones, had been aware for some time of his impending departure: at the age of seventy-six he could no longer fulfil his duties as actively as he should, and from now on he would have to curtail his activities. But sources "close to L'Oréal's management" told *Le Monde* that, on the contrary, the letter and the resignation were by no means unconnected. The troubles stemming from the Corrèze affair were only just behind them, and they were anxious that this new embarrassment should remain confined to Bettencourt himself and not taint the company or its principal shareholder, who was, of course, his wife.[44]

The tone Bettencourt took thereafter, on the rare occasions when he consented to speak about the affair, was one of sadness and indignation. He was, he asserted, the victim of a malicious conspiracy. But "the more I say, the more I stoke the polemic. . . . It's all a terrible trap," he complained to *Le Monde*. "Have some consideration for my dignity. It's appalling to imply that I could possibly have participated in genocide!"[45] And writing to Congressman Engel he reiterated the accusation that had so enraged Jean Frydman when he had first made it, saying that in his view, "this sudden revival of interest in articles . . . written half a century ago is at least partly due to the misrepresentation of events by people who want to make sure their financial interests prevail."[46]

V

IT SEEMS CLEAR THAT NEITHER André Bettencourt nor Jacques Corrèze felt guilty about what they had done during the war. Their regret was rather for the embarrassment their youthful acts caused them later. But that regret manifested itself quite differently in the two men, and had different roots.

Bettencourt's chagrin clearly stemmed from the sense that he had been unfairly picked out. Countless others—including, doubtless, many of his own acquaintances—had acted as discreditably as he. Even if they had not, as he had, actively promoted fascism, they had adjusted their lives to it without too much trouble. But the *épuration* was supposed to have dealt with all that. One of its important functions had been to act as an "exercise in the suppression of memory,"[47] so that France could step forward into the future, confident that the worst offenders had been punished. For private individuals, this amnesia took effect almost instantly. Thus, the journalist Merry Bromberger, profiling Schueller in 1954—only six years after his second trial—glossed over his wartime career with the comment "From time to time his enthusiasms have led him where he shouldn't have gone."[48]

All this meant that when Bettencourt said, "Everyone knew perfectly well what my position was during the war," the truth was in reality just the opposite. People *thought* they knew—and wanted nothing more than to go on thinking so. No one in the French establishment welcomed his exposure. It undermined the whole edifice. If Bettencourt was shown to be a liar, whose story could be believed?

For what made the Bettencourt case so disturbing (and what so infuriated him) was the certainty that it was not unique. His shameful trajectory had, after all, only been revealed by the sheerest chance. If Corrèze had not become obsessed with taking over Helena Rubinstein, if the Boycott Office had not intervened, if Dalle had not picked Jean Frydman as a partner for L'Oréal, none of his wartime activity would have come out. It was possible that the fates had picked the one rotten apple out of the barrel—possible, but not probable. What of the industrialists who had so enthusiastically funded La Cagoule, and whose names still remained household words in France? Would their stories, had they been forced to reveal them, have been so very different? And how many public figures had, like Bettencourt himself, transformed themselves into *résistants* at the last minute—as his friend François Mitterrand put it, "*mal embarqués, bien arrivés*"?[49] Were not their careers based, as his was, on lies and concealments?

One of the people most anxious that Frydman should not pursue his vendetta to the bitter end was Mitterrand himself.

"This story has gone too far," his aide Charles Salzmann told David Frydman. The president didn't want the affair discussed in the press because they might write "all sorts of things."[50]

But it was too late: they already had. As more and more of the L'Oréal story seeped out, Mitterrand's many detractors seized upon the Schueller connection, pointing up his far-right relations and questioning whether he had played the important part in the Resistance that he had always claimed. In particular, they pounced upon a decoration he had played down: the Francisque, the medal awarded for outstanding service to Vichy and Pétain. Mitterrand could hardly deny receiving it—when his party went into opposition, in 1962, the Gaullist deputies amused themselves by shouting "Francisque! Francisque!" whenever he rose to speak[51]—but he had hitherto explained it away by saying "When I received it in 1943, I was in England [i.e., on Resistance business]. That was really useful when I got back—it was the best possible alibi."[52] Now, however, when people looked into the issue more closely, they found that a photograph existed of him receiving the medal in person from the Marshal's own hand.

That Mitterrand should have been part of Vichy was no surprise. Of all the gang from 104, his background was probably the furthest right, and his family was intertwined, in many ways and on many levels, with La Cagoule. Not only was his sister, Marie-Joséphine, for many years the lover of Jean Bouvyer, who was involved in the Rosselli assassination, but the Mitterrands were actually related to the Deloncles via Mitterrand's brother, Robert, whose wife was Mercédès Deloncle's niece. During the days of La Cagoule and the MSR, the Mitterrands cut off contact with the Deloncles, but after Deloncle was killed they looked after his daughter, Claude, and her young children. And when, in 1949, Mercédès Deloncle finally married her long-time love Jacques Corrèze, the Mitterrands were present in force at their wedding. In 1984, when President Mitterrand, visiting New York, attended a party at the Hotel Pierre in New York given by the local French community, Corrèze's friends and colleagues were astonished to see the president greet him with a warm hug.[53]

But the point about Mitterrand's far-right connections, which he so fervently did not wish exhumed, was that *they had never been secret.* When he first emerged as a leader of the left, during the 1950s, the political scandal sheets made much of this sudden volte-face. "Our aim here isn't to determine the exact relations between M. Mitterrand and La Cagoule: everyone knows that that monster (by which of course we mean La Cagoule) had many heads and thousands of feet. We merely note that it's odd that an eminent member of the UDSR [Mitterrand's party] should be mixed up in the intrigues of [cagoulards] . . . who managed, during the Occupation, to construct a Vichyist/Gaullist/*collabo*/*résistant* synthesis before which the most persistent bloodhounds would lose heart," commented one in 1953; in 1954, another invoked "the political waters in which Mitterrand first met his friend Schueller, the father-in-law of Bettencourt, who's now a minister."[54] And the same was true of Jacques Corrèze. If anyone wanted to look, his beginnings with L'Oréal were an open secret. The latter article went on to mention "the cagoulard Jacques Corrèze, who owes his job in Madrid to Schueller . . . ." And later, as Lindsay Owen-Jones, Dalle's successor, said quite plainly, "This is not a guy who tried to hide in Argentina or Brazil. He never changed his name."[55] It was all out there—if you wanted to know it.

The truth was that most people did not want to know. They wanted to look forward, not backward. In the words of Mitterrand's Socialist Party colleague Laurent Fabius, whom he had made France's youngest-ever prime minister, "What did I care what he'd done thirty years ago?"[56] François Dalle, for instance, knew all about Corrèze, but decided to employ him nonetheless. In Dalle's eyes, he had paid his debt to society. "As a participant in the Resistance, I thought it was important to demonstrate tolerance at a time of reconciliation in France."[57]

But, then, neither Dalle nor Owen-Jones had ever suffered at the hands of Corrèze and his like. Those who had were not so blithe about letting bygones be bygones. And France's problem, in the postwar years, was that the two sides—the victims and the rest—could never agree as to the best way forward. One side wished to move on, the other—for whom closure was impossible unless the past was recognized—could not move on until it had seen justice done. The L'Oréal affair exhumed this split, which was why so many people found it so painful.

This problem was not unique to France. In one form or another it affected many countries after the war. But what made the French situation particularly edgy was that anti-Semitism had for so many years been one of the mantras of the anti-Republican right—and that for many, the differentiation this implied between French Jews and the "real" French had never really been effaced. Thus, in 1980, when a bomb exploded at a synagogue in Paris's rue Copernic, the then prime minister, Raymond Barre, commented, "This disgusting attack was aimed at the Jews who were going to the synagogue, but it actually injured innocent Frenchmen who were crossing the street."[58] If as late as 1980, in the mind of a moderate politician, Jews and "innocent Frenchmen" were still instinctively differentiated, then it was clear just how embedded in the national psyche Action Française's demonization still remained.

Obviously, there were real differences between a Bettencourt, who simply blew with whatever wind prevailed, and a

Corrèze, who had been a committed Nazi and who made a point of insisting that he had always acted on principle. The Senator Bettencourt of 1994 probably was genuinely different from the young man he had once been, just as the climate of postwar opinion was genuinely different from that in which he had been brought up. Admittedly his career was based on lies. But by the time Frydman resuscitated them he had told the official story so often that he had probably come to believe it. Had he truly been that young fascist cheerleader? His reaction to David Frydman's revelations showed that he knew he had. But how could that young man have turned into the person he was now? Was it really he who had inveighed against "the republic and her masks of parliamentarianism and liberalism," he who had called for "a leader who commands, not a crowd of clerks eternally discussing"?[59] It was impossible—yet it was true. A journalist who spoke to him on the phone after his resignation said he sounded "wounded and tormented."[60] "There's this incredible atmosphere of hate," Bettencourt said.

> *I had to withdraw from the only occasion I've been offered to put my side of things on television. . . . because I found out they were going to accompany it with images of the Germans marching up the Champs-Élysées. . . . You just have to put up with it; every time you talk about it you just fall into another trap. To say I'm an anti-Semite is shameful when my only daughter is married to a Jew who's like a son to me. After fifty years of an existence devoted to my country, am I only to be seen as an anti-Semite and anti-Freemason? It's horrible.*[61]

No such bitter regret was ever felt by Corrèze. He had never, as Bettencourt had, suppressed the person he had once been. On the contrary, he insisted that he did what he did when the MSR was in its prime "for a noble cause," haughtily declaring that although he had lost faith in the MSR some time before Deloncle died, he had not abandoned his old mentor while he lived because "I do not desert my friends."[62] Had his views changed simply because they were no longer admissible? It seems unlikely. Rather, his whole life had been a continuation of the same game, and when that game was exposed, he was not so much embarrassed as furious.

Naturally, he never went so far as to publicly glory in his past. When first questioned about his role in expelling Jews—including Georges Mandel, who until June 1940 had been minister of the interior, and Bernheim the well-known art dealer—from their homes and businesses, he, too, resorted to evasion, first denying everything. "I can't recall it—I don't think that can be true," he said first, then insisted that there was a difference between what he had done and actually maltreating Jews ("*faire des saloperies contre les juifs*").[63] Which was true enough: he had waited for others to do the dirty work, and then taken the profits. A few days later he issued a written statement asserting that "There's no one, among those hunted during the Occupation, Jewish or not, who can complain of having suffered, in his person or his goods, from my activity."[64] But in the end his actions were what they were, and he did not apologize for them.

The characteristic that struck reporters during the Cagoule trial in 1948 was his arrogance. He sat aloofly at the end of the row, leaning away from his fellow accused, his handsome head thrown back, viewing the proceedings from a distance down his well-shaped nose. He answered questions, when addressed, with a weary politeness. He was, journalists remarked, a romantic figure. He was also utterly unrepentant. And unrepentant he remained. Interviewed on television in June 1991, he was asked, "Do you feel you were a real anti-Semite?" to which he flashed savagely back, "I don't know if I was, but I'm about to become one!"[65]

He did not, like Bettencourt, try to cheat the gods. Rather, in a classic tale of hubris, he simply gave them the finger, pushing his luck, because he felt himself invincible. Given his past, and his defiant arrogance, it is hard to believe that Helena Rubinstein's Jewishness played no part in Corrèze's absolute determination to acquire her business. He never showed any interest in the very comparable Elizabeth Arden, who was an equally powerful player, who died only a year after Madame, and whose business went downhill in much the same way as Helena Rubinstein's. On the contrary, it seems in character that, having arrived in New York and sized up the situation, he should have decided to resume the old game he had so enjoyed in Paris—Colonel Corrèze redivivus, minus only the high boots and cross-belts. Everything he did points to his enjoyment of this underlying drama, his pleasure doubtless enhanced by the fact that only he was aware of it.

We have no way of knowing when he first set his sights on Helena Rubinstein's business, but since Madame was already over eighty when he arrived in New York, he must have realized even before he met her that Helena Rubinstein, Inc., would come into play sooner rather than later. He made a point of getting to know her; and to good effect. Dalle testified that it was Corrèze's personal friendship with Madame that enabled L'Oréal to acquire Helena Rubinstein Spain—the first step to the eventual takeover of the entire company.[66] When the boycott difficulties arose, it was he who insisted on conducting the Israeli end of the negotiations. He dropped hints to the Israelis regarding his past—which helped convince them that he was an honest broker—but as at the Cagoule trial this apparent frankness, whose effect was so disarming, in fact concealed far more than it revealed. And as the saga of the boycott became more and more tangled, his behavior became increasingly flamboyant. At one point he floated a crazy plan that might have come from Deloncle himself: a project called Operation Rocher to create a bogus company in Switzerland, apparently quite unconnected to L'Oréal, that would buy the Helena Rubinstein international operation.[67] He *would* control Helena Rubinstein—at, it seemed, any cost—and ended up occupying its chair in the same way as, during the war, he and his MSR cronies occupied the one-time offices of the Ligue Contre Antisémitisme, Georges Mandel's apartment, and the Bernheim art gallery. Would anyone realize who he was? Would they make the connection? Eventually, of course, someone did. And then he defeated them after all—by dying.

VI

THE STORY OF L'ORÉAL'S TAKEOVER of Helena Rubinstein, and the ensuing explosions, is an almost perfect dramatic construct. Had it not been for the vicious anti-Semitism of Schueller and his friends, Madame would never have rediscovered her Jewish identity and established the Israeli presence that gave rise to the boycott problems. Had Jacques Corrèze not been disgraced in France as an old Nazi he would not have ended up in New York, nor been so enchanted by the prospect of taking over a Jewish business. His and Schueller's eventual unmasking was a direct, if unforeseeable, consequence of their previous actions.

For the businessman who had to deal with the consequences, however, the scandals were nothing less than a nightmare. Lindsay Owen-Jones, L'Oréal's fourth CEO, assumed office in the autumn of 1988—just at the moment the boycott storm broke—and spent the next six years firefighting, as successive news stories rose from the dead to rip through L'Oréal's image.

A large part of his effort to repair the damage was directed at the reestablishment of that image with the Jewish community and Israel. American reaction to the boycott settlement had been angry, and L'Oréal faced a $100 million lawsuit alleging it had broken U.S. laws designed to prevent American firms from cooperating with the Arab boycott of Israel. In June 1994, therefore, L'Oréal announced that it had bought a 30-percent stake in Interbeauty (formerly Helena Rubinstein Israel) at a price of $7 million. Six months later, in January 1995, the company opened a factory in the Israeli town of Migdal Ha-Emek, producing Elseve shampoo, Plenitude antiwrinkle cream, and a line of products for export using Dead Sea minerals, called Natural Sea Beauty. That same year, L'Oréal agreed to pay $1.4 million to the U.S. government to settle its legal problems, and thanked the Anti-Defamation League "for its support of L'Oréal's business and community services activity in Israel." Bettencourt had resigned, Corrèze was dead, the Jewish lobby was happy. In 1997, the Union of Orthodox Jewish Congregations of America gave L'Oréal its International Leadership Award. Owen-Jones heaved a sigh of relief and prepared to turn his attention to other matters.

And then, in 2001, ten years after the Corrèze affair, six years after Bettencourt's exit, the Nazi past returned to haunt L'Oréal once more.

In the freezing winter of 1948, Eugène Schueller announced to his protégé François Dalle that they were going to visit L'Oréal's German subsidiary, which had its headquarters in Karlsruhe, just across the Rhine from Schueller's native Alsace. The company had opened its first German agency in Berlin, in 1922, but it did not do as well as expected, and its manager, Frau Kuhm, refused to produce her account books. In 1930 L'Oréal sacked her (to her fury—she sued, but lost) and opened another office under the management of a Frenchman, André Tondu.[68]

The Berlin premises were destroyed during the war, and after it Tondu, who remained in charge, moved the business to Karlsruhe. There, under the name Haarfarben und Parfümerien (Hair Dyes and Perfumery) he rented the ground floor and cellar of a house in the center of town, at number 18, Kaiserallee. The business at that point was "Lilliputian," Dalle remembered: its "factory" consisted of the cellar room, an area of about 300 square meters.[69]

When the business needed more space, in February 1949, Tondu signed purchase papers on its behalf for a property situated just round the corner, at 17, Wendtstrasse. This house and the one at 18, Kaiserallee, shared a common neighbor, number 19, Wendtstrasse, a once-luxurious mansion that had been bombed during the war, and which occupied the corner lot where Wendtstrasse met Kaiserallee. If Tondu could consolidate, and buy this property also, his business would then occupy an important and valuable site in the center of town.

In November 1951, he seemed to have received some assurance that he would indeed, sooner or later, be able to buy number 19. That month, Haarfarben bought the house at 18, Kaiserallee, whose ground floor and basement it had hitherto been renting—a move that only made sense if they now knew they would also be able to buy the ruined lot situated between the two properties they owned already. And in 1954 they duly did so.

The seller was a large insurance company, the Badischer Gemeinde Versicherung Verband (BGV), which had acquired number 19 in 1938 from a Frau Luise Dürr. The property, however, was not owned by Frau Dürr. Rather, it belonged to the family of a wealthy lawyer named Dr. Fritz Rosenfelder in whose name she was acting. Until 1936, Dr. Rosenfelder had lived there with his mother-in-law, his wife, Kaethe, and their young daughter, Edith. But the family was Jewish, and by the end of 1936 they knew they would have to leave Germany. Dr. Rosenfelder spoke French and had studied in Paris, and he therefore decided to move his family to that city, traveling on ahead to look for accommodations. They would join him there as soon as he had found somewhere suitable for them all to live.

By the time he was ready to receive them, however, the situation in Germany had deteriorated further. For Jews to leave was no longer a straightforward matter. There was now invariably a price to pay: in the Rosenfelders' case, this included their house. They would need exit visas, and to obtain them, Dr. Rosenfelder was told he must designate an agreed Aryan to handle all his business in Germany—which meant transferring "all the rights" to this person, including the right to dispose of property.[70] The holder of this power of attorney would be Frau Dürr. Dr. Rosenfelder had never met her and knew nothing about her. No one, least of all an experienced lawyer, would willingly sign over his property to such a person in this way. But as it was the only way to get his family out of danger, he signed.

The family duly came to Paris and in September of 1938 moved into an apartment in the rue des Saussaies, near the

Champs-Élysées (as it happened, just across the road from where the Gestapo would establish its headquarters). Meanwhile, on January 20, 1938, Frau Dürr transferred rights in number 19, Wendtstrasse on behalf of Dr. Rosenfelder "once of Karlsruhe, now of New York,"[71] to BGV.

For the Rosenfelders, as for so many Jewish families, the war was a time of unspeakable torment. In 1939, Dr. Rosenfelder was sent by the French to the first of a series of internment camps, where food was scarce and living conditions atrocious.* During intervals of freedom he managed to get visas for his family to emigrate to America, but his mother-in-law refused to go: America, she declared, had no culture. By 1941, however, it was clear that Paris, though doubtless cultured, was no longer safe for Jews. Fritz Rosenfelder was interned once again, this time at Les Milles, near Aix-en-Provence, and Kaethe, Edith, and Kaethe's mother, Emma, decamped to Allauch, a small town not far away, where they lodged with a family and Edith went to school.

So things went on for some months. Then one day, when Edith chanced to be at the beach with her teacher, her mother and grandmother were picked up by the *milice*. They were sent to the infamous internment camp at Drancy, a staging post for Auschwitz, where they died. Edith was saved by a young village girl who arrived before the gendarmes could find her, and who helped her hide.

Fritz, meanwhile, had escaped from Les Milles. When he

---

* Arthur Koestler, who also experienced these camps, said that fellow prisoners who had experienced both found the conditions in them worse than those at German concentration camps such as Dachau. The only difference, he thought, was that whereas in Dachau the intention was to kill, in the French camps death occurred by default. Conditions for Nazi prisoners of war in France were rumored to be—and were—far superior. (Koestler, *Scum of the Earth*, pp. 92, 114.)

heard what had happened, he realized there was no way of retrieving his wife and mother-in-law. He and his daughter made their perilous way to Switzerland, where, weakened by his successive ordeals, he died in 1945. Edith, then seventeen, ended up in a camp for Jewish displaced persons, where she stayed until an uncle who had made it to Brazil agreed to take her in. She traveled to Brazil, married there, and had two children. But she could never bear to talk about the war, or her dead mother and grandmother. She told her children she didn't remember.[72]

In 1951, the year Edith Rosenfelder married, BGV took full legal possession of 19, Wendtstrasse. Until 1949, regulations imposed by the victorious Allies had prevented any dealing in property stolen from the Jews by the Nazis. But on January 1st of that year these restrictions were lifted, and in August 1950, BGV began the process of establishing their legal right to number 19. In the absence of living claimants, all such matters were decided via the Jewish Restitution Successor Organization (JRSO), based in New York.

There were, of course, living claimants: not just Edith Rosenfelder, but an uncle, Fritz's brother, Karl Rosenfelder, who was then still alive. And it seems that Karl Rosenfelder was trying to lay claim to his family's property. But BGV made no effort to contact him—on the contrary: an internal memorandum dated June 4, 1951, records that a lawyer had phoned to say that Karl Rosenfelder had been in touch with a view to establishing his right to restitution of the property, but that if the matter could not be settled by negotiation via the JRSO, he (the lawyer) would not pursue the matter, as he had no wish to act against his friends in BGV.[73] As it turned out, this man had been chairman of the Association of National Socialist Lawyers for Karlsruhe during the 1930s and was personally responsible for the banning of Fritz Rosenfelder from practicing. He was unlikely, to say the least, to have been an enthusiastic advocate for Fritz's brother Karl.

The matter was settled, without reference to either Karl or Edith Rosenfelder, on November 5, 1951. On that day, BGV agreed to pay JRSO 5,000 deutschmarks as compensation, in return for ownership of the lot at 19, Wendtstrasse.[74] Later they claimed that Karl Rosenfelder had signed the document, but neither they nor anyone else have ever produced his signature.

Meanwhile, André Tondu's property purchases on behalf of Haarfarben progressed in close step with BGV's. In January 1949, as we have seen, the restriction on dealing in stolen Jewish properties was lifted, allowing BGV to begin the formalization of its ownership of 19, Wendtstrasse. In February, Tondu made the first of his purchases—number 17, Wendtstrasse. And he bought the property at 18, Kaiserallee on the very day—November, 5, 1951—that the BGV/JRSO matter was settled, that same day reconfirming his purchase of 17, Wendtstrasse.

Two and a half years later, on June 29, 1954, the Wendtstrasse saga was completed—at least as far as Tondu and Haarfarben/L'Oréal were concerned. That day Tondu, on behalf of Haarfarben, bought number 19 from BGV for DM 27,000. The transfer document noted that a restitution procedure had been initiated concerning ownership of this property, but that the file had been closed, entitling the present owner [BGV] to dispose of the property.[75] Haarfarben/L'Oréal now owned the entire corner site at the junction of Kaiserallee and Wendtstrasse. They would remain there for the next thirty-seven years, selling the property in 1991 (the same year, as it happened, that the Corrèze scandal broke).

Edith Rosenfelder, now Edith Waitzfelder, living in Rio de Janeiro, knew nothing of these maneuverings. But her daughter, Monica, noticed that the other Jewish families they knew in Rio, many of whom had arrived there in circumstances very similar to Edith's, had all received restitution payments from Germany. Edith had received nothing; and although she hated talking about her family's life in Germany, and what had happened to them, she said enough to indicate that they had been well-off and had owned a substantial property in Karlsruhe. Why, then, had she been neglected? What had happened to her rightful compensation?

Monica Waitzfelder determined to find out. She moved to Paris, found a job there, and set about unraveling her family's German affairs.

The task, which she carried out in the intervals of her busy life as an opera director, turned out to be difficult and complex. Papers that should have been available somehow could not be found. Bureaucrats were unhelpful. A clause in the November 5, 1951, agreement by which BGV acquired 19, Wendtstrasse, for example, stated that "The JRSO undertakes, inasmuch as the defendant (the BGV) acts in conformity with instructions from the JRSO, to compensate the defendant to a maximum of 5,000 DM if a situation arises where those with a priority right make themselves known and validly undermine the defendant's position."[76] But when Waitzfelder made inquiries regarding this clause, she was informed that the compensation had already been paid, and the matter was closed. Yet how was this possible? No one but Edith, her uncle Karl having now died, had a priority right, and she had never made herself known to JRSO, since by the time she found out what was going on in Karlsruhe, the JRSO no longer existed.

"L'Oréal is still very powerful [in Karlsruhe]," was the explanation offered by one nervous and unhelpful woman at the Karlsruhe town hall when asked why she could not supply copies of the relevant documents. Bit by bit, however, Monica

Waitzfelder accumulated the documents and pieced together the story. The 1954 papers recording BGV's sale of 19, Wendtstrasse to Haarfarben stated that "The compensation rights owed to victims of the war remain entirely within the possession of the vendor." That was to say, BGV—the people who had illegally acquired the property in the first place.

On June 18, 2001, Maître Charles Korman, acting for Monica Waitzfelder, wrote to Lindsay Owen-Jones, managing director of L'Oréal, detailing what his client had uncovered. Valuations of sales and rental income for comparable properties indicated that the Waitzfelders had been cheated, over the years, of a substantial sum. The amount named by Korman was DM 60,556,726, (roughly, €30,000,000, or $40,500,000). He made it clear that both he and Ms. Waitzfelder would prefer an out-of-court settlement, but failing that they would go to court.

However, in letters to the lawyer and, later, to Edith and Monica Waitzfelder, Owen-Jones rejected all notion of a settlement. He declined to acknowledge that L'Oréal had any responsibility in the affair, asserting that Haarfarben was quite distinct from L'Oréal and that L'Oréal had not bought a majority holding in it until 1961. If strictly true in a legal sense, in practice the company always regarded the German subsidiary as part of the parent organization. There is particular mention of Haarfarben as part of the L'Oréal family in staff magazines from 1948 and 1949, while a paragraph in L'Oréal Deutschland's website describes how André Tondu restarted the business in Karlsruhe after it was bombed out of Berlin.

Owen-Jones insisted that the JRSO transaction of 1951, in which due compensation had been awarded, had been signed by Karl Rosenfelder (though he, too, failed to produce any signature). He declared his "deepest conviction . . . that L'Oréal has done no wrong to Mrs. Edith Rosenfelder," and announced that L'Oréal had appointed its own lawyers to deal with the case. They were Michel Zaoui and Jean Veil, two well-respected Jewish advocates, one of whom (Zaoui) had been a leading prosecutor in the Klaus Barbie trial—a choice whose insulting implications were not lost on the Waitzfelders.[77] Owen-Jones had clearly been advised that the law was on his side, and, that being so, he was not inclined to give in.

L'Oréal did indeed win the case, both at the first hearing, when the Waitzfelders' complaint was declared out of time, and later, to Korman's great surprise, on appeal. But it is still hard to understand why Owen-Jones decided to fight rather than settle. From a publicity point of view, it would surely have been better for L'Oréal to portray themselves as prepared to right old wrongs rather than as legalistic skinflints upholding shameful Nazi theft. The Waitzfelders would doubtless have settled for less than the stated sum—not that €30 million would bankrupt a company of L'Oréal's size and wealth. In 1988, *Capital* magazine calculated that the Bettencourts, its main shareholders, were getting richer at the rate of €14.2 million *a day*, or €590,000 an hour, while in 2001 their share of the company's dividends amounted to more than €81 million.[78] As Owen-Jones presided over year after year of double-digit growth, the share price rose from $8 in 1990 to $76 in 2000. When he took charge, Liliane Bettencourt, the company's largest shareholder, was already the wealthiest woman in France; he made her the wealthiest woman in the world.

From its very inception, however, Owen-Jones's tenure as L'Oréal's CEO had been marked by rumblings from the Nazi past. When he took charge, in 1988, the Frydman affair was just about to explode. He spent seven years negotiating his way through that minefield, and succeeded in extricating his company without ever once actually admitting the various allegations. Perhaps the Waitzfelder case was simply one too many for him. To settle would be to acknowledge that L'Oréal really was tainted; and that, perhaps, was more than he could bring himself to do.

Whatever his motivation, the result has been hard on the Rosenfelder family. Edith Rosenfelder still lives, in difficult circumstances, in Brazil. Monica Waitzfelder has told her lawyers not to contact her unless they have good news to offer, as she otherwise finds the whole affair too upsetting. At the time of writing, she had not heard from them. The case is still unresolved, and it is before the European Court of Human Rights.

CHAPTER SIX

Consumers or Consumed?

I

For Owen-Jones, it is easy to see how these political scandals must have seemed like a never-ending, irritating diversion from his main job. These years saw the transformation of L'Oréal from a national treasure into a multinational giant. And from that point of view, the acquisition of Helena Rubinstein did what it had been intended to do. Corrèze and all he stood for represented a regrettable past. But the Helena Rubinstein deal represented the future. In 1988, when O-J assumed the chief executive's chair, the company was still a French hair-care group; when he stepped down in 2006, it was the biggest cosmetics business in the world, and readying itself to expand still further, into India, China, Brazil, and Russia. In such a context, recollections of ancient misdeeds receded into insignificance. "Not that old story," the family would sigh wearily whenever the old scandals resurfaced. The years, they implied, should have drawn the sting from that tale—and this hope, clearly, was shared by Owen-Jones.

But, on the contrary, the scandals remain relevant precisely because L'Oréal has become so large and powerful. The bigger the enterprise, after all, the bigger its capacity to bully. Huge multinational enterprises, with their enormous budgets and their ability to bestow or remove patronage, in the form of jobs or investment, hold more real clout than many nation-states. Their acts, therefore, take on a moral and political significance over and above the commercial. And L'Oréal is among them—number 346 in *Fortune*'s list of the world's 500 largest companies, with revenues in 2008 of nearly $26 billion. It is true that L'Oréal does not operate in such obviously edgy areas as power generation or banking. But the company's huge advertising outlay gives it immense influence over what we read in newspapers and magazines and watch on television. That advertising not only molds our sense of what we want to look like and who we want to be—in a very real sense, our perception of who we are—but also, as an essential source of revenue, enables the company to discourage unwelcome content in the media where it buys space.* Yet at the same time, as the Rosenfelder case shows, the company remains—as a commercial and not a political entity—politically unaccountable.

L'Oréal's founder would have been very much at home in this world where business and politics are inseparably twinned. Not that Eugène Schueller saw his company as a source of political power in itself. Rather it was a guinea pig upon which to

* In an earlier example of this kind of power, *Skin Deep*, the Consumer Research book on the beauty business, almost had its publication stopped when the editor of a women's magazine, *The Woman's Home Companion*, an old friend of the book's publisher, persuaded him that to destroy the cosmetics industry, as the book threatened to do, would remove too much valuable advertising from newspapers and magazines. Although the book was by then already at proof stage, its contract was canceled. Fortunately, the authors were able to find another publisher, and the book went on to be one of 1935's top best-sellers.

test out his theories and a provider of funds with which, subsequently, to buy the power to implement them. But in practice—and especially in France, where there has long existed a seamless interface between commerce and politics—such separations are almost meaningless. In Britain, where political power has traditionally been a perquisite of land ownership, the time-honored muckraking format is *Who Owns Britain?* with three books of (more or less) that title, by different authors, published between 1944 and 2001.[1] The same is true in America, where wealth has always ruled, and where four *Who Owns America?* books have been published since 1936.[2] But in France, the equivalent books—*Les 200 familles, Le Retour des 200 familles, Les Nouvelles 200 familles, Les Bonnes fréquentations*—are all about social networks. President Pompidou worked at the Rothschild bank and had numerous connections in the social and business worlds; Marcel Dassault, the aeronautical industrialist, was a member of the Assemblée Nationale; André Bettencourt was a senator and a member of successive governments, as well as being vice president of one of France's biggest companies.

By comparison with these far-reaching tentacles, Helena Rubinstein's concerns seem quaintly parochial. Never interested in political power, her extracommercial interests were solely personal and familial. And although she and Schueller were of the same generation, and set up shop within a few years of each other, this comparatively limited worldview meant that by the time of the takeover, his company represented the future, hers, the past.

Although the conjunction of the barber's hair-dye commission and Schueller's particular talents was undoubtedly fortuitous, it is clear that his combination of intellectual ability, obsession, and business acumen would have taken him to the top in whatever field he chose. For him, the vital factor was education. Once educated, he became unstoppable, able both to produce new products at the laboratory bench and to evolve a management philosophy that, like its inventor, could succeed in any industry.

Helena Rubinstein's success was far narrower, and was based almost wholly on her phenomenal talent for trading. Patrick O'Higgins once accompanied her on an afternoon's shopping in Paris. They started by visiting the painter Kees van Dongen, where she bought a canvas for $2,000 less than the price quoted by the artist, distracting Madame Kees van Dongen (who did the selling) at the crucial moment by observing that her skin was dry and promising to send her some products. They then continued on to Cartier's, who had developed a new double lipstick container that interested her, and which she acquired, after playing the manager like a hooked fish, for 700,000 francs ($14,000) rather than the official price of 800,000. The painting was sold, after her death, for three times what she paid; the lipstick case was "adapted" with great success, and as "Nite 'n Day" sold more than a million, at three dollars each. Nor was her interest limited to large sums. As a business associate observed, "If someone offered Helena Rubinstein a package of gum for a nickel she would say 'too much' in the hope that it was the only package of gum in the world that could be bought for four cents."[3]

Rubinstein's drive and marketing ability were so far above the ordinary that they enabled her to overcome both her lack of education and the social and commercial obstacles that confronted all would-be businesswomen. But even with all her business talents, she made it big only because her face cream hit at a crucial moment in social history.

Quite how fundamental this was may be seen in the very different fate of an equally determined Jewish entrepreneuse who tried to open a beauty salon in London's Bond Street forty years before Helena Rubinstein, and whose business, despite its great commercial success, crashed in humiliation and bankruptcy.

Mrs. Rachel Leverson, trading as Madame Rachel under the banner "Beautiful For Ever!" opened her salon in 1865. She sold the usual range of lotions, creams, powders, and paints, and did well. Within a few months of her salon's opening, she and her many daughters moved from the distant suburb of Blackheath to a fine house in Maddox Street, just around the corner from her shop, filled it with expensive furniture, and rented a pit-tier box at the opera, at £400 a season.

In the summer of 1868, Madame Rachel was sued for fraud and conspiracy by a middle-aged widow, a Mrs. Borradaile. Madame Rachel had sold Mrs. Borradaile a number of pricey products—cosmetics, a course of bran baths—promising that they would make her beautiful again and would enable her to catch a new husband in the person of Lord Ranelagh (whose role in all this remained unclear: he was a well-known and notoriously disreputable man-about-town). Mrs. Borradaile spent all she had on these treatments, and the results were not as promised. So she sued.

The case against Madame Rachel held little legal water. Admittedly, Mrs. Borradaile, stringy, middle-aged, with dyed yellow hair, had not become beautiful. Lord Ranelagh had not married her. And the sums charged by Madame Rachel—it was rumored £1,000 for the bran baths (around £62,000, or over $100,000, in current value)—were large. But nobody had forced the plaintiff to buy these products, and Madame Rachel had delivered what she had promised: namely, a course of baths. When the jury, after hearing much strange and muddled evidence, failed to agree on a verdict, the *Times* found its failure to acquit "only comprehensible on the supposition that they failed to see on which side the burden of proof lay."[4] Under English law Madame Rachel did not have to prove herself innocent. Mrs. Borradaile had to prove her guilty beyond all reasonable doubt, which she had failed to do.

That should have been that: case dismissed. But the prosecution appealed for a retrial, the judge allowed it, and this time the jury duly convicted. Madame Rachel, who had been denied bail while waiting for the retrial, was sentenced to an unusually harsh five years' hard labor; and the *Times*, despite its earlier pronouncement, applauded. "Whatever may be the differences of opinion about the prisoner's legal guilt, about her moral guilt we take it there can be no doubt whatever," it thundered—thus dismissing, in one sentence, the entire basis of the British legal system.

What was it about Madame Rachel that so rattled the British establishment? The prosecution made much of her Jewishness—but it was no crime to be Jewish in Victorian England: the prime minister in 1868 was the not-very-Protestant Benjamin Disraeli. There were hints of various unsavory doings: that the baths were taken in a room fitted up for voyeurs, that Mrs. Leverson's promise to "cleanse the system from many of its impurities" was code for performing abortions, whose providers often called themselves "Madame." But none of this hearsay was under scrutiny. That the real problem was the beauty salon was made clear by the prosecutor's declaration that he "wished all the ladies who had heard or read this case would learn that if once they crossed the threshold of such places they would come out with a taint upon them."[5] That was an extraordinary phrase. Men in nineteenth-century Britain clearly found the use of cosmetics highly threatening.

If asked to justify this attitude, the *Times* editorial writer would doubtless have taken his stand, as Victorian gentlemen did, on the Bible, where Saint Paul recommended that women should cover their hair—their "crowning glory"—while a man should not cover his, because "he is the image and glory of God, but woman is the glory of man."[6] In Victorian Britain as in Pauline Judea, women were second-class beings, inferior in the sight of God, and as soon as they married, the property of their husbands, who alone were entitled to enjoy their good looks. And Victorian men, like Saint Paul, further assumed that the only reason a woman might want to look good in public—and thus the only point of cosmetics—was to seem more attractive to the opposite sex: if unmarried, to catch a husband (in the words of a 1770 British law banning it, makeup was for "seducing men into matrimony by cosmetic means"); if married, to carry on adulterous flirtations.

This (invariably male) assumption still persists, as does the misogyny that informs it. In 2005, *Zoo Weekly*, a British men's magazine, ran a "Win a boob job for your partner" competition, offering all-expenses-paid breast implant surgery as a prize to the girl "who deserves it most." The magazine called for men, or their girlfriends, to send in shots of the woman's cleavage, to be voted on by readers. When BBC Radio 1 asked its listeners what they thought about this, some women objected that they found the idea of such a competition degrading. But this elicited aggressive replies from competition entrants. "Woah! Woah! Woah! Too much 'Girl Power' in here," ranted one. "Calm down, girls! I entered the competition not because I wanted to give my girlfriend a gift, if she wants bigger boobs she can pay for them herself. . . . Its [*sic*] not always about you girls. High horse . . . climb down off of."

Victorian England, Pauline Judea, and the readers of *Zoo* could hardly be more different. But they are all disturbed by the same idea: that women might choose to be something more than a support system for men. For them, the worrying thing about cosmetics is the inescapable sense that women do *not* wear them with men in mind, but on the contrary, for their own benefit. Just as on a bad hair day nothing will go right, so looking good is always a confidence booster. And self-confidence leads to self-assertion.

This was certainly Helena Rubinstein's view. One of her nieces once asked her what use cosmetics were in meeting people's real needs. Rubinstein replied: "If my products help one young worker feel better about herself that day, then I feel I have accomplished something worthwhile."[7] And making people feel better about themselves still remains the primary function of cosmetics and (more recently) cosmetic surgery. In a survey of 1,000 British women conducted in 2005 by the women's magazine *Grazia*, only 13 percent of those considering cosmetic surgery said they were doing so because they wanted to look more attractive to men, while 64 percent thought it would give them more confidence.[8] That confidence would of course help should they wish to attract a man. But it would also help them function without one.

Powder and paint, when worn by respectable women, were thus intolerable to the Victorians on two fronts. First, they bolstered the self-esteem of a class of persons supposed to be meek and subordinate; second, they represented a highly visible form of rebellion, an incontrovertible and unmissable statement that the wearer valued her personal satisfaction above the wishes of her husband. One might turn a blind eye to the receipt of a discreet parcel of beauty aids, or the digging-out of Grandma's recipe for rosy cheeks (though such activities were always noticed and remarked on: Mrs. X powders, Mrs. Y rouges.) But visiting a beauty salon too openly defied social taboos. As for running one, that was too much. It had to be stopped, and stopped it was.

Forty years later, however, the daughters of those Victorian wives had become lipsticked suffrage marchers who, as everyone knew, would sooner rather than later have their way. And Helena Rubinstein, rich, independent, self-made, eye-poppingly chic, and sheathed in a seamless shell of creams, powders, and paints, both offered an image of what was possible and provided the means of getting there—or at least of taking a step along the way.

The problem, however, with products that are of a particular moment is that they tend to date. Economically, today's women have never been freer. In that sense we are still living in Rubinstein's world. But cosmetics have moved on dramatically since Madame, in her heyday, was the constantly visible face of Helena Rubinstein. It was Eugène Schueller's scientific laboratory, not Helena Rubinstein's kitchen, that would hold the key to the cosmetics future.

II

During the twentieth century, dreams that had for centuries been the stuff of fairy tales one after another became reality. Airplanes gave us magic carpets; automobiles, seven-league boots. The telephone let us speak across continents; radio and television showed us all that was happening in the world, often at the moment it happened. Most recently, the Internet has granted us instant, universal knowledge. And although immortality is still beyond us, the beauty business offers a consolation prize. What (Freud famously inquired) do women want? Madame Rachel could have told him: to be beautiful forever. And today, beautiful forever is, up to a point, ours. When, in

1935, a reader wrote to the author of *Skin Deep* inquiring about Helena Rubinstein's "Herbal Tissue" cream, retailing at $1.25 and supposed to "prevent or heal lines, crepy eyelids and crows around the eyes,"[9] the answer was: "There is, alas, no cosmetic known capable of doing the things described." Today, however, that is no longer true.

Skin creams are still most people's first line of defense. And these days, they *can* have some slight effect. In April 2007, research carried out for the BBC television program *Horizon*, investigating the antiaging industry, found that although most creams left wrinkles wholly unsmoothed, one did, over time, make a slight, but measurable, difference: No. 7 Protect and Perfect Serum, a proprietary brand of the British pharmacy chain Boots, and at £16.75 ($27) for a 30ml jar, one of the cheapest products in the survey. Within twenty-four hours of the program being broadcast, sales jumped 2,000 percent. Customers queued outside branches of Boots at five the next morning. In Yorkshire, there was a near-riot when one woman bought a store's entire stock. Within two weeks what had been a year's supply of the lotion was bought up, and single jars sold on eBay for up to £100. Today, in time-honored style, the Protect and Perfect family has expanded to include day cream, night cream, beauty serum, intense beauty serum, and a range of products for men. Why stop at one product when twelve will do?

The secret of Boots' cream is a vitamin A compound called retinol, which increases the production of two important components of the skin, glycosaminoglycan and procollagen. Creams today also use hyaluronic acid, or hyaluronan, a component of connective tissue that cushions and lubricates, and their advertising heavily emphasizes scientific certainty. Thus, L'Oréal's Youth Code skin cream is "Inspired by the Science of Genes." But the scientifically active ingredients in such creams, although present, are a vanishingly small proportion of the whole—far less than the quantity required to produce any noticeable effect. As Liz Walker, proprietor of the House of Beauty in Barnsley, Yorkshire, put it, "A pampering facial or a nice cream is all very well, but it's not going to make those wrinkles completely disappear, is it?"[10]

If the cream doesn't do the trick, however, new and effective resources are now available. We can either go deeper, with plastic surgery, or iron out wrinkles with "cosmoceuticals." In 2006, the number of cosmetic procedures, both surgical and noninvasive, was estimated at well over 21 million worldwide. By 2015, the American Society of Plastic Surgeons expects its members to carry out 55 million such procedures annually in the United States alone.[11] The market, valued at nearly $14 billion in 2007, is growing at $1 billion a year.[12] On-demand shape-shifting has become one of the passions of the new millennium.

Plastic surgery is not new. As long ago as 2000 B.C., doctors in India repaired noses disfigured by disease or punishment. But until antiseptics and anesthesia made operations relatively painless and safe, it was used only in extreme cases. Toward the end of the nineteenth century, it gained ground: plastic surgery was one of the treatments Helena Rubinstein investigated on her whirlwind tour of European skin specialists in 1905, along with chemical skin peels and other such scientific innovations. But these treatments were expensive and often risky. In 1921, the American heiress Gladys Deacon, whom the press dubbed the world's loveliest woman, and who was certainly one of the richest, had paraffin wax injected into her face to correct a small indentation at the bridge of her nose. She hoped to achieve the profile of a Greek statue, but unfortunately for her the wax slipped, leaving her with an incipient horn on her forehead and a swollen neck where the wax had run down under the skin. It was a catastrophe from which neither she nor paraffin-wax treatments ever recovered.

As so often, military requirements nudged the science forward. Wars destroy many faces, and doctors such as Jacques Joseph in Germany during World War I and Archibald McIndoe in Britain during World War II were both made famous by their pioneering techniques in reconstructive surgery. Inevitably, these were soon co-opted by the beauty business. After World War I, another pioneering plastic surgeon, Sir Harold Gillies, wondered if it might be possible to make a living out of private plastic surgery. The answer, as he soon found, was yes. He neatly summed up the difference between his new field and his old: "Reconstructive surgery is an attempt to return to normal; cosmetic surgery is an attempt to surpass the normal."[13] But while comparatively few people, at least in peacetime, need reconstructive surgery, almost everybody would like to look better than they do, and many are happy to pay for the privilege.

Today, surpassing the normal has become so run-of-the-mill that to age unretouched seems almost a form of obstinacy. The website of one London cosmetic-surgery practice offers a body map: click on the appropriate part to choose your preferred procedure. Face, ears, arms, hands, breasts, abdomen, genitalia, hips, legs, skin—all can be altered, and, hopefully, improved. You can indulge in medical tourism: see Prague (or Warsaw, or Rio) and get your tummy tucked while you're there. The *New York Times* even published a restaurant-type guide to Rio doctors, giving prices, specialties, booking advice, and handy hints: "Dr. Müller is known for, among other things, sculpturing beautifully shaped breasts and performing body liposuction. If you're looking for an aggressive makeover this is not the place for you: Dr. Müller specializes in the natural look. . . ."[14] Doctors tout themselves online, publishing testimonials from grateful patients and employing media consultants to promote their public image—not only in America, where this kind of thing has always been allowed, but in Britain, where it very much has not. An old-school plastic and cosmetic surgeon I spoke to—he didn't want to be named, I'll call him Peter—thought advertising for cosmetic surgery "the pits: you used to get struck off by the General Medical Council for that kind of thing." However, even where there is a prohibition, doctors get around it: all they need do is belong to a clinic, which does the advertising for them.

So fundamental, indeed, has body altering become to our lives, and so fascinating are the possibilities, that watching it in action has become a component of prime-time television. In programs such as *Extreme Makeover, Nip/Tuck*, and *Ten Years Younger*, unreconstructed subjects undergo transformation by a team of experts—the dentist, the hairdresser, the boob man, the nose man, the stylist-cum-cheerleader—into another person altogether. The original subject—the clay, so to speak—exists only as raw material: the Before. The wizards do their stuff, and—shazam!—a new woman or man is born, all their own work. Pygmalion and Frankenstein live!

I asked Peter if he felt like a sculptor when remolding people's faces and bodies. He said he did. A lot of his colleagues, he said, are (as he is) painters or sculptors in their spare time—that was often what first attracted them to this branch of surgery. Indeed, he feels artistic skills so necessary to plastic surgeons that he set up a course called "Sculpture for Surgeons." In it, seven or eight plastic surgeons are given a ball of clay and told to model the head of a sitter—something they do not, at first, find easy even though, or perhaps because, they are so familiar with facial anatomy. One typical participant produced, in the words of Luke Shepherd, the sculptor who teaches the course, "what turned out to be an anatomical model, very hollow-looking, more like a skull. He said he didn't know how to fill in the soft tissue around the bone structure." That is, the shape of the end of the nose, or the eyelids—the details, in fact, that concern potential patients. "We try to give them a basic grounding in the language of form—what symmetry is, how the eye balances things," Shepherd said. "It's training the eye to ask questions of the form so when they come to surgery the eye is able to make those sort of decisions." He aims to teach the surgeons on his course to "see 3-D." It is also important that they see each patient as an individual problem. Plastic surgeons get known for a particular specialty, but with facial work this specialization can be dangerous: patients don't want a "signature" job, they want the nose, or chin, they themselves feel they need.

Plastic surgery is still not cheap. But easy terms are available, and the customers are happy to pay up. Fifty-four percent of the interviewees in the *Grazia* survey intended to have cosmetic surgery, expecting to spend on average $5,650 (£3,500). If they didn't have the necessary money available, they were happy to spend less on clothes and going out. If necessary they would take out a loan—many practices offer low-interest financing to their customers. And the market is not confined to women: a 2007 survey by the market-reseach organization YouGov found that a quarter of all men in the United Kingdom. would consider cosmetic intervention.

However, the great majority of cosmetic procedures these days do not involve surgery. On the contrary, the American Society of Plastic Surgeons predicts that 88 percent of the 55 million procedures anticipated in 2015 will be noninvasive. "You can do a lot of things with a needle now—you can compete with a knife," said Dr. Lucy Glancey, a specialist in cosmetic and antiaging treatments.[15] You can either plump out your face with collagen fillers, "redistributing volume," as Dr. Glancey put it, so that firmness returns without the deadly "windswept" look that can result from a face-lift; or you can simply smooth those wrinkles away with Botox, the registered name for an injectable solution of the botulinum toxin, which blocks the signals telling your muscles to contract. If you eat meat containing this poison, it attacks the muscles in your chest: you can't breathe and it kills you. But if a small amount is injected into your face, the facial muscles can't move—and so, can't wrinkle.

First used medicinally in the 1970s to relieve uncontrollable muscle spasms, Botox's possible cosmetic application was first recognized in 1987. Since then, its popularity has increased exponentially. In 2000, about 800,000 Americans had Botox injections, while nearly 2 million had cosmetic surgery; in 2008, 5.5 million chose Botox (one in eleven of whom were men), and 1.7 million surgery. L'Oréal, already part of the injectables market through its part ownership of the pharmaceuticals firm Sanofi-Aventis and its share of Galderma, a joint venture with Nestlé, in 2009 introduced its own botulinum toxin treatment, to be marketed under the name Azzalure in Europe, and Reloxin in the States. The market for these treatments, worth $1.2 billion in 2009, is expected to grow by 13 percent per year between 2009 and 2012—a tempting prospect, especially given that both 2008 and 2009 saw L'Oréal's profits fall: in 2008 by 27 percent, in 2009 by a further 3.2 percent.

Injections of Botox (as the treatment has become generically known, though in fact the name is a proprietary trademark owned by Allergan) are quick and virtually painless. The effects are almost instantaneous and involve no ugly scarring.

And if you don't like the result, no problem: it wears off. Since it works because of its paralyzing effect, it makes your face less mobile, producing a curious masklike look. But some users actively prefer this. Just as in eighteenth-century France, the cosmetic mask represents something so desirable—membership in the king's set, the defeat of time—that its very artificiality becomes a mark of status. "As the Botox wears off towards the end of three months, the movement returns to my face and I get really impatient for my next fix," said Jay Nicholls, a thirty-two-year-old model and dancer.[16] Jay has her Botox renewed every three months at £500 (about $700) a time. That's the financial equivalent of a face-lift every two years, on and on, into the foreseeable future.

Fillers are more dubious—or that, at any rate, is Peter's view. In fact, he thought they could sometimes be quite dangerous. Gladys Deacon–type disasters are by no means inconceivable even now. The "trout pout" that can result from having your lips plumped is a notorious risk. But, as with Botox, these treatments are not permanent, and since they are both cheaper, per treatment, than surgery, as well as far less time-consuming and daunting, more and more people want to try them. "Supermarket workers, dinner ladies, they're all saving up for [Botox]," says Liz Walker. "And there are no holds barred as to how far they'll go for all the other stuff, either. We're now using machines they don't even use in London in order to get more immediate results."

I asked Dr. Glancey if she had tried out her own treatments. She admitted that she had: several of them, in fact. "We're in a sweetie shop here—you can't resist," she said. And it's easy to see what she means. Once you take the first step—iron out your frown lines, whiten your teeth, plump out your cheeks or the backs of your hands—your body becomes a blank sheet.

What about those crow's-feet, those baggy upper arms . . . ? If something goes wrong, perhaps some further tweaking may improve it. Once you begin, the possibilities for discontent are infinite, perfection always somewhere around the next corner. And soon, in the excitement of redesign, you've forgotten what you looked like in the first place. Before-and-after photographs of surgery addicts show a terrifying disjunction between the presurgery face and the end result of serial adjustments. "Most surgeons have to convince people to have less," said Luke Shepherd.

For some, the procedure rather than the result is the important thing. In an extreme form, this pattern can be pathological: the feeling of constant discontent with one's body, and compulsion to change it, is a syndrome known as body dysmorphic disorder. But even for nondysmorphics, cosmetic procedures can be addictive. "I'm here for a wound check to make sure I'm healing properly," Lauren, forty-five, said as she waited for her appointment at a large London practice.

> *I had a tummy tuck, had my implants changed and I had a breast uplift. I had my first breast implants done 17 years ago after I had my son. My boobs went from a C to an A and I thought, "I don't like that, they look like pita breads." I was considering having a tummy tuck so I thought while I'm there I might as well have my breasts done.*[17]

Mostly, though, the treatments are a means to an end: feeling better about yourself. "I have completely re-invented myself and Botox has played a big part in that," said Lisa, thirty-seven, while Victoria, a widow, age forty-five, said Botox "has given me the confidence to restart my life after [my husband's] death."[18]

Workplace issues are also important. Particularly when times are hard, people feel that if they begin to look old they may lose their job to someone younger. When the beauty business began, this fear was not a woman's concern, as men were the principal wage earners and most women's chief preoccupation was to catch a husband—as in a typical L'Oréal ad from 1923, which showed a pretty girl sitting between two admirers: "The young are life's favorites. . . . Gray hairs don't attract admiring looks. And happy youth lasts longer for those who use L'Oréal."

But priorities soon changed—and the letters written by readers to the author of *Skin Deep* in 1935 and 1936, during the Depression, pinpoint the moment. These women's principal worry was no longer that they would fail to catch a man, but that they might lose their job. Their earnings, formerly, like their bright-red lipstick, a badge of newly gained freedom and independence, had become a vital part of the family budget; and cosmetics and hair dye (once carefree banners for emancipation) were now essential tools in the grim fight for employment. In those circumstances, cosmetics played a vital role—whether by preserving the illusion of youth, so that an employer would be less inclined to "let you go," or because the wearer felt—and so worked—better. *Skin Deep*'s researches revealed that all the synthetic hair dyes on the market in America during the 1930s were more or less allergenic, some seriously so; but the ensuing correspondence made it clear that many women felt they had to risk them, or else face unemployment. "Due to the fact that my hair is prematurely grey, and even more important, that if such a fact were known it would jeopardize my job, I have in desperation and with much fear and trembling been using Inecto Hair Dye," confessed a worried reader in 1935. Inecto had been found to cause acute dermatitis of the face, inflammation and irritation of the scalp, face, and nose, dermatitis of the scalp, sores on scalp and face, swelling of the eyelids and closing of the eyes, and "many other unpleasant consequences, including toxic absorption extending down over the face, back and arms, followed by acute nephritis, Bright's disease and anaemia."[19] Another wanted to know "if there is certain proof of injury to persons who have used Grayban for a long period. My work makes it important that I look as well as possible, and gray hair is not flattering to me, as many try to make me fancy."[20] Grayban was based on a salt of bismuth, and poisonous when absorbed. But many users would tolerate any discomfort to avoid being sacked.

Similar fears resurfaced in the economic crisis year of 2008. As always in a time of recession, the beauty business boomed. In America, a total of 12.1 million cosmetic procedures took place—despite the recession, a 3-percent increase over the preceding year. People were, however, less inclined to go for pure "bling": Dr. Richard Baxter, a plastic surgeon in Washington State, noticed a marked decrease in the size of breast implants as the economy started to go downhill. Before the recession, fewer than a third of his clients chose a B cup implant; after, about half picked a B. "People have turned to more natural-looking things," he said.[21] But men as well as women now turned to the beauty industry in hopes that it might make them seem more desirable to employers. In 2008's first quarter, one big U.K. cosmetic group reported a 17-percent rise in male face-lifts, while over 5,200 men consulted for other youth-enhancing procedures.[22] In the last three months of that same year, a time when thousands of workers in financial institutions lost their jobs, there was a 10-percent rise in face-lifts for men countrywide as sacked bankers used their severance packages to buy plastic surgery.[23] "There was this notion in the City [of London] where the older partners felt threatened by the younger partners," said Dr. Glancey (who also saw a marked increase in the number of men coming to her for treatment). "They didn't want to look too tired. That tells everyone you're not going to be as good as a young person. If your face doesn't give that message then perhaps they'll forget how old you really are."

Naturally this becomes even edgier if everyone else in the office has had the signs of advancing years removed. It's a classic example of positive feedback: once your competitors have had "work done," the notion of what's acceptable changes, and you're obliged to go down the same route merely in order to stay in the game.

For as youth increasingly becomes a necessary qualification for success, aging, even for the happily partnered and employed, has become frightening and unacceptable. "I'm not alone in thinking the idea of being 50 is an absolute outrage," confessed journalist Christa D'Souza. "If you were to look at [my] photograph and tell me you see an attractive middle-aged woman (for that technically is what I am at 46) I'd not be merely insulted, I'd feel, on some level, that I had failed."[24] But at what? At holding back age itself? Does looking younger make people feel younger? It is true that as longevity increases, forty will genuinely become, as we're constantly told, the new thirty. In 2000, the average German was 39.9 years old and could expect to live another 39.2 years; middle age could therefore be said to occur at age 40. But by 2050, the average German will be 51.9 years old and will live, on average, another 37.1 years, pushing middle age back five years.[25]

Face-lifts, then, may help reconcile people not only to the inevitability of getting older, but of being old longer. Writer Linda Brown said that when she first had her face-lift she felt her face no longer really belonged to her—it was simply "the face." "I wanted me back," she said. "I couldn't reconcile myself to the woman in the mirror—I just couldn't relate to this woman at all." That is easy to imagine, for we have all met that woman, and she is oddly unnerving: neither old nor young but rather, indefinably, outside age. Hers is the face of cosmetic surgery, the face of our times. And however familiar on others, to meet it in the mirror must inevitably be an odd experience. As the weeks passed, though, Brown got accustomed to it. "I now look like 'me.' I don't care about the red marks, I think for the first time in my life I don't have to compensate."[26]

I can personally attest to the irresistible allure of cosmetic surgery. I was brought up to assume that one made the best of what one had been given: in my case, large breasts. I've always hated them, but the thought of doing anything about them (other than wearing a good bra) never seriously crossed my mind. Perhaps that was stupid: Peter the surgeon thinks breast operations almost always leave the woman much happier than before. But my bikini-wearing days are over, nor do I any longer lust after strapless or spaghetti-strap dresses. It seemed inconceivable I would ever consider such an operation now.

In a spirit of inquiry, however, and for the purposes of this book, I arranged a consultation with one of the cosmetic-surgery practices whose ads, plastered throughout the London transport system, encourage travelers to "Shape up for summer!" Adorned with photos of improbably self-supporting cleavage, the advertisers imply that buying new breasts is no more problematic or significant (though a little more expensive) than buying a new swimsuit. The ad gave a phone number and urged tube-riders to call for a free consultation. So I did.

The practice was located in London's Harley Street, the traditional address of Britain's grander doctors, and one of the planet's most expensive parcels of real estate. A quick trawl through the Internet revealed at least thirty-two different plastic-surgery clinics and practitioners located there, and even more in the surrounding streets. Presumably Harley Street's aura of oak-aged respectability offers a counterweight to cosmetic surgery's still somewhat tacky image, compounded of dubious outcomes, tasteless advertising (one such ad, urging customers to "Make Yourself Amazing," offers £750 off breast augmentations if they take a late booking and fill a vacant slot), medical tourism, and easy finance.

The group with which I had my appointment started out twenty years ago with one clinic. Now it has sixteen nationwide. In the waiting area, which takes up the entire ground floor, every seat was occupied, with a six-deep queue at reception. Most of the patients were women, though there were a couple of young men. (In fact, I was told, 40 percent of this group's clientele is now male.) Many of those waiting were clearly habitués, in for a quick touch-up: "Vicky, you know your way downstairs—thank you, honey," the receptionist trilled. I had never met her, and was there to discuss what is in fact quite a serious operation, but I, too, was unhesitatingly greeted by my first name: "Hallo, Ruth."

When I got to see the nurse I was quite open about my reason for being there, and assured her there was little chance I would actually have the operation. But we agreed that she would nonetheless take me through the consultation as though I were one of her more usual customers—who generally, once they've saved up the money, can't wait to get it done. The booklet she gave me to take away urged patients to "take a period of 7–14 days to consider," which must mean that many don't. We began with pictures—befores and afters—and then the nurse explained what the procedures would be, and the costs. With one night in hospital, a breast reduction would cost me £5,720 ($9,180), with two nights, £5,990 ($9,600), plus another £300 ($480) for a subsequent necessary injection. That is serious money, for which I have other uses. But as we went on, and against all expectation, I found myself wondering whether, perhaps, I mightn't have the operation after all. Was it too late, even now, to release my inner Venus de Milo? If I'd still been in the spaghetti-strap market, I'd almost certainly have done it.

Vanity, vanity. But research shows that this desire to attain something nearer one's ideal physical self is more than that. Our preference for attractive people over plain ones is hardwired. When newborn infants as young as one day old are shown pairs of photographed faces, one judged attractive by adult subjects, one judged plain by the same subjects, the babies spend more time looking at the attractive face.[27] Such innate preferences must affect how others judge us, yet until now we have never been able permanently to alter our less attractive physical characteristics.

Which would seem to imply that the real gift is agency: the fact that we are now able to take the necessary action. A 1995 study of cosmetic surgery included one woman whose breast augmentation went disastrously wrong, leading to multiple correctional operations and scarring. But she was still pleased she had had the procedure done. Before it she had seen life as a downward spiral over which she had no control; after, she felt determined to keep going.[28] Next time, it would turn out better. In our age of infinite choice, a new and better possibility is always available, in bodies as in everything else. And there can always be a next time. And another. And another. . .

III

BUT IF NEW BODIES, AND new faces, are available off the rack, how will we choose which to select? Who sets the fashionable ideal?

The answer is: some enviable, powerful other. The look of the eighteenth-century French court, for example, was not only clownish but dangerous. Everyone knew that the skin-whitening paste called ceruse, made from lead, was a deadly poison that ruined the skin it covered and could cause death. But the king painted his face in this way; and rather than risk losing their social position by appearing outlandishly unpainted, members of the court made themselves up to match.

More recently the choice has often been a matter of race. Sometimes, as with those who sought urgent nose jobs in Nazi Germany, "passing" can be a matter of life and death. More often people simply want to look like the majority, because that majority holds the social and economic power. "Trying to succeed in a white world is very, very difficult," said Sami, a young Malaysian man living in Britain. "It's hard enough if you're white—but even harder if you're black." Sami was about to spend 40,000 euros on a leg-lengthening operation because he felt his present height—5'2", nothing unusual in Malaysia, where the average male height is 5'4"—made it impossible to be taken seriously in a society where the average man is 5'9" tall. And from mere practicality—aping the looks of the powerful because that will make life easier—it is a short step to finding those looks aesthetically preferable.

It is thus not surprising, though still depressing, that America's first black self-made millionaire, Sarah Breedlove, aka Madam C. J. Walker, made her money by developing hair-straightening products such as the hot comb. "Hair pressing was a ritual of black women's culture of intimacy," wrote the black author and historian bell hooks. "It was a world where the images constructed as barriers between one's self and the world were briefly let go. . . . I was overjoyed when mama finally agreed I could join the Saturday ritual." Later, hooks abandoned straightened hair, wearing her "natural" as a political declaration. But "For years I still considered it a problem. . . . It has been only in recent years that I have ceased to worry about what other people would say about my hair."[29] Similarly, flat-chested Asian girls living in Caucasian societies seek breast enlargements to conform to the white notion of what is beautiful, while big-bosomed black women seek reductions for the same reason.

Recently, L'Oréal has used two nonwhite women as its "face": singer Beyoncé Knowles and Freida Pinto, who starred in the film *Slumdog Millionaire*. In both cases, however, the pictures used in the ads showed them paler than in real life. When a storm of protest was raised by the sudden lightening of Beyoncé, L'Oréal said it was "categorically untrue that L'Oréal Paris altered Ms. Knowles's features or skin tone in the campaign." But the fact remained: the image they used was lighter than any other photo of Beyoncé. If L'Oréal Paris had not done the alteration, someone most certainly had. Presumably it was thought the main customer-base was not yet ready to emulate anyone more than slightly coffee-colored.*

Above and beyond the thorny issue of race, however, the lightening of Beyoncé raises interesting questions. They concern the relations between photography and the beauty industry; for not only do the age of mass cosmetics and the age of universal photography coincide, they are inextricably intertwined. Powerful new technologies inevitably affect our perceptions. The arrival of the gramophone changed the way we listened to music. And in the same way, the arrival of photog-

* It is perhaps worth noting that in 2007 the L'Oréal subsidiary Garnier was fined €30,000 for racial discrimination, when it stipulated (presumably for similar reasons) that hostesses recruited to hand out shampoo samples and discuss styling with customers should all be white.

raphy revolutionized the way we visualized ourselves. For the first time in history, we could obtain, at any moment, a record of ourselves as others saw us—and use that image to experiment with ways of improving what they saw. From then on, the camera dictated the way we wanted to look. And despite the camera's deceptive instantaneity, that look was always far from nature.

Photography has always been an art as much as a recording device. Because the earliest photographic films were more sensitive to blues than reds, and so didn't properly register fleshtones, the detail of early portraits had to be manually adjusted after the event. And when both films and cameras became more efficient, a new problem arose. The super-sharp images were wonderful for landscapes and buildings, and also for portraits when the intention was documentary, as in pictures of relentlessly weathered Native American braves or aging, bewhiskered prime ministers. But a pitiless record of every pore was not what a lady required. Often, therefore, photographers inserted a kindly blurring, softening the focus until blemishes were obscured in a gentle fuzz. After the small photographs known as *cartes-de-visite* became de rigueur in the 1860s, every woman visualized herself as she might be when posed in soft focus against a studio background.

It was this photo-face, painstakingly smoothed and prepared, that Helena Rubinstein presented to her customers, both in her advertisements and in all the other extensive publicity she engineered. Madame, as she appeared in those photos, was everything implied by the word *soignée*, her hair glossily in place, her skin matte, white, and flawless, her lips a perfectly outlined scarlet jewel, her face—even in her sixties and seventies—preternaturally devoid of wrinkles. Often pictured in her lab coat, she looked calm, dignified, smooth, youthful, elegant, an image of perfection that was far from the chaotic and substantial reality. "I had to airbrush *inches* from her waist!" moaned photographer Cecil Beaton after snapping the distinctly rotund Madame of the 1930s; and snapshots taken at less guarded moments show how much of this ideal look was achieved by a combination of skillful makeup and photographer's artifice. But the alteration had a significance over and above vanity. It was the photographs, not the unretouched reality, that defined the look women wanted to emulate; and the cosmetics those photographs sold gave them the means to do so.

Other cosmetics companies of course used their own endorsers, chosen from among society's enviable strata—which at first meant socialites. During the 1920s, Pond's Cold Cream divided these ladies into two classes—$1,000 people and $500 people—approaching them for endorsements around the twentieth of the month, when their allowances were getting depleted. They also recruited some genuine aristocrats from Europe—the Duchesse de Richelieu, Lady Mountbatten, and Queen Marie of Romania "a bargain [who] endorsed for $2,000, two silver boxes, and a miniature of herself by de Laszlo."[30] There, under a misty photograph, nestled the illustrious name; but you would have been hard put to identify its original if you passed her in the street.

Soon, however, these blurry socialites were supplanted by a new, specifically photographic aristocracy: film stars. Traditionally, actresses had been classed with courtesans, and had ranked similarly low in society. But photography—and, a little later, and definitively, cinematography—transformed them into goddesses, their images known and worshipped across the world. Constance Talmadge, one of the great stars of the silent screen, was said to have posed for 400 testimonial photographs in one day, "showing a set of white teeth due to the exclusive use of Pepsodent, Iodent, Kolynos, Dentyne, Ipoma, Squibbs, Lyon's, Colgate's or Pebeco."[31] Between takes, maids would help change her outfit, and stagehands would rearrange the settings.

These endorsement photographs were quite obviously posed. But soon a different class of pictures entered the public's photographic consciousness: the off-duty "snapshots" that became such an important part of Hollywood publicity. These photographs, the public was given to understand, represented the movie gods and goddesses in their casual, offscreen moments. The truth, of course, was that nothing could have been less casual: those perfectly clear complexions with their carefully graded highlights, those huge, mascaraed eyes, those big scarlet lips, that hair glowing with improbable brilliance and color, were the result of careful makeup, endless posing, skillful lighting, and, usually, extensive retouching.

And it was this denatured photographic "naturalness" that women tried to reproduce through cosmetics. You ladled on the foundation and powder, the eye shadow, mascara, and lipstick, and left the house camera-ready. Even in the most dimly day-lit offices and high streets, people felt undressed if they weren't wearing long black lashes, blue-shadowed eyes, bright red lips, and pancake foundation, as though imminently about to face the klieg lights. Traveling in the New York subway one day, I was struck by the unusually beautiful complexion of the young woman opposite—only to be confounded a few seconds later as she opened her bag, took out a makeup kit, and proceeded to cover her face with pink gloop. When she'd finished she looked just like everyone else, which, presumably, was the intention. Office life required this bland, smoothed-over, highly colored look. Even some men in the public eye—think Tony Blair, John Edwards—now feel undressed without the layer of artificial tan to which constant studio exposure has accustomed them—and us.

So people's notion of what constituted a "normal" appearance was rejigged to fit the movies. But the conspiracy was, on the whole, benign. Not only were the cosmetics companies happy, so was the woman in the street. At least the effect she sought was achievable. The Helena Rubinstein of the advertisements might be an artifact, but she was a self-created artifact. Artur Rubinstein the pianist, her friend, compatriot, and neighbor in New York (though no relation), would watch from his Park Avenue window, directly opposite her makeup room, as Madame, then well into her seventies, painstakingly constructed the face she wished to present to the world—a ritual he found touching, impressive, and, as a public performer himself, understandable.[32] And the final result, though heavily worked, nevertheless remained rooted in actual appearance. With time and expertise you, too, could construct a comparably perfect surface: a carapace that (if you followed wartime *Vogue*'s instructions, applying the color, blotting, powdering, reapplying, reblotting, repowdering . . .) would carry you through the day without cracking. The products were within most people's easy financial reach, and the effort was free.

Today, all is different. The fashion pages and celebrity magazines no longer represent living women and men but a sort of meta-world. In the film *The September Issue*, about *Vogue* magazine, there is a wonderfully self-referential scene where the cameraman is persuaded to become part of the fashion shoot he is filming. He is of normal shape—that is to say, his stomach is not perfectly flat. When Anna Wintour, the editor, views the resulting pictures, her immediate reaction is to call the Photoshop studio to have the offending inches shaved down. They are an intrusion: they have no place in the world *Vogue* sets out to create. In *Vogue*-world, as in the world of "procedures," reality is merely a starting point. Just when the universal takeup of cosmetic surgery, Botox, and the rest began to shift the boundaries of what could be achieved in recasting the body, Photoshop began to revolutionize the photographic image. Ever since, the two have been twinned.

The acknowledged master of Photoshop is Pascal Dangin, a Frenchman living in New York. He works for (among others) *Vogue, Vanity Fair, Harper's Bazaar, Allure, French Vogue, Italian Vogue, V,* the *New York Times Magazine.* Many photographers, including Annie Leibovitz and Steven Meisel, "rarely work with anyone else." For Leibovitz, he is a sort of validator of her craft. "Just by the fact that he works with you, you think you're good. If he works with you a lot, maybe you think, Well, maybe I'm worthwhile."[33]

Lauren Collins of *The New Yorker* spent several months shadowing Dangin for a profile, "Pixel Perfect." Here she describes him at work on some pictures of an actress:

> *"She looks too small because she's teeny," he said. On a drop-down menu, he selected a warping tool, a device that augments the volume of clusters of pixels. The dress puffed up pleasingly, as if it had been fluffed by some helpful lady-in-waiting inside the screen.*
>
> *Next, Dangin moved the mouse so the pointer hovered near the actress's neck. "I softened the collarbones, but then she started to get too retouched, so I put back some stuff," he explained. He pressed a button and her neck got a little bonier. He clicked more drop-down menus—master opacity*

> *stamp, clone stamp. [This] minimized the actress's temples, which bulged a little, tightened the skin around her chin, and excised a fleshy bump from her forehead. She had an endearingly crooked bottom row of teeth, which Dangin knew better than to fix. . . .*
>
> *Another time, Dangin showed me how he had restructured the chest . . . of an actress who, to his eye, seemed to have had a clumsy breast enhancement. Like a double negative, virtual plastic surgery cancelled out real plastic surgery, resulting in a believable look.*[34]

Even the recent Dove campaign, which uses larger women to model underwear in an attempt to counteract the relentlessly skinny ideal promoted by the fashion industry, was Danginized. "Do you know how much retouching was on that?" Dangin said. "But it was great to do, a challenge, to keep everyone's skin and faces showing the mileage but not looking unattractive."[35]

Routine retouching of this kind has created an ever-greater distance between what the beauty business tells us we ought to look like and what is achievable. The pictures of the possible and desirable that we carry inside our head are no longer based upon images of actual bodies. Jay Nicholls, the dancer who so loves her Botox, is thinking of using it to prevent underarm sweating. Not because sweating presents a particular problem: "I already use a roll-on solution that stops me sweating for two weeks." But she "would love to be able to stop it for longer."[36] What's sweating, after all? A mere bodily function. And who, these days, has any patience for those? Inside and out, we prefer the virtual ideal.

Of course people are aware of this disjunction. And the nervousness it arouses is reflected in their fury when the image of some well-known icon appears so heavily reconstructed that it is no longer possible to pretend these images reflect reality. With L'Oréal's Beyoncé and Pinto pictures, many of the protests were prompted by the perceived racism of the alterations. But race played no part in the controversy surrounding the heavily doctored images of actress Kate Winslet published by *Vanity Fair* in November 2008. "Those of us who are not legally blind will instantly realize that the woman on the cover looks *nothing* like the real Kate Winslet. Is the woman an imposter? An evil twin? Or just the result of hundreds of man hours of digital retouching? I'm going with 'alien,'" typically announced one blog.[37]

A video has recently been doing the rounds of YouTube. Marked "Every Teenage Girl Should See This," it shows a transformation scene: a normally pleasant-looking young woman Photoshopped before your eyes, her neck lengthened, her face thinned, her eyebrows raised, her complexion clarified: duckling to swan. Photographically, she becomes the beauty no "procedures"—and certainly no makeup—will ever make her in real life. How the girl in question feels, faced with so clear and unattainable an image of what she might look like if she only looked different, we are not told.

Unsurprisingly, the now habitual digital enhancement of fashion and glamour images has given rise to a good deal of agonizing. The British Liberal Democrat Party is so perturbed by its pernicious influence on young girls' self-esteem that it has proposed a new law. Just as cigarette manufacturers must print a warning on every packet announcing that tobacco is lethal, so they want every photographic image to be accompanied by a message saying whether or not it has been doctored.[38]

Our great-great-grandmothers encased their bodies in whalebone in pursuit of the eighteen-inch waist; our mothers covered their faces with paste and powder so that they might look like their favorite film stars. And today's women turn to the knife and the needle, liposucking off some inches here, tightening a jawline there, plumping out this fallen cheek, lifting that recalcitrant breast, in a never-ending, inevitably futile attempt to achieve the ultimate unreality: Photoshop.

IV

When Helena Rubinstein started out in business, men held the upper hand, financially and socially. And men decreed that respectable women should go unpainted.

Over the next half-century, the beauty industry ran hand in hand with women's progress toward an equal place in the public world. Painting one's face and cutting one's hair signaled a new universe of choice and possibility. It is no coincidence that lipstick, between the 1920s and the 1950s, was bright, bright red. Helena Rubinstein's motives were of course commercial: she wanted to be rich. But she also wanted independence, the right to control both her life and her money. And the cosmetics industry not only granted her wishes, it reflected her customers' similar aspirations.

Today the wheel has come full circle. Cosmetics and cosmetic "procedures," far from being unthinkable, have become almost compulsory. Who, now, dares be the only one in the room with wrinkles? Ironically, although women's independence and equality are enshrined in law, their appearance is once again under someone else's control.

And that someone is usually a man. Ninety percent of those "having work done," both in Europe and America, are women.

And 90 percent of cosmetic surgeons are men. Although the British Association of Plastic and Reconstructive Surgeons has 850 members, only 98 of them are women. In America, not one of *New York* magazine's nominated "Best Doctors" for cosmetic surgery in 2008 was a woman. An online trawl through plastic surgeons in New York and Los Angeles turned up only four women's names.

This gender imbalance does not mean that male plastic surgeons exercise some sinister power over their female patients. However, it does reflect the extent to which, in this world of supposed equality, men rather than women still tend to be the active agents. And nowhere is this truer than in the world the beauty industry now inhabits: the world of big business.

In her groundbreaking book *The Feminine Mystique*, published in 1963, Betty Friedan asked why so many highly educated American women were effectively abandoning careers. Instead, they were devoting their energies to homemaking, which, despite all the propaganda in its favor, left them bored, frustrated, depressed, and unfulfilled. Friedan concluded that in postwar America, women's "really crucial function . . . [was] *to buy more things for the home*." An entire industry of advertising and market research devoted itself to persuading them to do so. And since the marketing men had decided that "a woman's attitude toward housekeeping appliances cannot be separated from her attitude towards homemaking in general," it had become commercially imperative that as many women as possible spend time at home being what business labeled "true housewives." From the sellers' standpoint, career women were considered "unhealthy." And the persuaders had conveyed their message so successfully that the American career woman had become an endangered species.[39]

Partly as a result of Friedan's book, that changed. But the sellers still needed to sell. So they expanded their sights to include not just the home but the body—which of course accompanies you wherever you go and whoever you are. And although the beauty business, the industry concerned with bodies, had traditionally been a female enterprise, that now began to change. The structure of the market thus remained what it had been pre-Friedan. The buyers were mostly women, the sellers mostly men.

Helena Rubinstein, Elizabeth Arden, Estée Lauder, the great names in twentieth-century cosmetics, got where they did because men hadn't yet cottoned on to beauty's commercial possibilities. But by the time Friedan began her research, they had begun to do so. Patrick O'Higgins, offered a job by Helena Rubinstein in 1955, wandered uncertainly past the drugstore windows, eyeing the products. His first thought was, "Golly! Who ever buys all this crap?" and his second, "Women's names! Women's work?" Only when he noticed the other names—Max Factor, Revlon, Charles Antell—did he reflect that "The beauty business is an enormous industry."[40] And that made it suitable for men. Once the likes of Rubinstein and Elizabeth Arden had made beauty's commercial possibilities apparent, the boys moved in.

Now they have taken full control. The beauty business has become very big business indeed—and big business in the twenty-first century is a male preserve. A survey released in March 2010 found that only 10 percent of directors in Britain's top 100 companies are women, and twenty-five of the top firms had no women board members at all.[41] Whatever the potion, the firm manufacturing it will almost certainly be run by men. And that firm will likely be L'Oréal, which now owns more than 400 subsidiaries and 500 brands, spanning 150 different countries, including (in addition to Helena Rubinstein) consumer products Maybelline, Softsheen, Garnier, CCB; luxury products Lancôme, Biotherm, Kiehl's, Shue Uemura; the fragrance lines of Giorgio Armani, Ralph Lauren, Cacharel, Lanvin, Viktor & Rolf, Diesel, and YSL Beauté; professional products Kerastase, Redken, Matrix, Mizani, Shue Uemura Art of Hair; cosmoceuticals Vichy, La Roche Posay, Innéov, Skinceuticals, Sanoflore; The Body Shop; and Laboratories Ylang, the main producer of cosmetics in Argentina, where L'Oréal now controls 25 percent of the cosmetics market.

Seventy percent of L'Oréal's chemists are women. In Lindsay Owen-Jones's words, "the future of the company is in their hands at that level."[42] But the board is another matter. L'Oréal's board of directors contains three women—Liliane Bettencourt, her daughter Françoise Bettencourt-Meyers, and Annette Roux, whose family runs a yacht-making business in Brittany, not far from L'Arcouest. But none of these sits on the ten-strong management committee, where all the firm's real planning is done. At the time of this writing, the committee contained just one woman: the director of communications, Béatrice Dautresme—the same proportion as in the British survey and, as it happens, an exact echo of the proportions of males to females among cosmetic surgeons.

The constant concern of boards such as L'Oréal's—the ambition of all big business, as shareholders press for ever-higher dividends—is expansion: to increase revenues and profits. And as the main cosmetic market of mostly middle-aged women approaches saturation, new avenues are being explored. One highly controversial trend encourages very young women to start Botox treatment preemptively, to prevent lines before they form: a 2009 market research survey found that there was particular growth of interest in "procedures" among teenagers.[43]

There is also the still largely untapped pool of men. Helena Rubinstein's wartime cosmetics packs for soldiers developed into a postwar male market for such products as deodorants and aftershave. But despite breakthroughs (such as President Reagan's much-touted use of Grecian 2000 hair dye) men never went for cosmetics in a big way. However, today's fixation with youthfulness and attainable perfection affects both sexes. As the world gets fatter, and man-boobs ("moobs") proliferate, more and more men are opting for breast reductions. The British Association of Plastic Surgeons reported an 80-percent rise in demand for this operation in 2009.[44] And they're worrying about their wrinkles. Boots' "Protect and Perfect" line now includes a special range for men, while in a recent advertising campaign, a succession of aging male icons including Pierce Brosnan, the last James Bond but one, fronted for L'Oréal's tautening cream "Revitalift." If straight men can be induced to share what was once a dread exclusive to women and gays, the potential market at once grows by almost 50 percent.

Whatever the sex of the consumer, however, the world of cosmetics is still, as it always has been, associated with social control. In Madame Rachel's day, the argument was about keeping women in their place. For Helena Rubinstein, cosmetics were her route to emancipation; for her generation of women, they symbolized freedom. For Eugène Schueller, convinced that control and authority were essential aspects of a good society in which "Adam delved while Eve span," they paradoxically conferred the means to enforce dictatorship. And now, when Madame Rachel's "Beautiful For Ever" is literally and routinely attainable, the cosmetics world is the visible expression of a society in which anything is available to those with the means to buy it. The body has become a mere canvas, upon which the digital-age beauty business remasters our image of what is physically possible. But since perfection is ipso facto unattainable, what is really on offer, in the world of beauty as elsewhere, is infinite discontent.

CODA

Two Old Ladies

> Work has been my best beauty treatment! It keeps the wrinkles out of the mind and the spirit. It helps to keep a woman young. It certainly keeps a woman alive!
>
> —Helena Rubinstein, 1956

Helena Rubinstein died at ninety-two, in full command of her empire. At the time of this writing, Eugène Schueller's daughter, Liliane Bettencourt, is eighty-seven years old and still an active member of the L'Oréal board. Madame Rubinstein personified her own views of what a woman's life might be; Madame Bettencourt was raised in accordance with her father's quite opposite views. Which is the more successful life model? Or, to put it another way, which, if either, leads to contentment?

If money is the key, then these must have been the happiest of lives. Helena Rubinstein died before rich lists, but would certainly have figured on them had they existed in her day. And in 2007 Liliane Bettencourt, with a fortune of $20.7 billion, was, according to *Forbes*, the wealthiest woman in the world, and its twelfth-richest person. By 2009, both her ranking and her fortune had slipped, to twenty-first place and $13.4 billion, respectively (she was rumored to have lost "an undisclosed amount of money" in a fund overseen by René-Thierry Magnon de la Villehuchet, whose judgment was less impressive than his name and who committed suicide after losing $1.4 billion in Bernie Madoff's infamous Ponzi scam).[1] Her place as wealthiest woman had been claimed by a Walmart heiress. But although comparable losses would devastate public finances in the city-sized economies, sums like these more usually represent, at the level of individual lives they can make no conceivable difference. For a Bettencourt, the only real difficulty is in disposal. How can one spend even a fraction of that money? Solving that problem has been one of her life's chief occupations. "Fortune is an opportunity," she told *Le Figaro* in 2008. "You only need to look around—there are actions that impose themselves—and then go for it. Simply, without ulterior motives, without calculation, without waiting for a 'return on investment.'"

But money, however plentiful, cannot immunize its possessors against misfortune. And poverty, though always an inconvenience, is not always a fatal drawback. Helena Rubinstein was raised in poverty, but her subsequent instinct always to include her sisters in her good fortune attests to a strong sense of family solidarity. By contrast, Liliane Schueller, born to parents who had already become rich, suffered a cold and lonely childhood. When she was five, the rich little girl's mother died of an abscess on the liver. And this calamity would shape Liliane's life.

She has only once spoken publicly about this, in an interview with *Egoïste* magazine in 1987. "They came to fetch me in the middle of the night and I saw my father on his knees at the foot of my mother's bed. . . . When she died there was no more music in the house. She was a musician. A very beautiful woman, very tall, who got on easily with other people. . . . It meant my father was left to raise me as he wanted. When he had time, that is. . . . It isn't easy being raised by your father when your mother's gone. There's an absence of tenderness."[2]

Liliane's upbringing certainly presented her father with a problem. His wife's death occurred at a moment when he was diversifying in numerous directions—celluloid, photographic film, Russia, paint. There could be no question of looking after Liliane himself even had he wanted to (which he surely did not, being a man for whom child-rearing was doctrinally a woman's job). So he sent her to a Dominican convent school, where she remained for ten years. But the mother superior, though kind, was no substitute for the mother who had died. Nor did the holidays bring any respite from austerity. Home, Liliane remembered, was "all about the business, the economic climate, working hard."

This did not imply grimness—on the contrary, Schueller enjoyed luxury. He filled his houses with specially commissioned furniture, owned a yacht and a Rolls-Royce. But he was a particularly unsuitable lone parent for an only daughter. Business was his sole interest: "Work was how he communicated with me, and vice-versa. When he talked to me about a book or some other thing, he was still talking about work. . . . Psychology, action, ideas, that's still all business." Yet this fascinating world was one into which, on principle, Liliane could never be admitted. Although she was sent to work in her father's factory during the last three weeks of every vacation from the age of fifteen, starting by sticking labels on bottles, her father's writings made it clear that there was never any possibility she might succeed him. Admittedly his wife had kept the business going while he was away during World War I, but that was out of necessity. For Liliane there was no such necessity. Nor, despite her obvious intellectual capacities, did she attend university. It was her husband who became L'Oréal's vice president, her husband who, cushioned by his wife's money, became a senator and a minister. Her job was to support, partner, entertain, do charity work. That was what women did.

Of course it was not what Helena Rubinstein did—and her father disapproved of her quite as heartily as Schueller would have done in similar circumstances. But although Herzl Rubinstein hated what his daughter had become, the home he provided, and the Jewish tradition of strong women that underlay its culture, gave her (albeit unwittingly, and to his horror) the self-confidence to break away. And the consequence was a life defined not by money but by the business success that produced it. Like Eugène Schueller, of whom this was also true, Rubinstein enjoyed her money—the more so since, like him, she had once been poor—but it was their work, not their bank balance, that mattered most to them. This was something of which Rubinstein, to the end of her long span, was acutely conscious, and which she profoundly valued. Work was, as she said, the best beauty treatment.

The upbringing Schueller gave his daughter, however, meant that this satisfying life could never be hers. That would have necessitated rebellion, which for her was unthinkable. Her love and respect for her father were "visceral," a friend observed, her admiration for him, limitless. When he died, and she found herself owner of the business, she became, above all, the keeper of his flame—which included his values.[3] Yet that same upbringing, with its constant emphasis on achievement, also ensured that, paradoxically, she could never be satisfied by the life for which it destined her. "As far as people are concerned, if a woman's rich, she can't be intelligent," Madame Bettencourt told *Egoïste* defensively. "People park you in a corner and leave you there. Rich—it's not an agreeable word. In fact it's an ugly word. I prefer fortune. That implies luck."

The sense conveyed in that interview is of a life pervaded by an undefined frustration. Raised to consume, able to possess anything she might desire, consumption holds no glamor for Schueller's daughter. When an art critic cattily observed that Helena Rubinstein possessed "unimportant paintings by every important painter of the nineteenth and twentieth centuries," Madame retorted, "I may not have quality but I have quantity. Quality's nice but quantity makes a show."[4] "Making a show," though, is the last thing Bettencourt has ever wanted. "I like emptiness more than clutter," she told *Egoïste*. "Even if I fall in love with a painting, I'm quite happy to see it on someone else's wall." Rubinstein kept her jewels in a filing cabinet, sorted alphabetically, A for amethysts, B for beryls, D for diamonds, ready to hand for instant use. Liliane Bettencourt owns an equally astonishing collection of gems—bags of cut but unset stones, diamond necklaces, shelves of emeralds, rubies, sapphires—but they are kept in a bank vault whose contents rarely see the light of day,[5] while no photograph shows her wearing anything more extravagant than a pair of stud earrings. Rubinstein's New York living room, like everything else about her, was tasteless but full of gusto. It sported an acid-green carpet designed by Miró, twenty Victorian carved chairs covered in purple and magenta velvets, Chinese pearl-inlaid coffee tables, gold Turkish floor lamps, life-sized Easter Island sculptures, six-foot-tall blue opaline vases, African masks around the fireplace, and paintings covering every inch of wall space. But in Liliane Bettencourt's tasteful salon, gusto is conspicuous by its absence, the dead hand of the interior decorator everywhere apparent.

These contrasting styles are partly a function of milieu. Slender and terrifically elegant—in 2009 she was elected a permanent member of *Vanity Fair*'s best-dressed Hall of Fame—Liliane Bettencourt is a supreme exemplar of "bcbg," *bon chic, bon genre*, a style to which all Frenchwomen aspire and whose standards, of both *chic* and *genre*, are set by the couture-clad haute bourgeoisie of which Madame Bettencourt is a leading member. In bcbg, taste is all, excess is suspect, and a rather uniform, perfectly executed, expensive understatement rules. The whole point is not to draw attention to oneself. The Bettencourts' dislike of the public eye was legendary: for them, one of the privileges riches bought was total privacy. When Bruno Abescat, a financial journalist at *L'Express*, set out to write a book about "France's wealthiest couple," it was a year before he was able to get near them in the flesh—and then only at a public distribution of prizes financed by the Bettencourt Schueller Foundation.[6]

For Helena Rubinstein, by contrast, the whole point of spending money was to show you had money to spend. If nobody knew, half the pleasure was lost. In her milieu, wealth validated every eccentricity, and such was her status within it that even her ignorance was accepted as part of her personality. During a lunch in New York the conversation turned to the sad fate of Joan of Arc, burned as a heretic by an ancestor of Edith Sitwell, who was one of the guests. "Somebody had to do it!" cried Madame—an observation so stunningly crass that it would have barred her forever from bcbg circles. But the New Yorkers simply turned the conversation elsewhere.

The essentials of personal life, however, are unaffected by such details. And in that department Bettencourt, happily married for fifty-seven years, with a happily married daughter and grandchildren living just down the road in Neuilly, would seem to have beaten Rubinstein hands down. In 1987, after thirty-seven years of marriage, Liliane described her husband as "someone quite out of the ordinary"[7]; after his death in 2007 she remained in love with his memory. He was "charming, alive, intelligent. We were together fifty years, there was something indescribable between us, and then business and politics—it was so exciting."[8]

By contrast, Rubinstein's intimate life was a disaster. Her first husband, whom she married for love, constantly ran after other women. Her elder son bored her; her younger son, Horace, whom she adored, quarreled with her incessantly, made nothing of his life, and died in his forties. Artchil, whom she married for companionship, predeceased her by twelve years. So she blotted out the unbearable (Horace's death, Titus's infidelity) and compensated for the absence of real personal attachments with compulsive hyperactivity. And yet—despite this catalog of emotional catastrophes—her life was fulfilled in a way that Bettencourt's never has been.

There is one striking similarity in the lives of Helena Rubinstein and Liliane Bettencourt. Each, in old age, established a friendship with a much younger man. As the years passed, these friendships became the women's most important emotional focus. But the two relationships, apparently so similar, were quite different in emphasis. And those differences reveal, perhaps more than anything else in the lives of these two formidable women, their true vulnerabilities.

Helena Rubinstein's young man, Patrick O'Higgins, was the impecunious playboy son of Irish diplomats. He first noticed her in 1950, a tiny nexus of palpitating impatience barreling down the New York street ahead of him, furiously tapping her foot when lights forced her to wait before crossing the road. He had no idea who this vision might be, but soon afterwards ran into her at a cocktail party and was introduced. She was then seventy-eight, at the height of her power in the social and fashionable worlds. He was fifty years her junior, handsome, charming, and disorganized. She at once took a fancy to him, but although their conversation was noted by Rubinstein-watchers, nothing came of it until a year or so later, when out of the blue she asked him to lunch. After a copious meal ("I need to keep up my energy!") they went on to see *Ben-Hur* ("Most interesting! I'm glad the Jewish boy won!") then returned to her apartment, where, over a glass of whiskey, she asked him, "What do you really want to do with your life?" When he hesitated, she at once took over: "*Let Me tell you!*"[9] And tell him she did, from then on until the day she died, fifteen years later.

O'Higgins' role in Madame's life was to do and be whatever she required at the time. He accompanied her everywhere, as secretary, nurse, escort, interpreter, PR man, social director, and majordomo. Her strange and compelling personality mesmerized him. A floating bachelor (he may well have been gay, though he never openly admitted it—in the 1950s and sixties, when he knew Madame, homosexuality was still unmentionable), he received from her a focus his life had hitherto lacked. After first Artchil and then Horace died, they became increasingly close, until toward the end of her life he described their relationship as that of "a devoted son and a demanding mother."[10] "Who's your goy?" the Israeli prime minister David Ben-Gurion once asked her during a long and tedious dinner. "That's Patrick!" Madame beamed. "And . . . and, yes, *he is my goy*."[11]

Significantly, money played a relatively small part in their relationship. When she first employed him they agreed on a salary of $7,000 a year. To him, at the time, it seemed a fortune, though as the years went on he realized that others who did considerably less than he were paid considerably more. But although he often remarked on Madame's habitual tightness with money, O'Higgins never contemplated leaving her—or not on that account. Their one serious contretemps was emotional, when she refused to admit he might need to mourn the death of his mother. Her refusal was partly a jealous reaction—she hated the thought of sharing him, even with the dead. And partly, too, it reflected her horror of death and refusal to admit its existence. Her invariable response to bereavement was to pretend it hadn't happened, drowning grief in perpetual motion. But O'Higgins was made of less stern (one might say, more human) stuff, and her callousness brought on a nervous breakdown.

They were reunited in the end. Distraught at his absence, she wrote him letters: "I want to forget our differences. I hope you know that I love you *as a mother*. The mother you lost!" For a while he was unmoved—particularly since those letters somehow never enclosed promised checks. But eventually "I . . . realized that it was impossible for me to leave Madame. I couldn't escape from her. . . . Her letters had touched me and I longed to be by her side."[12] From then until the day she died, he was with her.

Rubinstein spent her last year putting finishing touches to her will. She left O'Higgins $5,000 in cash plus a yearly income of $2,000 "so he won't starve." He calculated that, should he survive twenty years (in fact he died thirteen years later, in 1980), this amount must represent a capital outlay of between sixty and eighty thousand dollars. Might she not have left him a larger sum outright? But then he recalled a conversation in which she'd said, "If I was to leave you twenty-five thousand dollars in cash, what would you do with it?" He'd replied, "Spend it! Have a lovely holiday!" at which she'd nodded sagely—and acted accordingly, in what she saw as his best interests.[13] Given his devotion and her great wealth, the bequest was far from generous. But that did not affect the love and respect he felt for her. They shine through the funny, affectionate memoir he left of their life together, a testament to the humanity that lay behind Rubinstein's overbearing and egotistical façade.

Liliane Bettencourt's young man was (and is) a different matter. François-Marie Banier is a well-known photographer, novelist, and all-round man-about-town twenty-five years her junior. As with O'Higgins and Rubinstein, the relationship is quasi-filial, with no hint of sex. Banier, unlike O'Higgins, is openly gay. "I see him with his partner, who is charming, cultivated, and intelligent," Bettencourt told the *Journal du Dimanche* in 2008.[14]

As with Rubinstein, too, the friendship is the more significant in that Madame Bettencourt has evidently found close personal relationships difficult. "I like to keep a distance between myself and other people," she told *Egoïste*. She had to be persuaded into marriage, and does not seem to have felt wholly at ease even with her own daughter, Françoise. "She was always rather an inscrutable child," Bettencourt told an interviewer in 2008, a year after her friendship with Banier had sparked a public fight between the two. "She got on better with my husband. Mother-daughter relations are very different from father-daughter relations."[15]

Banier has thus achieved an intimacy denied to anyone else. But where Patrick O'Higgins' attachment to Helena Rubinstein was independent of what she paid him (never, in any case, more than a very moderate salary), Banier's relationship with Madame Bettencourt appears to be rather different.

The two first met in 1969, at the home of the journalists

Pierre and Hélène Lazareff, Neuilly neighbors of the Bettencourts. Madame Bettencourt was then in her forties—as Banier remembered, "the most sought-after woman in society—very impressive and extraordinarily beautiful."[16] But they did not become close at that time. That happened eighteen years later, in 1987, when Bettencourt was sixty-five and Banier thirty-nine. He was assigned to photograph her for the *Egoïste* interview, they became friends, and the friendship flourished. Banier quickly became a habitué of the Bettencourt mansion; inevitably, Madame Bettencourt was at home much more than her busy husband. Soon he was not just her friend but her principal friend.

Ironically, during that interview, one of the questions was about whether she wasn't afraid of being loved just for her money. "How would one like to be loved, then?" she said. "Does one have to be ugly and undersized and fat before one can know that one's loved for oneself?"

That she loves Banier for himself is beyond doubt. And she is not alone in doing so. As he himself put it, "Wherever I go, I make waves" ("*Il y a toujours eu de vacarme derrière moi*").[17] Louis Aragon was besotted by him; he charmed François Mitterrand, Samuel Beckett, and Vladimir Horowitz. When he wanted to be an actor, Robert Bresson and Eric Rohmer gave him parts in their films. His novels—three published before he was twenty-five—were the talk of Paris. Diane von Furstenberg prefers his photographs to anyone else's; Johnny Depp insists Banier's portraits of him are unique and made Banier godfather to his daughter Lily-Rose.

Banier approaches all social encounters with the same all-consuming concentration. "Not many people are really interested in others. But I'm genuinely fascinated by everyone I meet, whether it's someone I know or a passer-by in the street.

I speak to them with my real voice. . . ."[18] It could almost be a definition of how charm works. The photographs, the books, the films, are all secondary: his real metier is to enchant. It is compulsive—and the compulsive is by definition compelling.

Banier's particular specialism, however, is wealthy and well-connected old ladies, whose pursuit appears to have been the first of his many careers. He embarked upon it at the age of nineteen, when he got to know Marie-Laure de Noailles, the maecenas of the Paris avant-garde, then sixty-four. "Didn't you have anything better to do at the age of nineteen?" asked an interviewer; to which Banier responded, "It's as though you asked me why I bothered to visit Leonardo da Vinci."[19]

Well, up to a point. Unlike Leonardo, wealth, not talent, had been Madame de Noailles's entrée into the artistic world. Banier, on the other hand, was poor: his father worked at the Citroën factory.[20] Both father and son, however, rejected the fact of poverty. Banier *père* hid his real life even from his family, pretending he was the bourgeois he dreamed of being; and his son, whom he ill-treated and who hated him, inherited this dream and singlemindedly fulfilled it. François-Marie followed the old precept: if you want to be rich, go where the money is. And it worked.

In 1971, when he was twenty-four, Banier published a novel, *Le Passé composé* (The Perfect Tense), which is in some ways transparently autobiographical. The hero, also called François (but whose surname, de Chevigny, implies membership of a class to which Banier did not, yet, belong), is poor but would like to be rich. He latches on to a rich girl from Neuilly, Cécile, and before their first date wanders through the Bois de Boulogne near her house, clutching a record he will give her as a present. "One day this boy, wandering around with a record in his hand, will have a big house with a big garden. People will say, 'Did you see? That's François de Chevigny! He's got lots of money. He has a house full of beautiful things, and a huge garden with enormous trees.' "[21] Now Banier, too, has all that. When speaking of his elderly lady friends, he never mentions their wealth. But it appears to have been the central fact of these relationships.

Of course, there were other attractions. Madame de Noailles knew everyone, and introduced Banier to her world. He repaid her with devoted attention. When she died of pneumonia in 1970, it was Banier who heard her last words. By then he had already made another conquest—Madeleine Castaing, the "diva of decorators." Castaing owned a smart shop on the corner of rue Jacob and rue Bonaparte and was famous, among other things, for her collection of paintings by Chaim Soutine, whom she had known in the 1920s. (When Banier's fictional François is courting Cécile, one of his lures is a promise to introduce her to Madeleine Castaing and show her the famous collecton of Soutines.[22]) When Castaing's husband of fifty years died in 1969, the young Banier obtained an introduction and stepped in to console her;[23] the friendship lasted until her death in 1992, at the age of ninety-eight. The photographs he took of her in extreme old age, nightgowned and wigless on her staircase, became famous. Her family detested them—saw them, indeed, as a form of abuse—but according to Banier it was she who initiated this photo shoot.[24] "You've got a nerve," he says Castaing said when she saw the photographs. "But that's fine: It's me."[25] They were exhibited everywhere, and launched Banier's photographic career.

Asked whether Banier "tried to use the friendship for material profit," Castaing's grandson said that thefts of family property had been a constant topic of conversation between his parents for as long as he could remember. A Soutine, he said, had disappeared during the 1930s, probably stolen by the famously light-fingered writer Maurice Sachs; another went—who knows where?—during the 1980s, along with his grandparents' letters from Picasso, Satie, and Cocteau. "And as it happens, I know that my grandmother gave François-Marie Banier a place with a conservatory in rue Visconti, in the 6th arrondissment of Paris. Things were just like that . . ."[26]

By 1987, when Banier met Liliane Bettencourt for the second time, Madeleine Castaing was already ninety-three. Clearly, this source of support could not last much longer. So it was a happy chance that, at the crucial moment, another generous friend should present herself. Pressed as to whether he didn't sometimes think his penchant for elderly ladies a little strange, Banier replied, "The young have fewer secrets than the old. It isn't just that they're old, they're loners. Also I find a person more beautiful at 108 than at eight years old. But I photograph young people too."[27]

What he did not add was that the old people who seemed most to interest him were also rich. Immaterial as this may be to Banier ("I don't take from people, I let them blossom, because I love and respect them,"[28]) this financial nexus is what the world chiefly sees. And in the case of Liliane Bettencourt, the pickings have been unimaginably huge. Beginning in 1996, there were regular outings when her chauffeur, under oath to tell no one, "particularly not M. Bettencourt," would drive Liliane the short distance from Neuilly to the Trocadero, where Banier would be waiting. Together they would continue to the nearby avenue Georges Mandel, where Banier's notary had his office; there she would make over money to Banier, and the notary would check the paperwork.[29]

As the years went on, the gifts got larger. In 2002, $14 million (€11 million) was handed over; in 2003, $315 million

(€250 million), mostly in the form of a life insurance contract of which he is the beneficiary; in 2004, $7.6 million (€6 million); in 2005, $71 million (€56 million); in 2006, $315 million (€250 million); in 2007, $2.5 million (€2 million). Nine paintings by Picasso, Matisse, Mondrian, and Leger have been signed over to Banier: they remain in Neuilly, but he will possess them after Bettencourt's death.[30] According to one account, he no sooner admired a Matisse painting hanging in one of her houses—its blue, he remarked, was "the color of our friendship"—than she said, "It's yours, François-Marie!" The Bettencourt Schueller Foundation, which supports both artistic activities, such as painting and filmmaking, and science, in particular medical research, has an annual budget of $160 million. That is a lot of money. But it is dwarfed by the untold wealth that has been lavished on Banier.*

"There have never been quarrels in the Bettencourt family, particularly not about money or power," admiringly declared their chronicler in 2002.[31] But this happy state of affairs was soon overtaken by events. If André Bettencourt remained unaware how attached his wife had become to Banier, as her instructions to the chauffeur would seem to indicate, their daughter Françoise both suspected what was afoot and was deeply disturbed by it. A few days after M. Bettencourt's death in November, 2007, Banier allegedly tried to get the new widow to adopt him as a son, which would give him the right to half her estate. A month later, Françoise Bettencourt-Meyers launched a criminal complaint accusing him of *abus de faiblesse*, arguing that her increasingly frail mother was no

---

* Piquantly, after Banier photographed Natalia Vodianova for Diane von Furstenberg, working "in silence, intense and intimate," he commented: "I am not accustomed to having somebody give me something."

longer capable of withstanding emotional pressure, and producing copious evidence from Madame Bettencourt's staff showing that Banier had bullied her.

Liliane Bettencourt indignantly denies that she is vulnerable. She argues, reasonably enough, that she is entitled to do whatever she likes with her own money. When the case first came to court there were rumors that she had even called in President Sarkozy, another Neuilly neighbor, to get it thrown out—a maneuver, if that is what it was, that failed (and which she denied, asserting, accurately enough, that Sarkozy "has other things to think about").*

And although it is unarguable that Banier has made a profitable career out of befriending rich elderly ladies, a habit some might find distasteful, the ladies themselves have not appeared to object. Why would they? Few old ladies are courted and made much of by glamorous younger men, and many might enjoy the experience. From their standpoint, Banier provided, and provides, the one thing money can't buy. Who can put a price on friendship? "I make Liliane rich, Banier makes her live," Lindsay Owen-Jones is reported as saying.[32] "He's an artist, that's what I like," Madame Bettencourt explained in 2008, after the friendship had become a matter of scandal. "Artists see things differently. Times change, everything's moving, you've got to stay in the swim . . . I was with him just a few days ago in the United States. We met some most interesting people. A big family, very artistic, with ten children. It's not much fun only seeing people like oneself, is it?"[33]

An interesting light has recently been shed on Bettencourt-Meyers' motivation in bringing this case. She is, after all, al-

* More recent events appear to indicate that this request may simply have been a quid pro quo for services rendered. See below for a discussion of recent developments.

ready unimaginably rich: Liliane Bettencourt has made over a large part of her estate to her daughter. Why, in those circumstances, would any daughter want to cause her aged mother such anguish, dragging her through the courts and making the family a focus for public prurience? In a similar situation Castaing's family drew back from this path. "As far as I'm concerned these aren't legal matters, they're about something else altogether," her grandson remarked.[34]

The answer, rumor has it, is business: the business in which neither Liliane nor Françoise Bettencourt, being female, play an active part. However, Jean-Pierre Meyers, Françoise's husband, is both a L'Oréal board member and (more significantly) a member of its management committee. He is also on the board of Nestlé; and there are hints that he "would like to do Nestlé a favour."[35] Nestlé owns 30 percent of L'Oréal, the Bettencourts, 31 percent; in 2004 Liliane Bettencourt signed an agreement freezing these holdings until six months after her death. It is common knowledge that Nestlé has for years wanted to acquire L'Oréal. If it can be proved that Madame Bettencourt was not competent when she signed that agreement, it is nullified, and Nestlé is free to move.*

Between Banier and Meyers, Liliane Bettencourt seems to be at other people's mercy. Or rather, at the mercy of the men in her life, starting with her father, whom she revered and could never contradict. Schueller brought up his daughter to do what he thought women were made for—to embellish the lives of her menfolk. And it has been the pattern of her life ever since.

---

* Once again, recent developments have shed a new light on events. Before they fell out, Mme. Bettencourt made over 30 percent of L'Oréal to her daughter, retaining only 1 percent. But that 1 percent of course represents the balance of power between Nestlé and the family, and its future is therefore of acute concern to a good many people who are anxious, lest it fall into the wrong hands.

Helena Rubinstein was no one's patsy: the self-effacing do not become captains of industry. Insufferable, selfish, bullying, crass, *she* did the exploiting, if any. For Schueller, this was the very reason why women should not aspire to the workplace. But Rubinstein showed, by example, and in a way that no woman had ever done before, that Schueller's prescription for the female sex was not just patronizing: it was—for those with ambitions beyond the home such as his own daughter might have nourished—actively cruel.

Rubinstein's astonishing self-confidence resounds through every word ever written about her. It was what enabled her to create the life she desired, and the fact of having achieved that life constantly reinforced it. And here, surely, is the core of the matter. For self-confidence is what the beauty business has always been about, has always been its true commodity. The creams, the paints, the injections, the operations, are merely routes to that all-important end. Self-confidence was what the Victorians wanted to deny their womenfolk. It was what Helena Rubinstein and her customers aimed to achieve through cosmetics. Selling it gave Eugène Schueller the riches to buy power. But in a nice irony, the company he used as a cash-cow now arguably wields more real power—trading, as it does, in self-confidence—than any political party, any economist, ever has or ever will.

The Banier affair, though it aroused a good deal of attention, seemed relatively trivial—if not to those concerned, at least to the world at large. But in the summer of 2010 it suddenly acquired a new and scandalous political dimension. Liliane Bettencourt's staff were already outraged by what they saw as Banier's bullying of their employer—the more so when he reacted to their criticisms by having several of them sacked after years of faithful service. Now the increasingly deaf and infirm Madame Bettencourt was, it seemed to them, being mercilessly manipulated by yet another interested party—her financial adviser, Patrice de Maistre. So her butler decided to take matters into his own hands and acquire proof of what was going on. He did so by bugging his cocktail tray—an item, in his experience, always central to these conversations. He then passed the memory card containing the recordings to Françoise Bettencourt-Meyers, who transferred them to twenty-eight CDs that she delivered, three weeks later, to the police.

What emerged was dynamite. The recorded conversations between Madame Bettencourt and de Maistre showed that Banier had not been the only one allegedly benefiting from the L'Oréal heiress's open purse. There had also, it seemed, been sub-rosa cash subventions to politicians, including the minister responsible for taxation, whose helpful inattention would of course have been highly advantageous to the Bettencourt interests, and whose wife was conveniently employed by de Maistre in the Bettencourt office. And although the legal limit for individual contributions to French political campaigns was €7,500, the election campaign of Nicolas Sarkozy, France's president (and a member of André Bettencourt's old party), appeared to have benefited to the tune of €150,000. It also transpired that André Bettencourt, while he was alive, had kept a chest full of cash conveniently at hand, cash that he doled out every election season to members of his political party, the UMP (Union pour un mouvement populaire), in unmarked envelopes.

There were other recordings, too, of telephone discussions between de Maistre and Fabrice Goguel, a tax lawyer and one-time official adviser to Madame Bettencourt on tax affairs. These conversations gave rise to allegations that Goguel was still involved with the estate—not advising on tax avoidance, which of course is legal, but on tax evasion and money laundering, which very much are not. Tens of millions had been stashed away in a Swiss bank account; other conversations seemed to show that de Maistre, worried about Switzerland's new openness on such matters, was anxious to transfer this money to Singapore, where it could be more securely hidden. There was also an island in the Seychelles that had never been declared to the tax authorities. Bettencourt's people asserted that the island no longer belonged to her and had been given to Banier, but Banier denied this: He had no use for it; there were too many sharks and mosquitoes. . . . Twenty years after the Frydman revelations, L'Oréal's owners were once again enveloped in controversy.

The parallels between the Nazi scandal of 1989–1995 and the *affaire Bettencourt* that began in 2007 (and which continues to fill the headlines at the time of this writing in summer 2010) are striking. In both cases, what began as something relatively banal expanded and metamorphosed into a huge political scandal. In 1989, the spark was a disagreement over a board meeting that may or may not have taken place and in 2007, a family quarrel over money. In both cases, the event that moved the affair onto a new, hotly political plane was a wholly unpredictable chance event. If L'Oréal's François Dalle had not decided to bring his old friend Jean Frydman into the business at what turned out to be exactly the wrong moment, Eugène Schueller's Nazi past, with all its ramifications, would have remained conveniently forgotten, as so many similar pasts were forgotten. And if Liliane Bettencourt's butler had not conceived the wholly baroque notion of bugging his cocktail tray, the *affaire Bettencourt* would have remained the comparatively innocuous *affaire Banier*.

For the public, the *affaire Bettencourt*'s chief scandalous revelation (perhaps less a revelation than a confirmation of what we always suspect but can rarely prove) was the way the very rich and very powerful casually assume that the laws governing everyone else are, for them, purely optional. Taxes need be paid only by the disorganized, limits on political contributions are routinely ignored, public servants can always be bought, and the happy recipients of cash-stuffed envelopes naturally do all they can to forward the interests of their paymasters.

The tax aspect, at least, would not have shocked Eugène Schueller. He was paranoid about taxation, ending his life as a supporter of Pierre Poujade, the anti-tax, anti-intellectual small shopkeepers' hero, whose protectionist Union de Défense Commerçants et Artisans gained fifty-three seats in the 1955 elections. In the perfect economic system, to which Schueller devoted his intellectual energies for the last thirty years of his life, taxation would be related not to income but to energy use. As for democratic accountability, he regarded it with contempt. A self-proclaimed authoritarian, Schueller thought government should be run in the same way as an efficient company, by those who had proved their fitness to lead by rising to the top. When political power was at the mercy of the popular vote—just as when a company found itself at the mercy of the trade unions—weak, inefficient leadership would invariably result. Few of today's public figures would actually utter such thoughts out loud. But one consequence of the *affaire Bettencourt* has been to show that many public figures actually conduct their lives upon such assumptions.

Both the *affaire Bettencourt* and the *affaire Banier* from which it sprang are about money—specifically, the huge fortune belonging to Schueller's daughter Liliane. But one can't help noticing that the one person who doesn't really figure in the drama is Liliane herself. She is simply a huge fountain of cash, which the various men in her life have tapped into in order to fulfill their desires. First there was her husband, André Bettencourt, whose political progress she financed and supported. Where did the cash come from, which stuffed those envelopes he kept ready, each election season, for the procession of political beggars? M. Bettencourt was a vice president of L'Oréal, but it was his wife who owned the company—and the money. Then there was François-Marie Banier, who befriended Liliane in 1987. Banier, a poor boy, dreamed of becoming rich; she fulfilled his dream. And now her financial adviser, Patrice de Maistre, appears to have his own ideas regarding her money.

The striking thing about Madame Bettencourt is that she seems to accept that this is simply how the world works. It is agreed by all that she is, or was, "a brilliant woman." Unlike other brilliant women, however, and despite all her apparent advantages, she never had a career of her own, but confined her role to furthering the careers of other people. The butler's recordings show a pitiful puppet whose strings are pulled alternately by Banier and de Maistre. According to Bettencourt's onetime nurse, emboldened by the recordings to testify, Banier uses his emotional thrall to get his hands on yet more of Madame Bettencourt's money; de Maistre instructs her, word for word, on what she must say when she meets the important politicians who are his friends, and he makes out checks for her to sign, impatiently explaining how the benefits they will buy are cheap at the price. For his pains, he has received the Légion d'Honneur. But no conceivable benefit accrues to Liliane Bettencourt.

Anyone who knows about Eugène Schueller and his ideas

will recognize that this fate—to have all the money and none of the power—might have been precisely, albeit unintentionally, designed by the father Liliane idolized. Just as the Nazi scandal was a consequence of his politics, so the *affaire Bettencourt* is a consequence of his social theories. Schueller, as we have seen, had decided opinions on many subjects, among them the place of women in society. Women, in his view, were there to support men. They were for making homes and breeding children; they should never compete in the man's world of work. This is the mold in which Liliane was cast, and she did not question it. First her widowed father's dutiful daughter, then her husband's supportive wife, she now, it seems, exists for the benefit of Banier, de Maistre, and their friends. It is for men to dictate the program. Liliane, true daughter of her father, merely facilitates it.

It is deeply ironic that the source of all this money should be cosmetics, the same commodity that constituted Helena Rubinstein's escape route from a similar situation. For Rubinstein and her clients, lipstick, powder, rouge, and the rest of the arsenal symbolized women's claims to an equal footing in public life. In this sense, the *affaire Bettencourt* is simply another episode in the standoff between Helena Rubinstein and Eugène Schueller. More than half a century after their deaths, it continues.

NOTES

Chapter 1 : Beauty Is Power!

1. *Vogue*, February 1915.
2. Yeb 63b, Ber 57b, see www.holysmoke.org/sdhok/jp-fem4.htm.
3. Greg, "Why Are Women Redundant?" *National Review*, April 1862.
4. Rubinstein, *My Life for Beauty*, p. 13.
5. Rubinstein, *The Art of Feminine Beauty*, p. 6.
6. Carter, *With Tongue in Chic*, p. 174.
7. O'Higgins, *Madame*, p. 246.
8. *Life*, July 21, 1941, pp. 37–45.
9. Quoted in Peiss, *Hope in a Jar*, p. 95.
10. All this detail—and everything else about HR's life in Australia—comes from Woodhead, *War Paint*.
11. Rubinstein, *My Life for Beauty*, p. 25.
12. Woodhead, *War Paint*, p. 41.
13. HR to Rosa Hollay, June 1915, Bulmer papers. Thanks to Ann Treneman for help regarding this source.
14. Advertisement from *Table Talk*, quoted in Woodhead, *War Paint*, p. 51.
15. O'Higgins, *Madame*, p. 151.
16. Rubinstein, *My Life for Beauty*, p. 26.
17. Ibid., pp. 28, 13.
18. Phillips, *Skin Deep*, p. 29.

19. Rubinstein, *The Art of Feminine Beauty*, p. 14.
20. Rubinstein, *My Life for Beauty*, p. 32.
21. Rubinstein, *The Art of Feminine Beauty*, p. 15.
22. Carter, *With Tongue in Chic*, p. 175.
23. Rubinstein, *The Art of Feminine Beauty*, p. 16.
24. Rubinstein, *My Life for Beauty*, p. 33.
25. Ibid., p. 34.
26. Ibid., p. 33.
27. HR to Rosa Hollay, July 20, 1915, May 1920, Bulmer papers.
28. Rubinstein, *My Life for Beauty*, p. 100.
29. Ibid., pp. 39–40.
30. S. N. Behrman, *Portrait of Max*, quoted in George Landow, "Max Beerbohm Creates a Great Fuss," http://www.victorianweb.org/authors/mb/rouge1.html.
31. Rubinstein, *My Life for Beauty*, p. 42.
32. HR to Rosa Hollay, December 8, 1914, Bulmer papers.
33. HR to Rosa Hollay, March 1923.
34. According to Fabe, *Beauty Millionaire*, p. 68.
35. Rubinstein, *My Life for Beauty*, p. 32.
36. Rubinstein, *The Art of Feminine Beauty*, p. 19.
37. O'Higgins, *Madame*, p. 92.
38. Rubinstein, *My Life for Beauty*, p. 70.
39. HR to Rosa Hollay, May 9, 1915, Bulmer papers.
40. O'Higgins, *Madame*, p. 104.
41. Figure given by the American Chemical Society; quoted in Woodhead, *War Paint*, p. 100.
42. *New York World*, September 11, 1910; Lillian Wald, *The House on Henry Street*, 1915, p. 192; both quoted in Banner, *American Beauty*, p. 217.
43. *American Magazine*, December 1922.
44. Gray, "People Who Want to Look Young and Beautiful," pp. 32–33.
45. HR to Rosa Hollay, November 12, 1914, Bulmer papers.
46. O'Higgins, *Madame*, p. 224.
47. Ibid., p. 233.
48. *Vogue*, May, 1, 1915.
49. Rubinstein, *My Life for Beauty*, p. 61.

50. HR to Rosa Hollay, July 13, 1915, Bulmer papers.
51. Quoted in Woodhead, *War Paint*, p. 122.
52. HR to Rosa Hollay, 1921, Bulmer papers.
53. O'Higgins, *Madame*, p. 181.
54. *Times* (London), March 20, 2002.
55. *The New Yorker*, June 30, 1928.
56. *Life*, July 21, 1941.
57. O'Higgins, *Madame*, p. 93.
58. All this detail from Woodhead, *War Paint*, pp. 166–70.
59. Rubinstein, *My Life for Beauty*, p. 72.

Chapter 2: The Authoritarian

1. 1936, *Skin Deep* correspondence, Rutgers University Special Collections.
2. There are two principal sources of information on Eugène Schueller's life. He gave a full account of his life history in evidence before the court that tried him for civil collaboration after World War I (Dossier instruit par la cour de justice du département de la Seine contre Eugène Schueller, Archives Nationales [cote Z 6 N L 11.108]). And some years later he told his story, differing slightly in some details, to journalist Merry Bromberger, who recorded the interview, along with others, in his *Comment ils ont fait fortune* (How They Made Their Money). Where no other source is credited, I have relied on these for what follows.
3. Abescat, *La Saga des Bettencourt*, p. 83.
4. Dalle, *L'Aventure L'Oréal*, p. 63.
5. Interview with Liliane Bettencourt, *Egoïste*, no. 10, 1987.
6. Ibid.
7. Curie, *Madame Curie*, pp. 305–10.
8. Abescat, *La Saga des Bettencourt*, p. 64.
9. Schueller, *De L'Innocuité des teintures pour cheveux*.
10. *Skin Deep* correspondence, Rutgers University Special Collections.
11. Interview with Liliane Bettencourt, *Egoïste*, 1987.
12. Bromberger, *Comment ils ont fait fortune*, p. 78.
13. Schueller, *Le Deuxième salaire*.

14. Testimony of Jacques Sadoul, Archives Nationales de France (CARAN): Dossier instruit par la cour de justice du département de la Seine contre Eugène Schueller (côte 26 NL 11.108).
15. Bromberger, *Comment ils ont fait fortune*, p. 78.
16. Ibid., p. 86.
17. Schueller, *L'Impôt sur l'énergie*, p. 115.
18. Corson, *Fashions in Hair*, p. 615.
19. Ibid., p. 619.
20. Schueller, *L'Impôt sur l'énergie.*
21. HR to Rosa Hollay, December 1915, October 1922, 1921, Bulmer papers.
22. O'Higgins, *Madame*, p. 28.
23. *Coiffure de Paris*, October 8–10, 1909. Translation is the author's, as are all translations not specifically attributed.
24. Schueller, *La Révolution de l'économie.*
25. Sadoul's evidence, Dossier instruit par la cour de justice du département de la Seine contre Eugène Schueller.
26. Schueller, *Faire Vivre*, p. 24.
27. Ibid.
28. Schueller, *La Révolution de l'économie*, p. 35.
29. Ibid., p. 6.
30. Schueller, *Le Deuxième salaire.*
31. Schueller, *La Révolution de l'économie*, p. 202.
32. Ibid., p. 35.
33. Ibid.
34. Ibid., p. 219.
35. Bromberger, *Comment ils ont fait fortune*, p. 91.
36. *Votre Beauté*, December 1934.
37. *Votre Beauté*, January 1936.
38. Lecture, Salle Pleyel, December 6, 1941, Archives Nationales, cote Z 6 N L 11.108.
39. Bromberger, *Comment ils ont fait fortune*, p. 73.
40. Schueller, *Le Deuxième salaire*, p. 5.
41. Dalle, *L'Aventure L'Oréal*, p. 23.
42. Charles E. Sorensen, David L. Lewis, and Samuel T. Wilkinson, *My Forty Years with Ford* (New York, 1956), p. 29.

43. Albert Lee, *Henry Ford and the Jews* (New York, 1980), p. 99.
44. Schueller, *Le Deuxième salaire.*
45. Ibid.
46. Dunlap, *Personal Beauty and Racial Betterment*, p. 20.
47. Ibid., p. 36.
48. Ibid., p. 58.

Chapter 3: What Did You Do in the War, Daddy?

1. Bromberger, *Comment ils ont fait fortune*, p. 73
2. Schueller, *Le Deuxième salaire.*
3. Koestler, *Scum of the Earth*, p. 32.
4. Dalle, *L'Aventure L'Oréal*, p. 20.
5. Potton, *On a trouvé un chef.*
6. Lecture, Salle Pleyel, December 6, 1941.
7. Schueller, *La Révolution de l'économie*, p. 219.
8. Ibid., p. 122.
9. Testimony of Georges Mercadier, Archives Nationales (cote Z 6 N L 11.108).
10. Lecture, Salle Pleyel, December 6, 1941, Archives Nationales (cote Z 6 N L 11.108).
11. Charbonneau, *Les Mémoires de Porthos* I, pp. 16–17.
12. Lecture, Salle Pleyel, December 6, 1941, Archives Nationales (cote Z 6 N L 11.108).
13. Addressing the political bureau of MSR, November 23, 1941. Abescat, *La Saga des Bettencourt*, p. 105.
14. Schueller, *La Révolution de l'économie*, p. 202.
15. This was true even though the Germans confiscated 42 percent of French GDP, and workers' buying power was halved by 1943. See Lacroix-Riz, *Industriels et banquiers sous l'Occupation*, p. 565.
16. Schueller, *La Révolution de l'économie*, quoted in Rochebrune and Hazéra, *Les Patrons sous l'Occupation*, p. 771.
17. Quoted in Lacroix-Riz, *Industriels et banquiers sous l'Occupation*, pp. 561–65.
18. Ibid., pp. 327–28.
19. Letter, Schmilinsky to Baron Dr. von Mahs, October 29, 1941:

Archives Nationales (cote AJ40 vol 775). Quoted in Lacroix-Riz, *Industriels et banquiers sous l'Occupation*, p. 436.

20. Charbonneau, *Les Mémoires de Porthos*, p. 334.
21. Péan, *Le Mystérieux Docteur Martin*, p. 249.
22. Amouroux, *Les Beaux jours des collabos*, p. 362.
23. Schueller interrogation, February 19, 1948, Dossier instruit par la cour de justice du département de la Seine contre Eugène Schueller (cote Z 6 N L 11.108).
24. "Un beau-père encombrant," *Le Monde*, February 12, 1995.
25. See, for example, Charbonneau, *Les Mémoires de Porthos*, p. 342.
26. Abescat, *La Saga des Bettencourt*, p. 103.
27. Abellio, *Sol invictus*, p. 213.
28. Schueller interrogation, February 19, 1948, Archives Nationales cote Z 6 N L 11.108.
29. Rochebrune and Hazéra, *Les Patrons sous l'Occupation*, p. 753.
30. Giesbert, *François Mitterrand*, p. 96.
31. Abellio, *Sol invictus*, p. 213.
32. Charbonneau, *Les Mémoires de Porthos*, p. 344.
33. Abellio, *Sol invictus*, p. 213.
34. Ibid., p. 215.
35. Schueller interrogation, February 19, 1948, Archives Nationales (cote Z 6 N L 11.108).
36. Archives de Paris, Comité régional industriel d'épuration d'entreprises de la Seine, affaire Schueller, 1946.
37. Peiss, *Hope in a Jar*, p. 242.
38. Woodhouse, *War Paint*, pp. 274–75.
39. *Current Biography*, 1943, ed. Maxine Block.
40. Gilman, *Making the Body Beautiful*, p. 180.
41. Guenther, *Nazi Chic?*, pp. 98–101.
42. Dossier instruit par la cour de justice du département de la Seine contre Eugène Schueller (cote Z 6 N L 11.108).
43. Evidence given in Schueller's trial for industrial collaboration, December 6, 1948. These of course were the official figures. They tell us nothing about the black market. Archives Nationales (cote Z 6 N L 11.108).
44. Archives Nationales (cote Z 6 N L 11.108).
45. Dalle, *L'Aventure L'Oréal*, p. 33.

46. Archives de Paris. Comité régional industriel d'épuration d'entreprises de la Seine, affaire Schueller, 1946.
47. Archives Nationales (cote Z 6 N L 11.108).
48. Archives Nationales (cote Z 6 N L 11.108).
49. Abescat, *La Saga des Bettencourt*, pp. 60–61.
50. Archives Curie, Paris: BnF Mss. Archives Joliot-Curie (déposées à l'Institut Curie) NAF 28161.
51. Ibid.
52. Archives of the Groupement des Industries Métallurgiques Mécaniques et Connexes de la Région Parisienne (GIMMCP), quoted in Vinen, *The Politics of French Business 1936–1945*, p. 196.
53. Berr, *Journal*, p. 204.
54. Charbonneau, *Les Mémoires de Porthos*, p. 345.
55. Archives Nationales (cote Z 6 N L 11.108).
56. Archives de Paris, Comité régional industriel d'épuration d'entreprises de la Seine, affaire Schueller, 1946.

Chapter 4: Family Affairs

1. O'Higgins, *Madame*, p. 183.
2. Bettencourt described their meeting in the preface to a souvenir book privately published by the family to celebrate Schueller's centenary in 1981.
3. *La Terre Française*, December 6, 1941.
4. Pierre Bettencourt, *Les Désordres de la mémoire*, p. 207.
5. Dalle, *L'Aventure L'Oréal*, pp. 14–15.
6. Ibid., p. 20.
7. Péan, *Une Jeunesse française*, p. 99.
8. Ibid., p. 76.
9. Dalle, *L'Aventure L'Oréal*, pp. 24–25.
10. Ibid., p. 62.
11. Ibid., pp. 84–85.
12. Péan, *Vies et morts de Jean Moulin*, p. 176.
13. Interview with Pierre Péan, in Péan, *Vies et morts de Jean Moulin*, pp. 470–71.
14. Ibid.

15. Archives Nationales (cote Z 6 N L 11.108).
16. Bromberger, *Comment ils ont fait fortune*, p. 92.
17. Péan, *Une jeunesse française*, p. 520.
18. *Votre Beauté*, January 1946.
19. Ibid.
20. Rubinstein, *My Life for Beauty*, p. 78.
21. Lewis and Wordsworth, *Miss Elizabeth Arden*, 86.
22. *New York Times*, February 2, 1944.
23. HR to Rosa Hollay, October 1, 1915, and late summer 1916, Bulmer papers.
24. *New York Times*, February 2, 1944.
25. O'Higgins, *Madame*, pp. 247–50.

Chapter 5: A Takeover and Three Scandals

1. O'Higgins, *Madame*, pp. 271–75.
2. Ibid., pp. 280–83.
3. Ibid., p. 45.
4. *New York Times*, April 3, 1965.
5. Dalle, *L'Aventure L'Oréal*, p. 231.
6. *New York Times*, May 19, 1968.
7. O'Higgins, *Madame*, p. 45.
8. *New York Times*, September 29, 1980.
9. Ibid., October 15, 1988.
10. *Le Monde*, June 4, 1988.
11. Ibid., December 21, 1991.
12. Bar-Zohar, *Bitter Scent*, p. 8.
13. *Le Monde*, June 6, 1991.
14. *Wall Street Journal*, June 7, 1991.
15. *Le Monde*, June 6, 1991.
16. Bar-Zohar, *Bitter Scent*, p. 37.
17. *Le Cri du Peuple*, October 14, 1948.
18. Ibid.
19. Corrèze papers at Le Centre de Documentation Juive Contemporaine, Paris.
20. Abellio, *Sol invictus*, 282.

21. *New York Times*, June 20, 1991.
22. *Lettre à un cousin*, July 27, 1954, quoted in Péan, *Une Jeunesse française*, p. 13.
23. Assouline, quoting Gide's secretary, Lucien Combelle, in *L'Épuration des intellectuels*, p. 74.
24. Dalle, quoted in *Le Monde*, June 6, 1991.
25. Bar-Zohar, *Bitter Scent*, p. 119.
26. *Le Monde*, June 6, 1991.
27. Conversation with the author, June 2008.
28. *New York Times*, June 27, 1991.
29. *Wall Street Journal*, June 7, 1991.
30. *L'Élan*, December 13, 1941.
31. *La Terre Française*, October 11, 1941.
32. Ibid., December 20, 1941.
33. Ibid., April 12, 1941.
34. Bar-Zohar, *Bitter Scent*, p. 203.
35. This is set out in two letters from "Grainville" (Bettencourt) to "Morland" (Mitterrand), dated August 9 and 11, 1944, published in *Le Monde*, March 9, 1995.
36. Frydman, *L'Affaire Bettencourt*, p. 23, quoting Alain Guérin, *Chronique de la Résistance*, p. 1585.
37. "Grainville" to "Morland," August 9, 1944, published in *Le Monde*, March 9, 1995.
38. Péan, *Une Jeunesse française*, pp. 439–40.
39. Trano, *Mitterrand, les amis d'abord,* 80.
40. Ibid.
41. Ibid.
42. *Le Monde*, February 12, 2005.
43. Ibid., March 9, 1995.
44. Ibid., February 12, 1995.
45. Ibid., March 9, 1995.
46. Letter, André Bettencourt to Congressman Engel, January 25, 1995, in Frydman, *L'Affaire Bettencourt*, p. 31–32.
47. J.-J. Roy, "Les Deux Justices," *Les Temps Modernes* 33 (June 1948), quoted in Judt, *Past Imperfect*, p. 47. Judt's discussion of the *épuration* is particularly perceptive.

48. Bromberger, *Comment ils ont fait fortune*, p. 93.
49. Benamou, *Jeune homme, vous ne savez pas de quoi vous parlez*, pp. 62–63.
50. Bar-Zohar, *Bitter Scent*, 173–74.
51. Abescat, *La Saga des Bettencourt*, p. 172.
52. Jouve and Magoudi, *Mitterrand. Portrait total*, p. 163, quoted in Péan, *Une Jeunesse française*, p. 288.
53. Bar-Zohar, *Bitter Scent*, p. 211.
54. Péan, *Une Jeunesse française*, pp. 12–13.
55. *New York Times*, June 20, 1991, p. D5.
56. Fabius, speaking in 1994, quoted in Benamou, *Jeune homme . . .* , p. 166.
57. Ibid.
58. Benamou, *Jeune homme . . .* , p. 195.
59. "The Revolution We Need," *L'Élan-Jeune Aquitaine*, December 13, 1941.
60. *Le Monde*, February 12, 1995.
61. Quoted in Trano, *Mitterrand, les amis d'abord*.
62. Testimony at the Cagoule trial, *Le Cri du Peuple*, October 14, 1948.
63. *Le Monde*, June 20, 1991,
64. *New York Times*, June 20, 1991.
65. Bar-Zohar, *Bitter Scent*, p. 145.
66. Dalle, testimony to examining magistrate Jean-Pierre Getti, June 19, 1991; quoted in Bar-Zohar, *Bitter Scent*, p. 158.
67. Bar-Zohar, *Bitter Scent*, p. 109.
68. Archives Nationales (cote Z 6 N L 11.108).
69. Dalle, *L'Aventure L'Oréal*, p. 208.
70. Waitzfelder, *L'Oréal Took My Home*, pp. 180–81.
71. Ibid., pp. 182–83.
72. Ibid., p. 55.
73. Ibid., pp. 204–5.
74. Ibid., pp. 192–93.
75. Ibid., pp. 184–85.
76. Ibid., p. 91.
77. Ibid., pp. 194–97 and 200–3.
78. Abescat, *Le Saga des Bettencourt*, pp. 90–91.

Chapter 6: Consumers or Consumed?

1. Two editions of *Who Owns Britain?* by Gordon Schaffer and Kevin Cahill, published in 1944 and 2001 respectively; and *Who Owns England?* by Peter Grant, published in 1991.
2. By Herbert Agar and Allen Tate, first published 1936; by Walter J. Hickel, published 1971; by Edmund Blair Bolles, published 1984; by Harvey M. Jacobs, published 1998.
3. "Madame Rubinstein, the Little Lady from Krakow," *Life*, July 21, 1941, pp. 37–45.
4. *Times* (London), August 22, 1868, p. 6.
5. Quoted in Miller, "Shrewd Woman of Business."
6. 1 Corinthians 11: 4–16.
7. Quoted in Woodhead, *War Paint*, p. 153.
8. *Daily Mail*, "Half of Women Will Have Cosmetic Surgery," July 13, 2005.
9. *Skin Deep* correspondence, Rutgers University.
10. Christa D'Souza, "My Name Is Christa. I'm an Age-orexic," *The Observer*, May 13, 2007.
11. *Plastic and Reconstructive Surgery*, June 2008.
12. Orbach, *Bodies*, p. 85.
13. Gillies and Millard, *The Principles and Art of Plastic Surgery* (London, 1957), p. 395.
14. Nessia Pope, "The Get: Body and Soul; Beauty Map / Rio de Janeiro," *New York Times*, October 22, 2006.
15. Conversation with the author, October 13, 2009.
16. Diana Appley and Cadie Nicholas, "We're Addicted to Botox," *Daily Mail*, September 18, 2006.
17. Laura Potter, "English Patience," *Observer Magazine*, October 21, 2007.
18. Appley and Nicholas, "We're Addicted to Botox."
19. Phillips, *Skin Deep*, pp. 78–79.
20. *Skin Deep* correspondence, Rutgers University.
21. Paul Harris, "Plastic Surgery in Decline as America Tires of Excess," *The Observer*, March 21, 2010.
22. The Harley Medical Group, report in *Sky News*, April 11, 2008.

23. John Dunne, "Redundant City Boys Opt for Facelifts," *The London Paper*, January 26, 2009.
24. D'Souza, "My Name Is Christa."
25. Warren Sanderson and Sergei Scherbov, "Average Remaining Lifetimes Can Increase as Human Populations Age," *Nature* 435 (June 2005): 811–13.
26. BBC, *Woman's Hour*, December 8, 2006.
27. Research by Alan Slater and colleagues at the University of Exeter, 2004, reported in *New Scientist*, September 6, 2004.
28. Davis, *Reshaping the Female Body*, p. 147.
29. bell hooks, "Straightening Our Hair," *Z Magazine* September 1988.
30. Alva Johnston, "Testimonials, C.O.D.," *Outlook and Independent* March 18, 1931.
31. Ibid.
32. His then wife recounted this to Lindy Woodhead; see Woodhead, *War Paint*, p. 200.
33. The discussion relating to Pascal Dangin derives from Lauren Collins, "Pixel Perfect," *The New Yorker*, May 12, 2008.
34. Collins, "Pixel Perfect."
35. Ibid.
36. *Daily Mail*, September 18, 2006.
37. Http://yeeeah.com/2008/11/04/kate-winslet-massively-photoshopped-in-vanity-fair/.
38. *Daily Telegraph*, August 3, 2009.
39. Friedan, *The Feminine Mystique*, 1982 edition, pp. 181–83.
40. O'Higgins, *Madame*, p. 29.
41. Ipsos Mori poll, cited in "Absence of Women from Top Boards Is Unacceptable, Says Gordon Brown," *Guardian*, March 8, 2010.
42. "No Fake Tan to This Story of Success," *The Independent*, February 19, 2005.
43. *Guardian*, May 14, 2009.
44. Ibid., February 2, 2010.

Coda : Two Old Ladies

1. Joshua Levine, "Une Affaire de Famille," *Forbes*, March 30, 2009.

2. *Egoïste* no. 10, 1987. All of Liliane Bettencourt's remarks on her upbringing and opinions are taken from this interview, the only one she ever gave until the Banier scandal erupted in 2007.
3. Abescat, *La Saga des Bettencourt*, p. 185.
4. O'Higgins, *Madame*, p. 65.
5. "The Bitter Family Battle for the L'Oréal Billion," *London Evening Standard*, July 20, 2009.
6. Abescat, *La Saga des Bettencourt*, p. 10.
7. *Egoïste* no. 10, 1987.
8. Liliane Bettencourt, "'Je n'ai plus envie de voir ma fille,'" *Journal du Dimanche*, December 21, 2008.
9. O'Higgins, *Madame*, pp. 26–28.
10. Ibid., p. 269.
11. Ibid., p. 250.
12. Ibid., p. 268.
13. Ibid., p. 290.
14. Liliane Bettencourt, "'Je n'ai plus envie de voir ma fille,'" *Journal du Dimanche*, December 21, 2008.
15. Ibid.
16. Michel Guerrin, "Il y a toujours eu de vacarme derrière moi," *Le Monde*, December 9, 2009.
17. Ibid.
18. Ibid.
19. Ibid.
20. Ibid.
21. Banier, *Le Passé composé*, p. 68.
22. Ibid., p. 66.
23. "La 'fausse camaraderie' du dandy-photographe," *Le Figaro*, February 13, 2009.
24. Banier on Castaing: www.fmbanier.com/madeleine_castaing_0.
25. Ibid.
26. "La 'fausse-camaraderie' du dandy-photographe."
27. Guerrin, "Il y a toujours eu de vacarme derrière moi."
28. Ibid.
29. Sworn statement, quoted in "Une Affaire de Famille," *Forbes*, March 30, 2009.

30. Levine, "Une Affaire de Famille."
31. Abescat, *La Saga des Bettencourt*, p. 250.
32. "Le sort de L'Oréal suspendu au procès pipole Banier-Bettencourt," *Canard Enchaîné*, February 24, 2010.
33. Liliane Bettencourt, "'Je n'ai plus envie de voir ma fille.'"
34. "La 'fausse camaraderie' du dandy-photographe."
35. "Le sort de L'Oréal suspendu au procès pipole Banier-Bettencourt," *Canard Enchaîné*, February 24, 2010.

BIBLIOGRAPHY

BOOKS

Abellio, Raymond. *Sol invictus, 1939–1947.* Volume 3 of *Ma dernière mémoire* (Paris, 1980).

Abescat, Bruno. *La Saga des Bettencourt: L'Oréal, une fortune française* (Paris, 2002).

Altick, Richard D. *The Presence of the Present: Topics of the Day in the Victorian Novel* (Columbus, Ohio, 1991).

Amouroux, Henri. *Les Beaux jours des collabos.* Volume 3 of *La Grande histoire des Francais sous l'Occupation* (Paris, 1978).

Anonymous. *The Lady's Toilette* (London, 1822).

Assouline, Pierre. *L'Épuration des intellectuels* (Paris, 1996).

Banier, François-Marie. *Le Passé composé* (Paris, 1971).

Banner, Lois. *American Beauty* (New York, 1983).

Barrett Litoff, Judy, and Judith McDonnell, eds. *European Immigrant Women in the United States: A Biographical Dictionary* (London, 1994).

Bar-Zohar, Michael. *Bitter Scent* (London, 1996).

Beevor, Anthony, and Artemis Cooper. *Paris after the Liberation 1944–1949* (London, 2004).

Benamou, Georges-Marc. *Jeune homme, vous ne savez pas de quoi vous parlez* (Paris, 2001).

Berr, Helene. *Journal,* tr. David Bellos (London, 2008).

Bettencourt, Pierre. *Les désordres de la mémoire*. Exhibition catalog (Rouen, 1998).

Bourdrel, Philippe. *La Cagoule, 30 ans de complot* (Paris, 1970).

Bromberger, Merry. *Comment ils ont fait fortune* (Paris, 1954).

Callil, Carmen. *Bad Faith* (London, 2006).

Campbell, Lady Colin (tr.). *The Lady's Dressing-Room* (London, 1892).

Carter, Ernestine. *With Tongue in Chic* (London, 1974).

Chapkis, Wendy. *Beauty Secrets* (London, 1986).

Charbonneau, Henry. *Les mémoires de Porthos* (Paris, 1967).

Coignard, Sophie, and Marie-Thérèse Guichard. *Les Bonnes fréquentations: histoire secrète des réseaux d'influence* (Paris, 1997).

Cooper, Wendy. *Hair* (London, 1971).

Corson, Richard. *Fashions in Make-up: From Ancient to Modern Times* (London, 1972).

———. *Fashions in Hair* (London, 1980).

Coston, Henry. *Le Retour des 200 familles* (Paris, 1960).

———. *Dictionnaire des dynasties bourgeoises et de la monde des affaires* (Paris, 1975).

Curie, Eve. *Madame Curie* (Paris, 1938).

Dalle, François. *L'Aventure L'Oréal* (Paris, 2001).

Davis, Kathy. *Reshaping the Female Body: The Dilemma of Cosmetic Surgery* (New York, 1995).

Delluc, Brigitte and Gilles. *Jean Filliol, du Périgord à la Cagoule* (Périgueux, 2006).

Désert, Joseph. *Toute la vérité sur l'affaire de La Cagoule* (Paris, 1946).

Dunlap, Knight. *Personal Beauty and Racial Betterment* (London, 1920).

Etcoff, Nancy. *Survival of the Prettiest: The Science of Beauty* (London, 1999).

Fabe, Maxene. *Beauty Millionaire: The Life of Helena Rubinstein* (New York, 1972).

Finkelstein, Joanne. *The Fashioned Self* (Oxford, 1995).

Friedan, Betty. *The Feminine Mystique* (New York, 1963).

Frydman, Jean. *L'Affaire Bettencourt* (Paris, 2000).

Frydman, Jean and David. *Pour servir la mémoire* (Paris, 1994).

Giesbert, Franz-Olivier. *François Mitterrand: une vie* (Paris, 1996).

Gilman, Sander. *Making the Body Beautiful* (Princeton, 1999).

Guenther, Irene. *Nazi Chic? Fashioning Women in the Third Reich* (Oxford, 2004).

Harris, John. *Enhancing Evolution* (Princeton, 2007).

Horton, Rosalind, and Sally Simmons. *Women Who Changed the World* (London, 2007).

Humphrey, Nicholas. *The Mind Made Flesh: Essays from the Frontiers of Psychology and Evolution* (Oxford, 2002).

Jouve, Pierre, and Ali Magoudi. *François Mitterand: portrait total* (Paris, 1986)

Judt, Tony. *Past Imperfect: French Intellectuals, 1944–1956* (Berkeley, 1992).

Kaplan, Alice. *The Collaborator* (Chicago, 2000).

Kitson, Simon. *The Hunt for Nazi Spies* (London, 2008).

Koestler, Arthur. *Scum of the Earth* (London, 1941).

Kolboom, Ingo. *La Revanche des patrons: le patronat français face au Front populaire* (Paris, 1986).

Lacroix-Riz, Annie. *Industriels et banquiers sous l'Occupation. La collaboration économique avec le Reich et Vichy* (Paris, 1999).

Lambert, Ellen Zetzel. *The Face of Love: Feminism and the Beauty Question* (Boston, 1995).

Levison, Sarah Rachel (Madame Rachel). *Beautiful for Ever!* (London, 1863).

———. *The Extraordinary Life and Trial of Madame Rachel at the Central Criminal Court* (London, 1868).

Lewis, Alfred Allan, and Constance Wordsworth. *Miss Elizabeth Arden* (New York, 1973).

McKnight, Gerald. *The Skin Game* (London, 1989).

Marrus, Michael R., and Robert O. Paxton. *Vichy France and the Jews* (New York, 1981).

Meade, L. T. *The Sorceress of the Strand* (London, 1903).

Meredith, Bronwen. *A Change for the Better* (London, 1988).

Milesi, Gabriel. *Les Nouvelles 2000 familles: les dynasties de l'argent, du pouvoir financier et économique* (Paris, 1990).

Monzie, Anatole de. *La Saison des juges* (Paris, 1943).

Nicholson, P. T., and I. Shaw, eds. *Ancient Egyptian Materials and Technology* (Cambridge, U.K., 2000).

O'Higgins, Patrick. *Madame: An Intimate Biography of Helena Rubinstein* (London, 1971).

Orbach, Susie. *Bodies* (London, 2009).

Ovid. *Ars amatoria*.

Paxton, Robert Owen. *Vichy France: Old Guard, and New Order. 1940–1944* (New York, 1982).

Péan, Pierre. *Le Mystérieux Docteur Martin* (Paris, 1993).

———. *Une Jeunesse française* (Paris, 1994).

———. *Vies et morts de Jean Moulin* (Paris, 1998).

Peiss, Kathy. *Hope in a Jar* (New York, 1998).

Perrier, Marc. *La véritable saison des juges* (Paris, 1944).

Perrot, Philippe. *Le Travail des apparences: les transformations du corps féminin XVIIIe–XIXe siècle* (Paris, 1984).

Phillips, M. C. *Skin Deep* (Garden City, N.J., 1934).

Poncet, Charles. *Nestlé, Bettencourt et les Nazis* (Vevey, Switzerland, 1995).

Potton, Ariste. *On a trouvé un chef* (Lyon, 1937).

Rochebrune, Renaud de, and Jean-Claude Hazéra. *Les Patrons sous l'Occupation,* volumes 2 and 3 (Paris, 1995).

Roughead, William. *Rascals Revisited* (London, 1940).

Rubinstein, Helena. *The Art of Feminine Beauty* (New York, 1930).

———. *My Life for Beauty* (London, 1964).

Rudofsky, Bernard. *Are Clothes Modern?* (New York, 1947).

Schueller, Eugène. *Le Deuxième salaire* (Paris, 1939).

———. *La Révolution de l'économie* (Paris, 1941).

———. *Faire Vivre—esquisse d'une economie proportionelle* (privately printed; Paris, 1945).

———. *L'Impôt sur l'énergie* (Paris, 1957).

Slesin, Suzanne. *Over the Top: Helena Rubinstein, Extraordinary Style, Beauty, Art, Fashion, Design* (New York, 2003).

Steiner, Wendy. *The Trouble with Beauty* (London, 2001).

Stevenson, Karen. "Hairy Business," in Ruth Holliday and John Hassard, eds., *Contested Bodies* (London, 2001).

Thomas, Martin. *The French Empires at War, 1940–45* (Manchester, U.K., 1998).

Tournous, J.-R. *L'Histoire secrète* (Paris, 1965).

Trano, Stéphane. *Mitterrand, les amis d'abord* (Paris, 2000).

Turner, Bryan. *The Body and Society* (Oxford, 1984).

Uzanne, Octave. *Etudes de sociologie féminine: Parisiennes de ce temps en leurs divers milieux, états et conditions* (Paris, 1910).

Vinen, Richard. *The Politics of French Business, 1936–1945* (Cambridge, U.K., 1991).

Waitzfelder, Monica. *L'Oréal Took My Home: The Secrets of a Theft*, Peter Bush trans. (London, 2006).

Walkowitz, Judith. *City of Dreadful Delight: Narratives of Sexual Danger in Late-Victorian London* (Chicago, 1992).

Webster, Paul. *Mitterrand: l'autre histoire, 1945–1995* (Paris, 1995).

Wilson, Elizabeth. *Adorned in Dreams: Fashion and Modernity* (London, 1985).

Wolf, Naomi. *The Beauty Myth* (London, 1990).

Woodhead, Lindy. *War Paint: Madame Helena Rubinstein and Miss Elizabeth Arden* (London, 2003).

ARTICLES

Helena Rubinstein

Sunday Telegraph February 1962, serialization of HR's memoir *Just For Luck*:

Feb. 4, pp. 12–13: "The Demons That Still Drive Me."

Feb. 11, p. 15: "M. Poiret Takes Offence—and Tears My Dress in Strips."

Feb. 18, p. 14: "Timing, Luck—and £2m. Profit."

Vogue (U.S.) February 15, 1915, pp. 20–23, "A Famous European 'House of Beauty' Announces the Opening of Its Doors in New York."

Vogue (U.S.) May 1, 1915, pp. 82–84, "On Her Dressing-Table."

Beerbohm, Max. "A Defence of Cosmetics," *The Yellow Book* 1 (April 1894).

Clifford, Marie J. "Helena Rubinstein's Beauty Salons, Fashion, and Modernist Display," *Winterthur Portfolio* 38 (2003), pp. 83–108.

Flügel, J. C. "Clothes Symbolism and Clothes Ambivalence: The Psychology of Clothes," *International Journal of Psychoanalysis* 10 (1929), pp. 205–17.

Gray, Allison. "People Who Want to Look Young and Beautiful," *American Magazine,* December 1922, pp. 32–33.

Johnson, Alva. "Testimonials, COD—Some Light on Big Names in Advertising" and "Testimonials, Wholesale," *Outlook and Independent*, March 18, 1931. pp. 398–99, and March 25, 1931, pp. 434–35.

Keiffer, Elaine Brown. "Madame Rubinstein, the Little Lady from Krakow," *Life*, July 21, 1941, pp. 37–45.

Miller, Elizabeth-Carolyn. '"Shrewd Woman of Business': Madame Rachel, Victorian Consumerism, and L. T. Meade's 'The Sorceress of the Strand,"' *Victorian Literature and Culture* 34 (2006), pp. 311–32.

Swerling, Jo. "Beauty in Jars and Vials," *The New Yorker*, June 30, 1928, pp. 20–23.

Schueller

Egoïste, no. 10 (1987), interview with Liliane Bettencourt.

Le Monde, February 1995 interview with Serge Klarsfeld.

Le Matin, August 27, 1941, interview with Eugène Deloncle.

La Gerbe, September 25, 1941, interview with Deloncle.

Coiffure de Paris, 1909, passim.

Noiville, Florence. "L'Oréal, une histoire au parfum de soufre," *Le Monde*, January 17, 1997.

Thomas, Martin. "Giraud," *French History*, 10, no. 1 (1996), pp. 86–111.

Tumblety, Joan. "Civil Wars of the Mind: The Commemoration of the 1789 Revolution in the Parisian Press of the Radical Right," *European History Quarterly* 30, no. 3 (July 2000).

Votre Beauté, 1929–45, passim.

ARCHIVES

Archives Nationales de France (CARAN): Dossier instruit par la cour de justice du département de la Seine contre Eugène Schueller (cote Z 6 N L 11.108).

Fonds Majestic (cote AJ40).

Archives de Paris: Fonds du comité régional interprofessionel d'épuration. Affaire Schueller (cote 901/64/1–282).

Centre de Documentation Juive Contemporaine, Paris.

Curie Archives, Paris: BnF Mss. Archives Joliot-Curie (déposées à l'Institut Curie) NAF 28161.

Letters from Helena Rubinstein to Rosa Hollay, 1914–28, now in the possession of James Bulmer.

Skin Deep correspondence, Consumers' Research Collection, Special Collections, Rutgers University.

INDEX

Page number followed by *n* indicates a footnote.